WALK
RIDE
PADDLE

WALK
RIDE
PADDLE

A Life Outside

TIM KAINE

HARPER HORIZON

To family and friends who've
adventured with me.

CONTENTS

PROLOGUE
2023

This book is an account of three journeys I undertook deep into Virginia nature from May 2019 through October 2021. I planned the multiyear experience in 2018 to commemorate turning sixty and reaching twenty-five years in public life. What I didn't know when I hatched the plan was that the adventure would coincide with two impeachment trials, a pandemic killing more than a million people in the United States and causing global economic meltdown, a violent attack on the Capitol with the intent to overturn the 2020 presidential election, and racial justice protests sparked by the murder of George Floyd and others. As a senator, I was in the middle of all of it.

I kept a journal each of the seventy-six days I was hiking, cycling, and canoeing across Virginia. Afterward, I added notes on each trip and planned the next portion. Each chapter is about the day's journey, the history—both human and natural—of the places I traversed, conversations with companions and passersby, memories of earlier trips, and thoughts occurring to me along the way.

The journal became an organic reflection of the extraordinary events occurring in America during the years of the journey. That daily turmoil filled my thoughts and came to play a larger part of the narrative than I would have predicted when I began. But the time in Virginia's wilderness also proved a balm for the chaos I was living.

Along the way, I've learned much about Virginia, America, nature, other people, and myself. I've resisted the temptation to revise sections of the journal based on what I now know about how these events played out. Instead, this is a real-time reflection of how I experienced these events, with only the knowledge I had at the moment, never sure what I would see around the next bend. Even now—more than at any time in my life—I'm not sure what I will see around the next bend.

INTRODUCTION
2018

Why embark on this odyssey?

I turn sixty this year, in the closing stretch of an exhausting two-year campaign to be reelected to the US Senate in 2018, following a tough year of campaigning for and with Hillary Clinton in 2016. I am approaching my twenty-fifth anniversary of public service in 2019. Life is filled with pressure: polling, waiting in lines at airports, endless fundraisers, eating standing up or in a car, leaving the house early, getting lobbied by interest groups, arriving home late, seeing my wife on weekends only, brief and often superficial interactions with huge numbers of people, partisan skirmishes in the Senate or on cable news. Politics seems more and more like an NHL game—point scoring surrounded by a crowd that's ready for a fight.

I am worried too; 2016 taught me some painful lessons about a country I thought I understood. While I have always been a preternatural American optimist, President Trump is a symptom of a national sickness. Indeed, a *global* sickness. And while his destructive traits are energizing for me and many others because they galvanize us into pursuing a better America, there is a level of dread and tension connected with everyday life as I struggle to minimize the harm he brings to a nation I love.

There is plenty of good—certainly enough to make me excited to continue running for office even after a quarter century of public life. Solving people's problems, witnessing the progress of my Commonwealth, getting more bills passed as I begin to master the quirks of the Senate, working with a wonderful staff of public-minded altruists, helping young candidates I've mentored along the way, meeting talented people with good ideas wherever I go, communicating in Spanish to our growing Latino population. These all bring me life.

But even with all the good that makes me feel lucky every day (well, most days), my job is like a treadmill going way too fast. And there is a paradox—despite being continually out in public, I feel as though I am living in an increasingly insular bubble where politics dominates everything and other realms of life are slipping far away.

I start thinking about what I might do after my reelection campaign to slow down, breathe a little, and reconnect. My brief foray into national politics in 2016 convinced me that I need not go higher in public office—but at the same time, it convinced me that I should try to go *deeper*. National politics is increasingly a branch of the entertainment industrial complex; a world that doesn't fit me. How can I moor my future public service to something more meaningful?

I love the outdoors. I've spent my life camping, backpacking, cycling, hiking, canoeing, trekking—with the Boy Scouts and boyhood friends, with my parents and brothers, with my wife and children, with law-school buddies and neighbors. My biggest sources of spiritual renewal are my small Richmond parish, playing and listening to music, reading, and being outdoors. Each of these—experienced alone and also shared with family and friends—has been a refuge.

In my thirty-five-plus years in Virginia, I've visited so many beautiful places: trails, mountains, marshes, campsites, beaches, historic homes, Civil War battlefields, streams and lakes, the Chesapeake Bay and the Atlantic, forests and swamps, gorges and meadows. And for all the places I have been—spring break hiking trips with adults and kids from my neighborhood, a long-running Memorial Day camping tradition, summer canoe trips on Virginia rivers, bike rides all over the state—I still have so many more I want to see. But unlike church or music or reading, the things I love to do outdoors grow harder with age. Aches and pains subtly multiply. Sleeping on the ground—a bizarre specialty of mine—gets less attractive. How much longer before day hikes will be the extent of what I can attempt? Why not tackle bucket-list outdoor adventures in Virginia—seeing new things but also reliving great trips from my past? I need to do it soon, while I still have a reasonable chance of actually finishing what I start.

The plan quickly forms—create and then complete an epic Virginia outdoor quest: hike the whole Virginia stretch of the Appalachian Trail, cycle the Skyline Drive and Blue Ridge Parkway in our state, and canoe the entire James River. I have done small portions of each over the last thirty-five years: a section here and a stretch there. But why not tackle all three as a project?

Some states have these big outdoor challenges. New York has the Adirondack 46ers, where people climb all forty-six peaks with an elevation greater than four thousand feet. Our sister and brother-in-law from Syracuse did this with their kids when they were growing up and we joined them for three—Marcy, Algonquin, and Whiteface. There's a similar quest in Colorado to climb all the 14ers—peaks higher than fourteen thousand feet. Iowa has RAGBRAI—the Register Annual Great Bicycle Ride Across Iowa—sponsored by *The Des Moines Register* every year, where cyclists travel five hundred miles from the Missouri to the Mississippi in seven days, thousands of people each year riding through small towns and farms. I did this with law-school friends in 1996.

Virginia deserves a quest like this. Every state deserves a quest like this.

It strikes me—this should help me do my job better. All kinds of pressures are threatening our natural beauty in Virginia and elsewhere: climate change, accelerating development, deforestation, interstate pipelines, diminishing air and water quality. I have battled for open space preservation, Chesapeake Bay cleanup, resilience against rising sea levels. But the threat levels are escalating. By getting more in touch with our natural beauty, I hope to be a better advocate for new ideas to ensure that our environmental bounty is available for coming generations.

And I want to talk to folks along the way. Many senators do state tours by car, RV, or plane, using days out of Washington to hear from citizens. Why not tour by foot, bike, and canoe, stopping in communities and visiting with people to hear about what matters to them?

It's decided: during weekends and in Senate recess weeks, I will create a Virginia Nature Triathlon. I don't know of anyone who's done it. In 2019, I'll hike the 559 miles of the Appalachian Trail that cross Virginia from Harpers Ferry to the Tennessee border. In 2020, I'll bike 321 miles along the crest of the Virginia Blue Ridge on the beautiful parkways built during the Depression to create jobs and give everyday people on the East Coast an accessible place to vacation. And in 2021, I'll canoe the entire James River, 348 miles from its headwaters in the Allegheny Mountains to its entrance into the Chesapeake Bay near Fort Monroe, where the first English settlers arrived in 1607 and the first enslaved Africans in 1619.

I need to spiritually recharge, reconnect to Virginia's outdoors, and clarify new public-service challenges for myself. And I hope to rope others into joining me, especially those who have been with me on outdoor trips throughout my life.

Maybe I'm looking for something. Or trying to escape something. There is no clear goal in my mind other than that I need to tackle something unique and difficult—and, as I push myself, learn something along the way.

Thank God for a wonderful wife. Anne also loves the outdoors. We had our three kids sleeping in tents as babies, and now that they are grown, they still jump at the chance to camp. Anne is supportive from the moment I mention the idea, even though we are already apart a lot as I work in DC (two-plus hours from our home in Richmond) during the thirty-six or so weeks a year that the Senate is in session. She is interested in joining me for some stretches of the journey. And when my will falters along the way, as it surely will, I know I can count on her to gently encourage.

On paper, it sounds great. But I have to admit—I have major doubts about whether I can actually do it. Hiking, biking, and canoeing 1,228 miles? To find out if I have what it takes, I'll have to start walking.

WALK

2019

On a Thursday afternoon in May, I walk to Union Station in DC after our last votes of the week and hop a train to Harpers Ferry to start hiking south on the Appalachian Trail. My primary emotions—excitement and nerves. I look forward to this but am not sure I can do it.

Harpers Ferry is a tiny town at the confluence of the Potomac and Shenandoah Rivers separating Virginia, West Virginia, and Maryland. It's barely more than an hour west of DC but feels worlds away from the congestion and self-importance of our political epicenter. Yet few small communities have played such an outsized role in American history.

This is the site of the John Brown raid in October 1859 that ignited a spark leading to the Civil War. In an attempt to initiate a revolt among those enslaved, abolitionist John Brown and twenty-two others captured a US arsenal. Over the next three days, they fought a fierce battle before being defeated by US Marines commanded by Robert E. Lee. Many of Brown's racially diverse followers—whites, free Blacks, escapees who had been enslaved, two of his sons—were killed in the battle. Brown was captured and then executed a few weeks later. His public reputation quickly morphed from violent fanatic to religious prophet, calling down judgment upon a nation proclaiming equality as its cardinal virtue but acting to preserve and expand slavery as its daily practice.

Brown chose Harpers Ferry for two reasons: there was a lightly guarded US arsenal with thousands of weapons and stockpiles of ammunition he could seize to fuel his revolt, and the town was situated along the mountain range running from Alabama to Newfoundland. This was known by different names along the route—the Smokies, Alleghenies, Blue Ridge, Adirondacks, Poconos, Catskills, Berkshires, Whites, Blacks, Greens, Notre Dame, Mégantic—but they were all lumped together as the Appalachian Mountains.

Brown's plan was to win a decisive strike in Harpers Ferry, declare a new government where all were free, and encourage Southern enslaved people to flee their homes, farms, and plantations and make their way to the Appalachians, which would be an overground railway to freedom in the North. There was a connection in his mind between the wildness of the mountain range and freedom.

Today, Harpers Ferry is near the midpoint of the Appalachian Trail and contains the headquarters of the Appalachian Trail Conservancy (ATC), the nonprofit network of individuals and organizations who—together with the National Park Service—maintain the trail.

The trail was an idea proposed in 1921 by forester and urban planner Benton MacKaye. Like Brown, he also saw a wilderness trail that would serve as a spine along the mountains of the American East. Like Brown, he connected these mountains with an idea of freedom—freedom from overcrowded cities, industrialization, the dominance of the automobile.

MacKaye especially wanted East Coast workers to have access to outdoor recreation, believing that they needed "relief from the various shackles of commercial civilization." Hiking and nature clubs labored for years, under the leadership of Myron Avery, one of the early leaders of the ATC, to capture MacKaye's vision, completing the trail in 1937.

The 2,190 miles of the AT cross fourteen states, beginning at Springer Mountain, Georgia, and ending at Mount Katahdin, Maine. One-fourth of the trail is in Virginia. Over the years, the trail route has changed often, as land was acquired by the National Park Service and Forest Service.

Someone hearing about my hike gave me an early set of AT guidebooks from 1959–60, published by the DC-based Potomac Appalachian Trail Club. PATC does amazing work, maintaining more than 240 miles of the AT (plus hundreds of miles of other trails) and dozens of cabins and shelters in Virginia, Maryland, West Virginia, Pennsylvania, and DC. It is one of numerous trail clubs that have adopted portions of the AT. I will refer to the advice from these sixty-year-old PATC books as Old Guide. Old Guide informs me about the frequency of trail changes with a warning that also serves as a general life lesson: "The chief difficulty of guidebooks is that they become obsolete so rapidly." Don't we all?

1

I should have figured I would wake to rain. It's 6 a.m.; I am planning to depart on my hike around 7:30, and the drizzle is steady across the town. After a hot breakfast, with rain falling faintly, I begin.

The start of my hike could not be more picturesque. Wet, worn stone steps climb steeply from the lower town. These are the Bloody Stone Steps of lore, running red with blood during a Civil War battle in 1862 when eleven thousand Union soldiers were captured. I climb toward St. Peter's Catholic Church, built in the 1830s to serve the migrant Catholic laborers who flocked to Harpers Ferry to work in the then-thriving munitions plants.

Just past the church, the trail immediately enters a deep wood. Hundreds of feet above the Shenandoah River is Jefferson Rock, a stone outcrop named after Virginia's quintessential conflicted public servant, who once surveyed this spot and wrote: "You stand on a very high point of land. On your right comes up the Shenandoah having ranged along the foot of the mountain a hundred miles to seek a vent. On your left approaches the Potomac, in quest of a passage also. In the moment of their Junction, they rush together against the mountain, render it asunder, and pass off to the sea." This Jefferson, reflecting on slavery, later wrote: "I tremble for my country when I reflect that God is just: that his justice cannot sleep for ever."

From the rock, I can survey the town where Brown helped ignite the war Jefferson trembled over. And I can look across the river to where I will soon be climbing: Loudoun Heights, nearly one thousand feet above the town below.

As I hike south, I find for the next few days that I am practically alone in going that direction. Thru-hikers are working their way north, nearing the halfway point on their 2,190-mile journey. But I see very few people, even day hikers, hiking south. Brown was right about this trail—it is for northbound sojourners.

I haven't hiked with a pack for nearly six years, since a birthday trip with neighborhood friends in the Dolomites in Northern Italy. And that hike was hut to hut—with no need to carry a tent or sleeping bag or stove or much food. Clothes, water, lunch, a harmonica, the card game Quiddler, a Wiffle ball and bat—the pack was probably seventeen pounds. Now, as I cross the Shenandoah River by bridge and start ascending Loudoun Heights, I am carrying it all: clothes, multiple days' worth of food, water, bivy sac, sleeping pad, sleeping-bag liner, other stuff. Plus—of course—the harmonica, although no Wiffle ball or bat this time. Probably thirty to thirty-two pounds total.

I feel the weight of the pack more intently than before and also realize that I am six years older. In that time, I've suffered a minor meniscus tear in my right knee. My self-rehab was sufficient for Senate work, but I start to feel the knee throb as I slowly climb through the humid forest. The rain has stopped now but I must have entered the low-lying clouds based on the quiet fog surrounding me.

My hope is to hike from Harpers Ferry to Ashby Gap in my first two and a half days on the trail. It's a shakedown hike—seeing how I feel and how fast I can go, checking to see whether I am bringing the right gear. This part of the trail contains a twelve-mile stretch known as "The Roller Coaster" for its continuous up-and-down as the trail was relocated off the ridge of the mountain to make room for a US government weather observatory.

The first miles, tracking the state line between Virginia and West Virginia, pass smoothly, silently, slowly. I see two to three folks max. We nod, say, "Good luck," and pass each other quickly. I make my first real stop at Keys Gap around 10:30 a.m.

The mountain ridge is interrupted by gaps where the elevation declines just a little. Some gaps are water gaps, cut by still-flowing streams. Others are wind gaps, originally cut by vanished streams and now dry. These gaps became the original footpaths to cross the mountains, and then trails for horses and wagons and eventually paved roads. My first week on the trail will be Harpers Ferry to Keys Gap to Wilson Gap to Snickers Gap to Ashby Gap to Manassas Gap to Chester Gap to Thornton Gap. I love these names.

At Keys Gap, I shed my pack, gulp water, and eat a tasteless health bar. A guy pulls into the small parking lot and I notice a "2190" bumper sticker, a sign of a thru-hiker. I ask him about it and he says he just finished his hike two days ago. He was hiking sections over the past couple of years and completed his last stretch in Damascus, Virginia. Just done two days ago and already back on the trail? He was there to do some "trail magic"—leaving surprise gifts (in this case, cold beer and soda) on the trail for the thru-hikers. He offers me a soda, but I am chugging water and don't want anything carbonated so early and set off.

As I walk, a new pain to accompany my right knee returns like an old friend. As the miles pass by, my shoulders start to ache; I've had this pain before but had forgotten about it. I first dislocated my right shoulder in college in a rock-climbing accident—later dislocating my left shoulder as well. And a cycling accident twenty years ago added a broken right collarbone to the list of minor injuries I have suffered over the years. One thing I love about the outdoors is that I tend to remember the good parts of hiking and camping trips while the annoyances are quickly forgotten—but now I remember how the same ache bugged me while hiking in the Dolomites in Italy six years ago.

I have thought about that trip many times over the last few years but never once recalled that my shoulders were sore at all. As I hike today, the memory returns. I center more pack weight on my hips, adjusting the shoulder straps every hour or so to vary the position of the pack. Both the knee and my shoulders will remain moderately painful no matter what, but as soon as the pack is off, the pain disappears and causes me no trouble.

I stop for lunch at an empty shelter along the trail, one with a great porch swing where I slowly rock in the sun while eating an apple. I am amazed that I am not very hungry. I am working very hard—maybe just a little too hard—but instead of working up an appetite, I feel slightly nauseous. Thirsty, yes, but without much of a desire to eat.

By 3:00 p.m., I reach the Blackburn Trail Center, a hikers' center about half a mile off the trail and operated by PATC. I am not planning to stay at the center, where there are tent sites, tiny cottages, and a free bunkhouse for hikers. But I definitely need water and want to rest a little. The caretaker, Dave, who is retired military, recognizes me and we talk a little about operating this outpost. He loves the fact that he never knows who'll show up next.

By 3:45, I am off again, although darkening clouds make me wonder whether leaving is a good idea. I am still trying to make another three to four miles today and am hoping to set up camp around 6:00 p.m. But halfway to my desired camping spot, the thunder I have been hearing off in the distance draws closer and raindrops start to fall. I press on for a bit along the east side of a rock ridge, but when the trail starts to climb the ridge and the thunder increases, I calculate that being on the ridge in a thunderstorm is a bad idea. I set my aluminum hiking poles down next to the trail, hike twenty yards off trail to the base of the ridge, put a poncho over myself and a trash bag over my pack, and sit down to wait out the storm.

For an hour, there I am, all by myself, the lyrics to the old hymn "Rock of Ages" running like a loop in my head. Thunder and lightning, a cool pelting rain. Normally, this would go on for about twenty minutes, but today's storm has more staying power. I don't mind hiking in rain, but lightning has earned my respect over many years, and I sit tight. Eventually, the thunder has moved farther away and I jump back up, anxious to get to camp before it gets dark.

My campsite isn't an AT shelter or anything official. My trail app tells me that a side trail branches off toward a cell tower shortly after a stream and spring. I finally get to the rain-drenched stream, fill up on water, find the side trail, and climb up toward the cell tower, seeing some flat areas where campers have created four to five obvious sites. I have about forty-five minutes of light left to set up camp, eat, hang my food out of bears' reach, and collapse.

All goes well and I am soon in the bivy (a superlight waterproof sleeve big enough for one sleeping bag and elevated a few inches above one's face with a half-hoop pole). I fall asleep on top of a cloud-soft sleeping pad and a fleece sleeping-bag liner. And then the second thunderstorm begins. Thunder, lightning, drenching rain. And I realize that, though the bivy is waterproof, I haven't set it up right; water is coming through the bug net over my head and I cannot seem to get it adjusted to keep dry.

I hunker down, thinking the storm will pass, but it doesn't. At some point, water pouring in, I briefly contemplate the chances of drowning high on a mountain. Eventually, against all my animal instincts, I get out of the bivy and figure out how to fully close it. I lift the bivy up to dump out all the water that has collected, strip off all my soaked clothes, pull dry clothes out of the pack hanging under a tarp on a nearby tree, and jump back inside to hopefully get some sleep. It's damp inside but there are no puddles. And thank God it's not too cold—maybe the high fifties. With the rain still falling, I finally drift to sleep.

2

I wake before sunup as birds announce the start of the day. I am completely alone, no one camping anywhere near me, and most of my stuff is soaked. At least the rain has stopped, though, so I start draping gear and clothes over the nearby trees to get them drying as the sun rises.

It has been a long time since I camped by myself. In fact, though I am pretty sure I have, I can't even remember when I might have done it last. All night, as I was battling the elements and then finally finding sleep, I kept speaking aloud to imaginary companions as I tossed and turned, my family members floating through my mind:

"Are you soaked, Woody?"

"Nat—what kind of animal do you think that is?"

"Annella—should we just break camp early and start walking? We can dry stuff out later."

I would speak these questions out loud, a habit from family trips, and then realize that no one was in the tent. Or the campsite. Or, likely, within miles. An eerie feeling.

I am a lot slower today. Part of it was overdoing it yesterday but the bigger reason is that the trail is soaked. Mud, rocks, tree roots. All are slippery when wet, and I walk much slower to avoid slipping. After the first thunderstorm yesterday, I fell twice in the final hour of the hike. I was lucky and had nothing more than a few scrapes, but I don't want to take a worse fall today.

There is a short section today near a rock formation called Bears Den where day hikers are common. I am switchbacking up a trail and hear a group coming down toward me. It is five to six male voices and, surprisingly, all are speaking Arabic. When they round the corner and pass me, the last looks at me and says, "Aren't you Senator Kaine?"

"I sure am."

"You and your team helped my mother get cleared to come and visit me after the Muslim travel ban blocked her!"

We talk for a few minutes. He's a proud Syrian-American dentist and hoped to get his mother to the US after the atrocious civil war in Syria turned his country into a humanitarian disaster. But the administration's Muslim travel ban had blocked his mother for nearly two years. My Senate team had been working with him for months, and we had all just received news the day before that his mother was now cleared to come be with him. What are the odds that, less than twenty-four hours after he gets the good news, he meets me—unshaven and soaked—on the AT and gets to say thanks in person?

The second day-hiker encounter is not nearly as good but is my own fault. I am looking for a turn off the trail to get to a hostel where I can refill water bottles when some day hikers coming down the hill tell me I have passed the turn and need to backtrack a half mile. Sure enough, I *had* passed a side trail a half mile back, so I follow their advice without checking my map. After hiking a half mile back down the trail, and another half mile down the side trail, it dead-ends into a road and I realize they accidentally steered me wrong. I waste nearly two miles due to the mistake. Should have checked my map rather than merely relying on advice.

I have been climbing and descending a bit but things take a turn as I now hit the Roller Coaster section of the AT. It's a fairly monotonous but intense pattern—climb up four hundred feet or so and then drop down. Repeat for twelve and a half miles. And because the trail has been routed off the ridge, the peak of each climb is still shrouded in the forest with no killer views to make you feel that you have achieved anything.

On this stretch, with my knee and shoulders still throbbing, the effort of climbing and descending while avoiding slips and falls works over time to chase out any conscious thought about anything. And I start to notice three phases of mental awareness during my hike: clear thinking, mental meandering, and—believe it or not—an increased awareness of songs.

The first phase is when I can clear my head. When the day starts, or after a long stop on the trail to restore energy, I think about the ten thousand things on my mind—family, work projects, memories of other hikes. I am directing and in control of my own thoughts. And the pace of a hike allows for high-quality thought. I solve some problems this way, make resolutions to tie up loose ends, and have insights about things to do once I am off the trail. But as I start to tire, especially during a tough climb or as the heat rises, I find myself less able to direct my thoughts. The sheer effort needed to keep moving starts to take all my attention and my mind empties.

As this mental emptying begins, I start reciting basic incantations to push myself ahead. Instead of looking up and being depressed by how slowly I am reaching the next summit, I look down at my feet and do a kind of mental rosary, reciting slow cycles of Our Father, Hail Mary, Glory Be, the Pledge of Allegiance—one phrase with each breath. Another incantation, delivered slowly—especially when I am breathing hard—is from Vietnamese Buddhist Thich Nhat Hanh. "Breathing in, I relax. Breathing out, I smile." It's a great phrase, turning the effort of a hike into a walking meditation. At the end of each cycle, I look up and see that I have progressed quite a bit.

But these intentional efforts eventually give way to a near-fugue state where I slip into a free-form mental meander. It's like my brain is turned off, not affirmatively trending in any direction—simply open to whatever thought or impression slips in. First is what I call "joy shocks" at seeing pure nature. Box turtles, orange mushrooms sprouting on the base of a sodden tree trunk, butterflies, sounds of swollen streams, a fiery-red salamander, birds and other small animals creating ripples in the green curtain of foliage all around me. I am cut off from nature in much of my life, so an immersion like this, when I get out of my own head to truly experience it, is therapy.

Finally comes an increased awareness of song snippets. I will catch myself singing a lyric under my breath—have I been singing for thirty seconds or five minutes? I didn't consciously decide to start singing anything but I find myself doing so. Some songs' provenance seem clear enough: "Rock of Ages" while sitting backed up to a rock and trying to avoid a thunderstorm; "Ribbon in the Sky" as a description of the AT; "Inca Roads" as I trek by foot; "500 Miles" as I think about how far I have to go; "Big-Eyed Rabbit" a few minutes after I see one scamper across my path. Many are songs from my gospel-choir days: "We've Come a Long Way, Lord" ("We've borne our burdens in the heat of the day . . ."); "I Have Decided to Make Jesus My Choice" ("The road is rough, the going gets tough, and the hills are hard to climb"); "I Don't Feel No Ways Tired" ("Nobody told me that the road would be easy"). The inspirations for other songs are harder to figure except that music is deep memory for me and, when other thinking has stilled, thousands of songs are there to bubble up and enjoy.

I reach an AT shelter midway through the afternoon and break for a late lunch. The shelter is standard issue—I will see dozens of them. Three sides (wood or stone) and a tin roof, open side usually facing east, the floor a simple raised wooden platform where folks lay out sleeping bags safe from the elements. The real fancy ones might have two levels for sleeping with an upper deck.

The weather looks a little iffy. I had hoped to go a few miles farther today but then remember the same dilemma from yesterday and what a drag it was to get blasted by a thunderstorm while out on the trail. The shelter, surrounded by flat ground for tents in a hollow at the confluence of two tiny creeks, is shady and inviting. I decide to set up camp early and skip the extra miles.

What a difference this makes on my mental state—not just for today, but also as I think about the rest of the hike. If you feel like you *have* to hike a certain number of miles, that's a form of mental pressure. I get enough of that in my day job; I'm looking to this hike for respite from mental pressure.

As I am setting up the bivy, still a little damp from last night, I form rules for my journey: walk when I want; rest when I want; camp when I want. Why press it if I'm sore? Why risk bad weather? Why skip an opportunity to camp in a nice place? I'm here to see and enjoy, not kill myself. And I am not trying to set any speed records—just hoping to do the whole Virginia stretch on my own time.

A few northbound thru-hikers arrive for the night. They all use trail names—Magic, Tracker, Underdog. They have just passed the thousand-mile mark and are feeling good about that. We talk a little about what they've seen. A fourth hiker arrives, looks at me, and says, "Senator Kaine?" This surprises the others, and they break out laughing once they figure out who I am. They ask, "Where's your security detail?"

"They blend in pretty well back in the woods, don't they?" I deadpan. They look around for a microsecond before they realize I'm joking.

Since I am getting off the trail by noon the next day, I offer them extra food I know I will not use. A twelve-ounce pack of summer sausage, divided four ways, is a great add to mac and cheese and the other hiker staple meals that they've grown tired of by now. But as we turn in, they amply return the favor. Noting my bivy, they ask whether I have seen the weather report. When I say no, they say that it looks bad and point out that there's more room in the shelter. But having screwed up the rain fly the night before, I am determined to get it right tonight. So they make a genius suggestion and point out the picnic table pavilion a few yards from the shelter. They help move the table out and I reposition the bivy under the roof.

Not five minutes after I am set up, the skies open and it pours all night. The combined sounds of rain on the tin roof overhead and the two streams rushing by—together with the comfort of sleeping completely dry—is heaven.

3

Today will be a short day. Doing the hike while serving in the Senate means interruption of trail time—and even though it's Sunday, duty calls. Nights, weekends, and holidays are the norm for a senator. I have to finish hiking by late morning to get to Orange, Virginia, in time to speak at the centennial celebration of the Dolley Madison Garden Club.

The rain lasted all night and is still falling as I break camp. Luckily, all my gear stayed dry under the picnic shelter roof so I can pack quickly, bid farewell to the thru-hikers, and head south. The sound of the rain falling through the dense leaf cover is hypnotizing as I maneuver the wet trail early in the day. I see only two people before I get to my pick-up spot.

The physical challenge of hiking is exceeded only by the mental challenge. Since I am not in a race, the reality of pain and age can be overcome by hiking slowly and resting when I want. My realization yesterday that I don't have to stick to a fixed mileage plan is comforting.

But the mental challenge is trickier. As I hiked yesterday, and even a little bit today, I find myself thinking, *Is this really a good idea? I am not sure I can do the whole trail. And why do I need to do the whole trail anyway? Why don't I just do a series of day hikes?* I am a little embarrassed at these thoughts. I wonder whether they will gnaw at me every day for the rest of this trip, and whether I will succumb to them.

I am also figuring out some things about the hike. The bivy sac instead of a tent seems like it will be okay. Not bringing a stove and relying on cold food is still a questionable call. I will keep trying, but I definitely brought the wrong food on this trip—too much, too heavy,

15

not appetizing enough. I make some mental notes about what I will change for the next hiking stretch.

The Garden Club speech seems like a fitting way to mark the end of my first stretch. It is still raining as I hit my road crossing and exit the trail. I am soaked, tired, and dirty. While the Garden Club is all about natural beauty, they expect me to be in a suit and tie, not shorts and muddy hiking boots. I get to the town, shower and change, and step into a celebration that is pure Americana.

Local, state, and federal officials along with Garden Club members from Orange County, Virginia, and elsewhere have gathered in a town park to commemorate the centennial and inaugurate a fountain. There are speeches, music, and ice cream. The purpose of the event is to reflect upon the centennial—not only of the Garden Club, but also of the passage of the women's suffrage amendment to the Constitution in 1919. As Alice Walker explained in "In Search of Our Mothers' Gardens," gardening was an artistic outlet, sometimes the chief artistic outlet, for women for centuries.

The women who started what became The Garden Club of America in 1913 and the Dolley Madison Garden Club in 1919 wanted to promote gardening, friendship, and environmental stewardship. They became active in opposing billboards in 1919 and were testifying in favor of the national park system as early as 1921. In the 1930s, garden club members all over the US mobilized to save California redwoods. When I was governor, our garden clubs helped us preserve four hundred thousand acres of open space and fight development near Civil War battlefields.

America's wilderness will not survive if we leave it alone. The incremental expansion of humanity will whittle down our natural bounty unless there are sustained and intentional efforts by government, organizations, and individuals to preserve it. I tell the Garden Club members and alums who gather that they are part of a vast network of engaged people who are needed every day to preserve wilderness gems like the nearby AT.

4

Yesterday was the twenty-fifth anniversary of my being sworn into my first public office—the Richmond City Council. It seems fitting that I'm back on the trail again, about two months after my first shakedown hike to test the trail readiness of my equipment and supplies. Now, it is not a cool and rainy spring anymore, having been replaced by a hot, humid summer.

At 10:30 a.m., Anne drops me off where the AT crosses a gravel road near Mount Weather. She is on the way to spend four days with her older sister, Tayloe, who was diagnosed with early Alzheimer's about ten years ago. Every few months, Anne goes to upstate New York to spend long weekends with her, partly to visit and partly to give a caretaker's break to Tayloe's amazing husband, Jon.

As I say goodbye to hike south for four days, one of my old hiking poles breaks, leaving me with just one. I am pissed off. Anne, ever the problem solver, says, "Maybe you'll like hiking with one pole better. If not, you can find a stick the same size as your pole and have a pair." I am lucky to have such a practical wife—and I end up using only one hiking pole for the rest of the trip.

Anne will be joining me for stretches of the trail when I get farther south. She is a great hiker and camper, a legacy from her childhood summer camp and Girl Scout days. We met in law school and built our relationship enjoying the outdoors: picnics, bike rides, taking public transportation to the beach. When we graduated in 1983, we took a three-week camping trip in New Mexico and Colorado to celebrate, punctuating days in the wilderness with stops in Santa Fe, Taos, and Boulder to eat good food, hear local music, and visit friends.

But our outdoor adventures really hit their stride when I moved to her native Virginia to get married in 1984. Since then, we have made so many trips—adventures and misadventures—within the Commonwealth. And we've hiked, biked, canoed, and camped elsewhere—the Rockies, the Adirondacks, the Sierras, the Ozarks, the Tetons, the Pyrenees, the Yucatán, state and national parks wherever and whenever we can.

Camping together is a reflection of marriage: there's fun, yes, but also arguments and moments of exhaustion. A mentality of *You lean on me and I'll lean on you*. On our first big trip after graduation, our camp stove burst into flames as we started to make dinner. I backed away, wanting to avoid a fireball, and told Anne to do the same. Instead, she whipped off her flannel shirt and smothered the fire. I yelled at her, "That was so dangerous! The fuel in the stove could have exploded!" And she yelled back, "And if someone didn't smother the fire, how were we going to prepare food for the rest of our trip?" Good save.

But when we crossed a dangerously angled scree field, where every step caused you to slide five or six feet down with the threat of a rock avalanche, her intermittent fear of heights kicked in and I had to coach her through every single step of the traverse.

Our joint love for the outdoors has passed on to our three kids: a Marine infantry commander, a visual artist and pre-K classroom aide, and an actor and server. They are each strong, different from each other and us. Our love of nature is still a unifier for our family, something that can cause each of us to drop what we are up to and reunite for another adventure. My memories of our family trips together would fill volumes.

With my late start, I am trying to do about thirteen miles today. The temperature is in the mid-nineties with humidity to match. Within the first four hundred yards, I am drenched with sweat—and will be for the next five hundred miles.

Today I finish the Roller Coaster stretch and move into a more traditional run of long climbs and descents. I cross Ashby Gap—Route

50 near the town of Paris, population two hundred. My sixty-year-old companion Old Guide has this quaint description: "Lodging and meals obtainable at Paris of Mrs. O.T. Adams (next to public garage). Tourist cabins and light lunches available at Blue Ridge Service Station, .1 mile east of Trail crossing in Ashby Gap. At Linden, lodging and meals are available at house of Miss Nellie Heflin." I see the ruins of an old service station and reason that, after sixty years, hostesses Adams and Heflin may be unavailable. I press on.

The AT climbs a mountain and crosses the upper reaches of a beautiful state park, Sky Meadows. I emerge from under the tree cover and enter a bizarre sun shower—rain pouring down for twenty minutes with no apparent clouds. A trail from the state park—the Ambassador Whitehouse Trail, named after the father of my Senate friend and environmental champion Sheldon Whitehouse—intersects the AT and veers off into a beautiful valley.

Earlier, I wrote about the mental zen state that settles in when you are working so hard that any thoughts of work or daily life are chased out of your mind. It sounds nice and positive, right? But there is another side to it that isn't so benign.

Hiking in the heat—and this is the hottest weather I have ever backpacked in—can bring you close to the bonk—extreme fatigue, usually caused by dehydration—if you are not careful. This is when you are drinking a lot of water but sweating out so much more. Your pee turns from clear to yellow and then won't even flow because all your liquids are sweated out. You start to feel loopy; you drift on the trail in a stupor until a stumble breaks you out of your reverie.

The hike ahead—most of which will happen in August—could be treacherous. I know to never pass a water source without filling up my two bottles. Add electrolytes—fizzing tablets or some other additive—for flavor and a boost of what you are quickly losing in the heat. Sharing is also important—give water to other hikers if they need it and you can spare it.

I reach my stop at the Whiskey Hollow Shelter. It is one of the nicest shelters I will see in my weeks on the trail—a double-decker with a front porch that is also under roof so you can eat dinner at a picnic table without getting soaked. And despite a big crowd of north-bound thru-hikers on the trail today, I am alone when I arrive at 6:00 p.m. I am still alone at 8:00 p.m., so I skip the bivy and set up my pad and fleece liner in the shelter's upper deck, where I spend the night by myself. Every noise—mice climbing the bear pole to attack my food bag, acorns falling on the roof, wind through the hollow, branches falling, off and on rain—is magnified tenfold. And it is so dark. When I wake periodically, I cannot even see my hand in front of my face. But I am so tired that sleeping is a cinch.

5

Today—another hot and muggy sweat fest—is wildlife day. All day long, I am seeing animals and birds. I round a bend and hear commotion a few yards from me at the foot of a rock ridge. I see a big black shape that I am sure is a bear but on closer inspection is two massive buzzards. I have never seen ones so large. They seem to be eyeing my hike with a mixture of skepticism and delight.

I get to a shelter midday and stop for lunch. As I walk down a side path to a spring, a massive black snake sunning on the trail uncoils and slithers into the grass. The snake is easily six feet long and doesn't move very fast—clearly not too scared of me but not wanting to get stepped on either.

This is bear season. As northbound hikers pass, they occasionally warn about seeing some up ahead, and as I round a curve in the mid-afternoon, a cub scampers across the trail about fifteen yards ahead of me. I stop, sure that a mother bear is nearby. After three or four minutes, it becomes clear that the mother must have been ahead of the cub and already crossed before I arrived. I start hiking as fast as I can, singing "Leaning on the Everlasting Arms" at the top of my lungs, the lyric "safe and secure from all alarms" assuming special importance. As it turns out, I don't see any more bears for the next few days. Just saying.

In some ways, the best wildlife on today's hike is heard but not seen. I am nearing Front Royal, a town where there is a massive Smithsonian compound, almost a modern-day Jurassic Park, where endangered species are nursed back to health. Originally used as a site for horses training for service in the cavalry, the facility now serves as one of the premier wildlife biology research centers in the world.

I had toured the place a year or so ago, seeing various compounds used for Burmese deer, cheetahs, exotic bird species, unusual horses. Some of these animals go to the National Zoo in DC or other zoos. But the ultimate goal is to revive species that are extinct in the wild and reintroduce them into their natural habitat. This little-known facility in the Blue Ridge Mountains obtained a herd of scimitar-horned oryx from the estate of a Middle Eastern royal with a private zoo and patiently raised them until they were hardy enough to be introduced back into Chad, following decades of extinction in the wild.

The AT runs along the compound's fence for a few miles. I keep hearing animals moving through the thick brush on the other side, but I can't see the animals so my imagination runs wild. For some reason, the word *coatimundi* comes to mind. I don't even know what a coatimundi is. In a few places, the eight-foot-high chain-link fence has been torn down or knocked over by a falling tree. I immediately wonder about escapees but I later find out that the downed fences are dangerous for the opposite reason: bears and coyotes know that there is prey *inside* the compound. There have been several instances of them breaking in and killing exotic species.

I am making good time today and keep going past where I originally thought I would camp, eventually working my way down to Mosby Gap where the AT crosses Route 522. I am now on the outskirts of Front Royal, a great trail town.

Trail towns are godsends to long-distance hikers. After days in the sun and rain, sleeping in a tent or shelter with food supplies dwindling, a trail town offers the chance to rest, restock, and maybe get a bed and shower. Front Royal is the first easily accessible trail town south of Harpers Ferry and it has a lot to offer. In addition to the AT, Front Royal calls itself the Virginia Canoe Capital because it is on the banks of the Shenandoah River, with many outfitters equipping folks to canoe, tube, and fish. It is also the northern gateway to Skyline Drive and thus attracts day cruisers, camping families, Harley riders, and road cyclists. My own favorite spot is Bing Crosby Stadium, home to a team in the Valley Baseball League ("Gateway to the Majors"). The League is a collegiate summer wooden-bat league sponsored by Major League Baseball.

I have read about a hikers' hostel, the Mountain Home Cabbin (not a misspelling!), right where 522 crosses the AT. I hit the road and there it is, one hundred yards to the south, an old cabin next to an equally old main house. I walk up the driveway to see if there's a vacancy. I'm in luck.

Lisa and her husband, Scott, had bought the vacant and derelict 1840s buildings after Scott did an AT thru-hike in 2012. Months on the trail with his son convinced him that he wanted to move out of the congested DC area and open a haven for hikers. He and Lisa first renovated an old cabin that can now sleep eight hikers and then renovated the main house to serve as their home and a comfortable B and B.

Lisa recognizes me and we decide to have dinner together. We get takeout Thai food from a local restaurant (trust politicians on one thing without hesitation—good places to eat—we've tried them all). She and Scott regale me with the saga of renovating the house and the characters they meet every day. I even get laundry done and afterward sink into a hot bath. No law says I have to rough it every night!

6

Today will be a long hot day with a lot of climbing. I start at about nine hundred feet elevation and climb to Compton Peak at 2,900 feet in the first five miles. Then after a long and generally downhill stretch, I climb Mount Marshall at 3,400 feet before finishing with a downhill into a hut at Gravel Springs. Early in the day, I will enter Shenandoah National Park, where I will be for the next eight or nine days of the trip.

Scott's sunny-side-up eggs, with toast and fruit, are good fuel for the day. And the other hikers around the table—Choo Choo and Redbush—are funny in recounting their tales and appreciative of the hiker hospitality at Mountain Home.

I stagger/climb in the heat for ninety minutes and reach a shelter where I get water and am able to rest a bit. A day hiker with her dog comes up, complaining of being stung by a wasp a few yards up the trail. As we talk about our respective hikes, we get into a discussion of paper maps versus trail apps. I have always been a paper-map person and so is she. But to navigate this hike, I am using a trail app. (There are many—I use Guthook, since renamed FarOut.) She asks to check it out. We pull up our location, which includes notes that other hikers have uploaded. Multiple notes from the last few days complain of stinging hornets at this shelter. Despite my love of paper maps, there are definite positives to trail apps.

I enter Shenandoah National Park about half an hour later. This two-hundred-thousand-acre park, opened in 1936, is the natural jewel of Virginia. The park contains the AT, Skyline Drive, and numerous side trails, overlooks, and campgrounds. As I hike, I will be following the ridges of innumerable mountains that crisscross Skyline Drive until the southern end of the park at Rockfish Gap.

The trail immediately improves since maintenance responsibility is now not just by the PATC but also the National Park Service. Perhaps as a result, the number of hikers picks up, with many families parking their cars along the Drive to hike, picnic, and experience wonderful views. The ease of reaching this park from the DC area and other East Coast cities generates nearly 1.3 million visitors a year.

My family and I have had some of our best outdoor memories in this park. Anne and I spent part of our honeymoon hiking here. For years, I had an Election Day tradition of voting first thing, driving up to hike Old Rag Mountain with family and neighbors—an eight-mile round trip with a memorable rock scramble and a 360-degree view—and then heading to whatever victory party we chose to attend that year.

But my favorite memory is spending a cold January night here several years ago, camping with my oldest son at his request to celebrate his twenty-first birthday. With snow on the ground and temperatures in the teens, we had set up a camp far off the trail, in a flattish space that clearly used to be someone's home based on the still-visible outlines of an old stone foundation. We may or may not have violated the "no fire" policy before turning in early. Lying there, listening to the wind, it was amazing to realize that we might have been the only folks sleeping outdoors in the entire park that night—and yet we were only seventy-five minutes away from a massive metro area. In the middle of the night, we heard a large creature walking around our tent. I softly asked Nat if he was awake—he was. We eliminated possibilities. It couldn't be a bear—there was no heavy breathing, and it was hibernation season. It couldn't be a crazed mountaineer—we were so far off the trail that none could easily find us in the dark. A settler's ghost? Unlikely.

It must have been deer. I flicked on my flashlight, waved it around in the tent, and heard the animal clatter off. Poking my head out of the rain fly, I saw two white-tailed deer (*Odocoileus virginianus*) and realized what had happened: when we cleared snow and rocks to set up our tent, we exposed plants; the deer were trying to find a midnight snack. As soon as we were back in our sleeping bags, they returned and kept nosing around all night until we exited the tent at daybreak.

In the 1930s, when Virginia worked with the federal government to take this land and turn it into a national park, the entire Shenandoah National Park was thinly populated. You can still find stone ruins and other signs of the life and death of the people forced to leave their homes—there are a few small cemeteries, still lovingly tended, high on some of these mountains. A poignant book by Katrina Powell, *The Anguish of Displacement*, tells the stories of these families through the letters they wrote during the process of the park's creation. Sue Eisenfeld's *Shenandoah: A Story of Conservation and Betrayal* examines their displacement through a modern-day search for cemeteries and ruins, interspersed with interviews of those whose families were kicked off their land. The beauty of the park and the oasis it provides for millions was purchased at the cost of others losing their longtime homes. As is so often the case, progress for some is pain for others.

As I continue to hike during this hot July stretch, each of my three rules are taking shape. I mentioned earlier that my trail mantra was "Walk when I want; rest when I want; camp when I want." Since I don't have a fixed date by which I have to finish the Virginia AT, why stress out about how many miles I do each day?

"Walk when I want" is how I start the day. Usually, I am up with the sunrise—although a bit creaky after spending a night on the ground. Even a nice sleeping pad leaves you stiff when you wake up. I'll putter around for about an hour, taking my time with eating breakfast and packing my gear. After an hour or so, I am stretched out and ready to start walking. If I am near a shelter, an hour of motion gives my digestive system time and inclination to use the privy—so much easier than breaking out the trowel along the trail.

"Rest when I want" is easy. I *always* want to rest, especially when

I am climbing a hill. I stop whenever I feel like it, but usually for only about two minutes at a time—and I have figured out the ideal stopping spot. A log or rock on the side of the trail that is about thigh-high is the perfect place to sit without having to take off my pack. And this becomes a little motivator for me. If I am climbing and want to stop, I wait to look around the next bend to see what's up ahead. If I don't see the right kind of rock or log, I go on to the next bend, or the next after that, until I find my perfect spot. It is amazing what a two- or three-minute rest and a sip of water will do for your energy.

The longer rests are when I take off my pack. I usually do a mid-morning stop of about twenty minutes, an hour-long lunch stop, and a midafternoon stop. When the pack is off, I stretch out, check my phone for messages, take a picture or two, and think about my progress.

For the third rule—"Camp when I want"—I always start the day with a basic idea of where I will spend the night. But that basic idea can easily change. Weather, fatigue, my pace, the pace of folks hiking with me, trying to coordinate a meeting spot with someone joining me, the quality of the campsites I pass during the day—all these factors could make me stop sooner or go farther.

And to be clear, "Camp when I want" is a bit of a misnomer. I sleep in my bivy sac many nights. But other nights, I will be in cabins, ATC shelters, motels, or hiker hostels when the AT intersects a town. And even the camping has variety—sometimes I'll be in the wild, some-times in a state or federal park along the trail, sometimes in or near an AT shelter where I know I will find water. The variety of where I sleep each night is part of the diverse experience of a long hike.

I reach the Gravel Springs shelter (Old Guide says it used to be called Gravelly Springs) at about 5 p.m.—an early bird. No one is in the shelter yet but there are two or three tent campers already set up. A Ridgerunner, hired by PATC to hike between shelters, help folks out as needed, and enforce trail rules along the way, is also here. I set up my bivy as the weather worsens rapidly.

By 6:30, even though there is much daylight left, the sky is dark as night as a massive thunderstorm rolls through. It is July 4, and the lightning and rain are the only fireworks display for the night. I zip the bivy closed and run fifty yards to the now-full shelter to sit under the eaves and eat my dinner with the others who will overnight here. There must be ten people inside talking; most are northbound thru-hikers who know each other well after weeks of hiking together. It is so dark that no one can see each other's faces.

Tonight's stories are about weird people they have met along the way. Some think other hikers are weird. But tonight, the stories are all about non-hikers, and the unifying theme seems to be that, most of the time—no matter how odd or how shocking their behavior or language or political opinions are—people are very willing to help hikers. The best story is a hiker who had a moped rider pick her up near Roanoke while she was hitchhiking to a local bar. Seconds later, the rider was stopped, handcuffed, and arrested for a hit-and-run just a few minutes before he'd picked her up. Imagine fleeing the scene of a moped hit-and-run accident (itself a novel concept) and then stopping to pick up a hitchhiker while the police are in hot pursuit. Now that's kindness to a hiker!

The rain never really stops, but when it lets up a little, I race back to my site. The rain has poured down so hard that the drops striking the ground have kicked up mud all over the outside of the bivy. It is dry inside, though I can feel the pressure of the raindrops pounding the outside. But being dry is all that matters.

7

All my gear is soaked when I wake in mist after a night of hard rain. Today, I am hiking fourteen miles to Thornton Gap where Virginia Route 211 crosses the Blue Ridge Mountains, intersecting the trail. Anne is returning from a four-day trip to her sister's, and we are supposed to meet up around 5:00 p.m. Because I will finish the day by meeting Anne, packing is pretty easy. If I were hiking on, I would want to get my gear dry and clean, taking some time early on to get things set because I would be camping again tonight. But since I am getting off the trail at day end, I can just stuff everything in my pack, knowing that I will have time this weekend at home to clean and dry everything.

This part of hiking has always struck me as a good metaphor for life, one of many lessons from time outdoors. Some mornings, you take your time and pack everything just right. But when conditions are bad, you stuff everything in the pack and start walking. My son Woody is the master of this. While he will sleep till noon if you let him, you can wake him in bad conditions and say, "Weather's bad, let's go," and he'll be walking with a hastily stuffed pack in five minutes—perhaps not fully awake, but truckin' on. There is hardly a better trait when camping.

After being on the ticket with Hillary and losing in 2016, I had a million emotions. For about 105 days, I had experienced the particular brand of chaos that is a presidential campaign—and what an experience. When Hillary asked me to join her, I started to say yes, but she wouldn't let me answer until she told me why she wanted me on the ticket:

"There may be better political picks than you. But if something happens to me, you would be a good president."

Obviously, the compliment touched me deeply. It also said

29

something very important about Hillary, something that spoke to her character but was arguably a detriment to her campaign: she is a person of substance and the politics are less important to her.

During the 2016 campaign, I went to 140 cities in forty-one states. Anne and I did nearly one thousand events and media appearances. The original plan was for us to travel together, but when the team saw how good Anne was, they gave her a separate itinerary so we could cover more ground. The entire experience was a blur, with days and nights running together. But some experiences stand out—good and bad.

Because of my time working with missionaries in Honduras after law school, I was able to do Spanish-language media everywhere. Once, a radio interviewer—hearing me answer questions in Spanish from the hosts and callers—said, "We've never had anyone on the ticket who could listen to us in our own language before." That stuck with me—not "*speak* our own language" but "*listen to us* in our own language." Most people don't feel listened to.

I found that my work as mayor, governor, and senator gave me the ability to always connect a question from anyone anywhere to something I had worked on before. I inspired dozens of dad jokes and then—proving the point, I imagine—had to be told what a dad joke was. And because I also play the harmonica, I frequently got opportunities to play music during the campaign with bands all over the country. (Jon Batiste, John Popper, Jon Bon Jovi—and that's just the Js!) These are some of the happy memories of the campaign.

But I also remember the October day when the WikiLeaks dump included my cell phone number. My voice mail immediately filled up with disturbing messages.

I remember my debate with Mike Pence. My goal was to forget about myself during the debate and keep the focus on Donald Trump, while also trying to stop Pence from opening up new attacks on Hillary. Reviews were decidedly mixed. Folks who knew me best hated it. Folks who had been on the receiving end of Trump-style bullying liked it fine.

I remember the precise spot in Tallahassee where I was standing when I heard that Jim Comey had publicly announced that he needed to reopen the FBI investigation into Hillary's emails ten days before the election. I watched our lead drop every day as those inconsequential emails became the closing story in the campaign.

As I went to my neighborhood polling place in Richmond on Election Day, I still thought we would win but was less confident than most on the team based on a simple data point: in 2008, with the chance to make history in electing the nation's first African American president, the early voter turnout of Black voters was amazing. People wanted to do all they could to see Barack Obama in the White House. In 2016, when we hit late September and early voting started in key states, I looked for a similar surge of women voters hoping to make history—Hillary would, of course, be the first female president—but I didn't see that same surge and it worried me.

And then election night. It was clear within thirty minutes of Virginia's polls closing that we would win the state by more than President Obama had won it in 2012. Having spent so much time trying to help Virginia catch up to the rest of the nation on issues of equality and inclusion, that helped me relax a bit. But Virginia was not the only state undergoing change. While our state is growing younger and more diverse, others are not following the same trend. We ended up winning the popular vote by millions but lost the race. (Ever since, I've called myself an "Electoral College dropout.") We conceded the next morning. I was inspired by Hillary's patriotic message urging all to accept the result but press forward on the values we hold dear.

Hillary could have made history by being the first woman president. She could have done something very rare in American history by winning a third Democratic presidential term in a row. She could have overcome the Russian disinformation campaign designed to help Donald Trump. She could have succeeded despite the FBI's shocking intrusion into the race at its most critical moment. She could have done any three of these four things. But she could not surmount all those challenges at once.

Five days later, I was back in the Senate. The first colleague who came to see me was Senator and former presidential candidate John McCain. He knocked on my office door early Monday morning, and I remember the conversation like it was yesterday.

"Tim, I'm the only person in the Senate today who knows exactly how you feel," he said. "We've both been on a national ticket and lost. And you know what? The only medicine is to just go right back to work. Now give me Hillary's number so I can call her."

I've worked hard to follow John's advice. That same day it occurred to me: "The Senate might be needed to save this country." I decided right then that I didn't need to sort out all my feelings right away. Just like at the end of a hike, I simply needed to stuff them in my pack and carry on, knowing that I would have time later to sort it all out. This walk—nearly three years later—is part of that process.

I start early and it is a fine day for walking—it's in the nineties again but seems a bit cooler because of breeze and shade and there is no prospect for more rain today. At some point, I reach Elkwallow Wayside along Skyline Drive and splurge on a cheeseburger and chocolate shake.

Splurging is always good to do when working hard, and it is especially good because I am going so minimal otherwise. Two of my vices are coffee and bourbon, but I am bringing neither on the hike. The heat of hiking in the summer makes coffee seem unnecessary. And while bourbon always seems welcome and necessary, extra liquid just adds too much weight. So I save coffee and bourbon for trail towns where they can be part of something special when I stop.

I have been feeling good about no shoulder or knee pain on this stretch, but after four days of intense heat, I experience a problem common in others that I have never felt in all my years of hiking: blisters. My boots are fine; there is no problem with friction on my heel or toes. But sweat and rain have left my socks perpetually damp. And wet socks have produced sizable blisters on the bottom of both heels and the balls of both feet. I am walking pretty fast, but with increasing pain each step. I'll need a consult from my Marine son when I get home.

I encounter a solo hiker called Boomer at an empty shelter mid-afternoon and we talk about her northbound thru-hike. She has been with a group of people for weeks but they have now moved a couple of days ahead of her and she's clearly a little down. The physical part of a thru-hike is tough enough; the mental part is even harder. With a group of people, she felt buoyed along the way. Now that she is hiking solo, that motivation is sorely missed. And the feeling is compounded by the Virginia Blues—the feeling that you *never* get out of Virginia. Thru-hikers get a rush crossing state lines. But with nearly 560 AT miles in Virginia, even the fastest hikers take weeks to get through the Commonwealth. One more hot day on a trail with no milestone in easy reach can make your spirits sag.

I think about an old motto that University of Virginia men's basketball coach Tony Bennett uses with his team. UVA won a national championship a few months back, and Tony frequently said: "To go fast, go alone. To go far, go together."

I have done eighty miles with a full pack in rain and heat in five full days and two half days at age sixty-one after not carrying a backpack for many years. I have proven to myself that I can go fast alone—or at least fast enough. But as I think about how far I still have to go after my finish later today, I am elated that friends and family will join with me for significant portions of it later on. It makes it easier to contemplate the rest of the trip to know that I will be with people I care about for much of it.

I hobble the last few miles on blister-sore feet. Anne and I set a tentative meeting time of 5:00 p.m. I exit the AT at Thornton Gap at precisely 5:03 and don't have long to wait. Anne has driven hundreds of miles from Syracuse and hits the trailhead at 5:15. Thirty-five years of marriage have given us well-synced internal clocks. She sees me shuffling toward her like an old man, and I can't tell whether the look on her face is alarm or amusement.

8

Okay. Now this thing gets serious.

I did two long weekends—three days in May and four days in July—to see if this hike was doable. On each day, I found myself thinking, *I don't think I can do the whole Virginia AT*. But I pressed on. Eighty miles down—479 to go.

I am starting a big stretch during an unusually long August Senate recess. I will hike for sixteen days, take a weekend off for Senate responsibilities in Hampton Roads, and then hike another twelve days. This won't get me all the way to Tennessee but it will get me into far Southwest Virginia—probably within a week of the finish.

And I will do the next twenty-eight days during a summer of intense heat. Most Virginia communities are shattering records with the number of ninety-plus-degree days vastly exceeding those in any previous year. Rainfall is low, water sources are starting to dry up, and many folks are staying off the trail.

There are some major changes since the earlier days of the hike. First, Anne has been asked to assume the presidency of George Mason University—the biggest public university in Virginia, with nearly forty thousand students—for one year, starting August 1. It's a bolt from the blue—she has been on the faculty, teaching education policy, but the abrupt move of the current president to another university led the board to ask her rather than a provost or dean to assume the interim leadership role. I am very proud of her. She needs to be a workaholic for the first month or so, meaning that she is glad to have me out of her hair for a few weeks!

The second change is that I have worked to solve the pain issues from my first two hikes—knee pain, shoulder pain, and blisters. Advice from my infantry-officer son should be helpful. We'll see how I do.

Third, I have adjusted my food and drink. Eating cold food for the early days of the hike meant I hardly ate. I now carry a Jetboil stove and dehydrated food. My diet remains simple: oatmeal and instant coffee in the morning (after giving in to my coffee vice, the quality of my hike immediately improves); no lunch; minor snacks along the way (Hershey's Kisses, trail mix, etc.); a two-serving backpacker meal for dinner. I still have no bourbon but will gladly accept the kindness of strangers.

Finally, the remainder of my hike will be a mix of solo and accompanied. I did the first seven days entirely by myself so I could focus on my body, my gear, and whether this hike was even in the realm of possibility. Plus, I didn't want loved ones to hear me cry, curse, or pray to be put out of my misery.

Today's stretch picks up at Thornton Gap. I am shooting to get about eighty miles to Rockfish Gap, the southern end of the Shenandoah National Park, by the end of the week. For the first three days, I will be hiking with my friend Ned, probably the best hiker I know.

I am blessed with good friendships and have two regular groups of outdoor companions. Ned is part of the same Richmond group I'm in. It is a loose bunch of eight to ten neighbors who hike and travel together; we meet Tuesday mornings at a local diner in a tradition of more than fifteen years. The group has done multiple hikes around Virginia. We also have circuit-hiked Mont Blanc in the Alps and walked along the Alta Via 1 in the Dolomites of Northern Italy. Four of the Richmond crew, starting with Ned, will join me for portions of my AT hike.

Ned is a great hiker, spending a lot of time over the years on the nearly five hundred miles of trails in Shenandoah National Park. People often think of politicians as natural conversationalists, but Ned is the master talker between the two of us, keeping up a steady stream of gab about the trail, sports, music, family, politics, anything. He will pull anyone into a conversation, meaning that we have extended chats with each person we pass on the trail for the next three days.

But Ned doesn't camp. To be more precise, he does not like sleeping on the ground. With Ned, it is either day hikes or figuring out how to find a bed every night on a multiday hike. This complicates my third rule of "Camp when I want," but it's worth it. We will hike south from Thornton Gap to Swift Run Gap in three days, stopping the first night at a PATC cabin and the second night to stay in a cabin at Lewis Mountain Campground. He will drop off midday of the third day when we hit Swift Run Gap, and I will continue hiking solo.

Our fifteen-mile stretch today is punctuated by a stop at Skyland, a resort run by a Park Service concessionaire right on the trail, and multiple crossings of the Skyline Drive. We have reached out to Jennifer Flynn, the superintendent of Shenandoah National Park, to ask her to lunch so we can quiz her about the park. Over burgers, we talk about the big maintenance backlog they are experiencing, the changing patterns of how people use the park, and the already notable effects of climate change on the flora and fauna. Warming temperatures affect the ability of species to reproduce and live. Some move to higher and higher elevations to stay cool. And when the temperatures warm enough even at the highest peaks, they simply disappear from the park.

Jennifer also talks to us about bears, repeating multiple times that "there has never been a bad human-bear interaction in the history of Shenandoah National Park." But she goes on to tell us about bears clawing their way into tents at the Gravel Springs and Blackrock Huts in the last few weeks, making me wonder how she defines a "bad human-bear interaction." I camped at Gravel Springs in July and will be at Blackrock in a few days.

After our lunch, Jennifer presents us each with a small AT pin that we put on our packs. She asks where I will stay and whether I have a reservation for a tent site later in the week when I get to the Loft Mountain Campground. When I say no, she says she will make one for me and I can pay when I arrive.

As we near the end of the day, I am hiking well ahead of Ned on a stretch of trail where there is a sheer cliff going up on my left and a sheer drop on my right. I round a turn and there is a very large male black bear about ten yards ahead of me, standing directly in the middle of the trail. Between the cliff and the drop-off, neither of us has anywhere to go.

I assume my largest posture—standing up straight so my pack makes me look bigger, my arms and hiking pole stretched out—and start whistling loudly. The bear looks at me for a while and then starts ambling away on the trail, going the same direction that I am trying to go. I follow slowly, whistling as I walk. We round a few bends like this, the bear leading and me following, until the sheer cliff face on the left gets a little less steep. I am amazed at how this enormous bear becomes so agile, climbing a fifty-foot cliff lightning fast to get to the woods above. He is gone in seconds and I realize why they tell you that you can never outrun a bear going uphill. If you have to, you should go downhill because bears can have balance problems on a downslope. Regardless, the streak of no bad human-bear interactions in SNP remains intact. I guess Jennifer was right.

Ned and I reconnect after that and finish for the day at the PATC Rock Spring Cabin that Ned reserved. He is a longtime PATC member. I have never joined but I should. Old Guide says that the rules for membership, circa 1959, include a positive vote by two-thirds of the club members, or around 67 percent. I have never gotten more than 58 percent in any election in my life! (Fortunately, you can join today without a membership vote.)

The cabin—built in 1936—is simple: no electricity or running water, with a privy nearby and a spring just yards away. We spent a night here many years ago in a howling sleet storm—ten people, a mix of adults and kids from the neighborhood, packed in like sardines on four double bunks and the floor, tending a woodstove all night to keep warm. I was governor then and two of our cabinmates were Virginia State Police from my security detail, reminding me often that other governors didn't make them come out to hike and camp in awful weather. Ned designed a goofy trivia game that kept the group laughing until our sides hurt.

We talk about that memory as we eat dinner outdoors in the ninety-degree heat. I fill a collapsible dog bowl I brought along with cold water from the nearby spring and we use it to wash up before turning in. With only two of us, the cabin feels empty. We hit the bunk beds, which are nothing more than wooden platforms with a gym mat–style pad for a mattress on each. No matter the circumstances, hiking wears you out enough that any bed will do.

9

The hike today is one I have done a number of times—thirteen miles from the Rock Spring Cabin to Lewis Mountain Campground, a National Park Service campground that is right on the AT and Skyline Drive. Per Ned's "no sleeping on the ground" rule, we have reserved a cabin at Lewis Mountain. A real cabin with electricity and running water!

This stretch of trail in Shenandoah National Park is delightful. It's better maintained than most of the AT, and dozens of side trails bisect it to facilitate the many day hikers visiting the park. You get great views both east into the Virginia Piedmont and west into the Shenandoah Valley. And, since you are in a national park, there are more amenities than on other stretches. After a few miles, the trail goes through Big Meadows, a large natural meadow on the top of the mountain ridge with campsites, an old lodge, cabins, horseback riding, and popular day-hiking trails. Not ones to miss an amenity, Ned and I buy sandwiches from the coffee bar in the lodge and stake out two rocking chairs on the porch to eat lunch and watch hikers and tourists come and go.

Afterward, we hike the day's relatively easy stretch. We take our time and catch up on family and work. Ned and his wife, Patty, are godparents to our son Woody. Between the two of us, we have six kids, and now that they are spread here and there, there is always news to report. We both are feeling somewhat in transition, with Ned about to switch jobs and me looking for new inspiration to power me in my next chapter of public service after twenty-five years in office. The leisure to talk about these things over the course of a few days, instead of needing to cram all topics into an hour or two, is very pleasant.

Conversation tends to be quite natural on the trail—short talks and much silence while walking, followed by lengthier discussions during rest stops or at day's end.

One of my favorite books is Thoreau's *A Week on the Concord and Merrimack Rivers*, his account of a river trip with his brother. It is equal parts reflection on nature and exploration of male friendship. I am blessed with many longtime friends, and it strikes me that most of my best friends—my two brothers, three brothers-in-law, my Richmond neighbors, my law-school circle—are those with whom I have spent significant time outdoors.

When I grew up, my parents had wonderful friendships with couples they knew from church or the neighborhood. But I don't remember my dad doing things by himself with male friends very often—his social life was as part of a couple. That seemed normal then. But even with a busy schedule—back and forth from Richmond to DC two-thirds of the year—my time together with guy friends has been a pillar of my life during all thirty-five years of my married life. (The same is true for Anne—she is in a book club with seven other women that is approaching thirty years of monthly meetings.) The days of solitude on the trail make me think about how thankful I should be for time with friends.

Ned and I make Lewis Mountain and check into our cabin before 5:00 p.m. The camp store sells cold beer, so I buy two tallboys for us to drink with our freeze-dried dinner. The campground's history—which the Park Service has only recently begun to tell—is equal parts sad, inspirational, and fascinating. When both the Skyline Drive and park were built during FDR's presidency, Virginia donated the land on the condition that the amenities must be segregated. Lewis Mountain Campground was the place set aside for African American tourists. It had cabins and tent sites, a camp store, and a well-loved restaurant that also featured entertainment during peak tourist times. While African Americans were shut out of the lodges and other campgrounds, Lewis Mountain was a very popular destination for Black tourists from around the country. And the food and entertainment proved so notable that white diners also found their way to Lewis Mountain.

The campground, originally called the Lewis Mountain Negro Area, was segregated until 1950, when the National Park Service integrated all its facilities. (They first started with an experiment at the Pinnacles Picnic Grounds—we walked through it yesterday—where they observed whether white and Black folk could picnic together without the world coming to an end!) Even after desegregation, SNP official maps steered Black visitors to Lewis Mountain and white visitors to other facilities until the 1960s. Old Guide just talks about the AT "skirting east of Lewis Mountain campground," with no mention of the cabins, camp store, or other amenities—just "water here in picnic grounds." Old Guide is glad to describe the meals and lodging offered by Miss Nellie Heflin of Linden, but apparently this campground didn't deserve an encouraging word.

My hike is very segregated, now that I think about it. It is a healthy thing to see campgrounds generally full of people diverse in age, race, income, and nationality. Certainly, the day users of SNP are a diverse group. But once you get on the AT, the racial diversity drops substantially and immediately. I again think about John Brown and Benton MacKaye. Brown envisioned the Appalachian range as an overground railway for enslaved people freeing themselves from Southern plantations. I wonder whether MacKaye's dream for a trail for Eastern workers to escape "the various shackles of commercial civilization" had an assumption that they would be white.

With a few exceptions—for example, my Syrian-American day-hiking dentists from day two—I hardly see any minorities on the AT. Outdoor magazines and park officials fret over this—and they should. So should policymakers like me. We need to be more proactive in ensuring everyone feels welcome on the trail. Users of a natural resource become stewards of the resource. As the nation gets more and more diverse, we need increasingly diverse stewards to protect our natural assets from the many pressures they face.

10

It feels good to wake up in a real bed rather than on the ground or a wooden platform. Just outside the cabin, a female deer is scavenging near trash cans. The deer are smart and know there is no hunting allowed in the park, so they are not very afraid of humans. She lets me watch her up close for a while before she wanders off.

Ned and I are hiking a long, hot stretch today, mostly downhill toward Swift Run Gap. Then Ned will drop off to retrieve his car and head back to Richmond. I will do a long climb up Hightop Mountain and hope to spend the night at Hightop Hut.

Our hike is fine but we are at an emotional imbalance; the end is in sight for Ned, while I am left thinking, *I have to go on by myself.* This is the first time on my hike when I have had someone drop off and leave me solo; it's an experience that will be repeated often in the weeks and miles to come.

Everyone always leaves the same way. It's inevitable, I suppose. You work some logistical magic to have them join you on the hike for a while, and then they drop off at a point where it is easy to retrieve a car or get a shuttle or rideshare of some kind. That drop-off point always seems to be where the trail descends to a road located in one of the gaps. Which means that the first thing you confront after losing your hiking buddy is having to climb back up from the gap—usually a long climb, by yourself.

Ned and I hit Swift Run Gap about noon. His car is parked a few miles away and he will hitchhike to it. We sit and eat a snack in the tiny bit of shade we can find. I refill my water bottles at the park entrance station and say my goodbyes. I definitely have the blues as I trudge by myself in the noonday sun up a sharply climbing path.

But the sheer effort of the climb quickly chases away any lingering loneliness. It is hard, getting my body and pack up these mountains—the weather is sticky and hot. Soon all my attention is just focused on the hill and whether I can make it. Each turn promises some relief—at the very least a gentler grade—but the false hope vanishes like a mirage as I round each bend. I can tell by looking at the tree line that I still have a long way to go.

I laugh as I remember a line that Ned and his son Tommy always use on hikes, an all-purpose incantation to lighten the mood when the going gets tough: "There's no *way* we'll make it . . . Where's the helicopter?" (My own incantation for times like these is Samuel Beckett's: "I must go on. I can't go on. I'll go on.") When I finally make it to the crest of Hightop Mountain, the feeling of accomplishment is also a powerful antidote to any blues.

The rest of the trail before Hightop Hut is downhill, and I arrive by 4:00 p.m. I set up my bivy but a steady rain starts at about 5:00 so I move all my gear into the simple three-sided shelter where I am alone all night. Before this trip, I would always choose a tent or bivy over a shelter. There is little privacy in a shelter, and the snoring can be intense when others are there. (That's why most hikers carry earplugs.) Plus, hikers smell bad, a toxic mix of multiple days' body odor, sweat, dirt, damp, and grimy clothes and caked-on bug spray and sunscreen—so bad that anyone farting in a shelter should be thanked for improving the air quality. Finally, shelters have a way of attracting mice and other small creatures who know they can find food there. Nothing like having a mouse run across your sleeping bag—or your face—in the middle of the night. It's happened to me, and I shudder even as I write this sentence.

But it's amazing how your standards change at the end of a long day when you are tired. If I arrive at a shelter and no one is there, I default toward staying in the shelter and saving the five minutes it takes to put up my bivy. And if it's raining or likely to—like tonight—there is enough room in the shelter for my pack and gear and I don't have to worry about putting a poncho around everything and hoping it all stays dry. The rest of the trip will be more shelter and less bivy as a result. But the bivy—weighing less than a pound—is great as backup because it can be set up anywhere and sometimes shelters are full or so unevenly spaced that you can't count on finishing the day anywhere near one.

As I turn in a little after sunset, I hear a "yip-yip-yip-howl" about six hundred yards away. It takes me a minute to realize that it's a coyote. It doesn't sound too menacing though, and I drift to sleep. A little after 2 a.m., I am suddenly awoken by small animals scurrying around in front of and under the shelter, which is built, like most are, about eighteen inches off the ground. I hear the coyote again, no more than fifty yards away at this point. I have never heard a coyote that close and it definitely gets my attention. I turn on my headlamp, wave it around, and hear the coyote scamper off. I slowly fall back asleep and hear nothing more until morning.

11

Up with the sun and all by myself. Breakfast and packing are leisurely—sleeping on the wooden shelter platform makes my joints creaky. Taking things slow helps me limber up. I think of the great nature poet Theodore Roethke and his poem "The Waking."

This poem is full of meaning for me. Here is a motto for my walk: "God bless the Ground! I shall walk softly there. And learn by going where I have to go." And such a hopeful line—"Great Nature has another thing / To do to you and me." Please let it be so—and let me recognize it!

My goal today is Loft Mountain Campground, a sizable National Park Service campground on the AT and Skyline Drive with dozens, maybe hundreds, of RV and tent sites. It is midweek and there is virtually no one else on the trail. The next twenty-five days, in the heart of a heat-blasted summer, will be notable for the absence of other hikers. I pass PATC Ridgerunner Sabine; I saw her several days ago at Gravel Springs. She gives me a backcountry hiking permit to hang on my pack. I guess it will help identify me in the event of an accident. Easier than matching dental records!

As I near Loft Mountain, I can tell from my map app that I am near Skyline Drive. There is a nearby café that is reputed to have a milkshake machine. I exit the trail stage right and bushwhack through the forest to get to the paved road. A mile or so later, I come upon the simple café, although in the pounding summer sun it looks more like the Emerald City in the Land of Oz to me. But I must have been punished for seeking such creature comforts—the milkshake machine is broken. I settle for a cheeseburger and Dr Pepper.

Afterward, I climb nine hundred feet up a long path to the Loft Mountain camp store—and then climb even farther to the ranger station where campers check in. I arrive and wait in line behind two large black minivans. When they are done, I amble up and say, "I think the park superintendent made a reservation for me. My name is Tim Kaine."

Ranger Samantha and campground hosts Mike and Scott break up laughing. "We've been waiting for you all day. Jennifer said you would come but we were sure you would be in a black Suburban. And then you arrive, a backpacker on foot standing in line behind two black Suburbans."

I pay my thirteen bucks and am directed to the tent site Jennifer had reserved for me, which offers the best view in the park. (For those who want to experience this bliss, it is tent site A-20.) I set up the bivy and make dinner, watching a beautiful sky darken at day's end. People keep coming by wanting to look at the view from my camp.

After enjoying the zen of a magnificent mountaintop view for a while, I am delighted when Mike and Scott drop by with camp chairs and cold beer. They tell me about themselves—retirees who serve as volunteer campground hosts in national parks nine months a year. They drive their RV to a park and get a free site for three months in exchange for taking care of the campsites and campers. After the three months are up, it's on to another national park. I ask what they do the next three months of the year. Drive the RV to a vacation spot, of course. This has been their life for more than twenty years.

Why do it? "We love this country—and as retirees, volunteering in national parks is our way of saying thank you to the US."

Used to RV living, they eye my bivy skeptically. And when the breeze picks up, they take their leave. The wind howls all night and it rains off and on.

12

The wind blowing all night and into the morning was scary, threatening to topple trees and dead branches—they're called "widow-makers" because people have been killed by falling branches and trees in the wild. Some close friends of my sister-in-law and her husband were killed long ago when trees toppled after a microburst struck their tent during the night while they camped in the Adirondacks.

When I wake, random gear from other campers has blown into my campsite. My stuff has stayed put in the bivy and bear box but the wind is blowing so hard that I have a difficult time getting the Jetboil fired up for coffee and oatmeal. At least the driving wind dries my bivy out quickly, and I hit the trail for one of my shortest days—eight miles to Blackrock Hut. I am going easy today because I hope to do twenty-plus tomorrow to meet Anne in Waynesboro at the southern end of the park.

I have been walking for only fifteen minutes when I round a curve and come nearly face-to-face with an adolescent bear, standing right in the middle of the trail and foraging something off a tree. Whatever he's eating must be good because, though he sees me and clearly hears my obnoxious whistling, he does not want to move aside. We stand our ground for a long time this way and he finally finishes breakfast and ambles off the trail as I speed by.

The hike goes quickly but I am a little worried by the notes I am reading in my trail app about the Blackrock Hut being beset with wolf spiders. I do not like spiders, which is a continuous challenge on a hike. Since I often start early in the morning and many spiders spin webs overnight across the trail, I have to get used to breaking spider webs with my body and face as I walk. A night in or near a hut with wolf spiders—they look pretty fearsome—is not my cup of tea.

When I arrive in the early afternoon, I scour the shelter and surroundings and find that either the wolf spiders have vanished or, more likely, the hiker writing about them didn't know the difference between a wolf spider and the innocuous daddy longlegs, which are indeed plentiful here.

The shelter log does confirm another problem that Jennifer hinted at when we had lunch a few days back. About ten days before my arrival, a hiker wrote in the log that a bear pawed its way into his tent looking for food—he had to yell and poke the bear to get it to back off. He was spooked enough by this that he packed up and hiked on in the middle of the night after leaving a warning note in the log. A large Sharpie-drawn note from a park ranger then follows: "Tent sites closed till further notice due to bear activity." And then a new note from three days ago: "Tent sites reopened."

Somehow, the all-clear from three days ago doesn't assuage my bear anxiety. With no one in the shelter, I decide to forego the bivy once again and sleep in the hut. It strikes me that there are many things to be scared of out here. I'm reminded of another Roethke line: "I feel my fate in what I cannot fear." How about feeling your fate in all the things that make you afraid?

When I began this journey in May, there was a murder on the AT in Southern Virginia: a deranged guy wielding a machete killed a veteran who had been thru-hiking as therapy for his PTSD. Anne spotted an article about the murder in the newspaper and made sure I saw it one morning at breakfast.

I do meet some oddballs in the wild, many with visible big knives hanging from their belts, a few with sidearms, and more than one carrying a machete. A few clearly are hiking under the influence, as one note in a shelter log makes clear: "Alcohol, caffeine, methadone, nicotine—then hike again!" One hiker threatens friends of mine staying at a shelter by repeatedly asking, "Do I scare you?"

And it's not just the people: bears, bats, coyotes, spiders, and snakes—black snakes, timber rattlesnakes, and copperheads—are legion here. One shelter is beset with ravenous and possibly rabid raccoons. Big vultures and buzzards gnawing chunks of dripping red flesh from carcasses are common.

Even things that are supposedly inanimate are deadly: dead branches fall all the time—a big one dropped with a loud crash ten yards ahead of me on the trail in the middle of a still, sunny afternoon just as I had stopped to drink some water. Like I said earlier, they call them widow-makers for a reason.

There are so many ways to hurt yourself. Falls are common and can do serious harm, especially when you are far from a road or other hikers. Cell reception is spotty, so you can never be sure you will be able to call for help if you need it.

Lightning threatens often in summer storms that turn the sky pitch-black. One of our scariest family camping memories is when, many years ago, we were forced to race down from a peak way above tree line during a lightning storm. And the rain can pound down—I stop at one AT shelter by a tiny pastoral creek in a steep hollow that has multiple signs warning of flash floods.

But the real water problem is *not too much*. Water is getting scarcer and scarcer, and sometimes my thirsty self needs to drink it immediately upon arriving at a stream, not really giving my purification tablets the three hours they need to do their magic. What parasites or brain-eating amoebas lurk in the cool water I have been hoping for hours to find? Norovirus—a nasty intestinal bug caused by poor hygiene and bad water—is a common fear on the AT. The shelter logs are filled with stories of hikers diverted off the trail by cramps, vomiting, diarrhea.

Sunburn and heat exhaustion are a real possibility in the summer. But Old Guide overdoes this worry, saying that "shorts should be worn with much caution." Didn't they have sunscreen in 1959? I wear my shorts with casual insouciance, indeed abandon. But hey—I always walk on the wild side.

Mosquitos and other swarming insects are unlikely to be that dangerous, but they are annoying as hell. In the higher elevations, the wind and cooler temperatures keep them away, but as you descend toward water sources, they find ways to feast on you.

The biggest danger is the smallest thing—ticks. Lyme disease from deer ticks is common in Virginia and northward along the trail. Rocky Mountain spotted fever is also a risk in the East with the prevalence of American dog ticks. The Longhorn tick has a bite that confers an allergy to red meat—I have friends who have been so stricken while hiking in the Commonwealth. Another tick that feeds off mice and chipmunks carries Powassan virus, which can cause encephalitis. One of my Senate colleagues and friends, Kay Hagan of North Carolina, got Powassan virus after a 2016 hike and suffered a stroke-like brain injury a few weeks later. She never fully recovered and died of her condition in 2019. I use DEET-based tick and bug lotion liberally and check myself for ticks every day, but some are smaller than a freckle and very hard to spot.

And then there's the fear of failure. Will I get lost? Am I too old to finish this? Can I handle this much time by myself? Will I look like a fool if (when?) I scrap the whole thing after telling folks that I was going on this adventure?

If you stop and think about any of this stuff, it can drive you nuts. More than one of my Senate colleagues, when I tell them about my hike, expresses disbelief and urges me not to do it. Most of my staff feel the same way. (When they don't succeed in talking me out of it, they give me laminated cards with contact information that I am to carry in case any passersby come across my expired or expiring body.) My hiking-expert buddies unsuccessfully urge me to invest in a satellite phone for constant ability to communicate in the event of an accident. My eighty-five-year-old parents in Kansas City worry about me every day and chart my progress on a map based on my periodic photos from the trail. Should I take it as a good or bad sign that my wife and kids are uniformly supportive? Come to think of it, my life insurance is paid up. . . .

Enough of this pleasant reverie. If I am scared, what about the young teacher who arrives an hour or so after I set up in the shelter? She sees that there is plenty of room inside, but like many solo hikers, she has a tent that she can use on her own. Maybe she likes a tent or maybe she is wary of strangers, especially solo hikers like me, in a shared space like a shelter.

We talk later at the picnic table, and after she is apparently satisfied that I am not *too* weird, she tells me that she's trying to complete a hike that she began last year. She came within two hundred miles of completing a flip-flop thru-hike (Maine to Harpers Ferry and then Springer Mountain to Harpers Ferry) but then fell and broke her ankle. Getting so close but then having an injury is a common thing—hugely disappointing. But she is back this season to wrap it up.

As we talk, a mother and daughter arrive, leading a big, friendly dog on a long leash. The daughter—an intercollegiate cross-country runner—thru-hiked the AT when she graduated from college two years ago. The two of them are now training for a hike on the Pacific Crest Trail next year with a younger sister who is about to graduate from college. When I naively ask the mother about how much hiking she has done, she starts reeling off the names of trails and mountains in Southern Virginia, most of which I have never done. And the dog, Django, is a major source of entertainment with a bizarre appetite for daddy longlegs which he amply satisfies as we talk.

Mom and daughter ultimately set up a tent as well and I fall asleep comforted with the knowledge that Django will bark loudly if the Blackrock bear returns in the night—and that I no longer have to worry about daddy longlegs.

13

More Old Guide wisdom, this time an epigraph from Myron Avery at the start of each volume: "Remote for detachment, narrow for chosen company, winding for leisure, lonely for contemplation, the Trail leads not merely North and South but upward to the body, mind and soul of man." Who wouldn't want to do the AT with that description?

Today will present three challenges—heat, distance, and vanishing water sources. The heat is now my daily hiking companion, with most days topping ninety degrees. I have varied my mileage with a low of four miles on a partial day early in the hike and a high of eighteen miles. Today, I am trying to push myself to do twenty-one miles. The reason? Anne will drive to the southern end of Shenandoah National Park, where the AT crosses I-64 at Rockfish Gap, and hike in a few miles to meet me. We will then drive to Waynesboro, a well-known trail town just a few miles away, to have a date night.

The teacher hiker I met yesterday has just done the same stretch coming north and tells me that water is scarce. I fill up my bottles with the knowledge that two liters will have to last me for thirteen miles until I reach a hut with a slow trickling spring where I can restock.

The hike has ups and downs and a number of Skyline Drive crossings. I cross many water sources that have gone dry in the August heat and watch my supply dwindle first in one bottle and then the other. But the prospects of seeing Anne, staying in an air-conditioned motel with a shower, and going out for a non-freeze-dried dinner eaten off a plate instead of out of a bag are good motivators.

Meeting up with Anne, a strong woman in hiking and all other categories, makes me think of how many strong and independent women

52

I am meeting on the hike. The teacher and the mother-daughter team from last night are good examples. Cheryl Strayed's book *Wild*—about her solo hike on the Pacific Crest Trail—is a motivator as well. Many use a long hike to test themselves, celebrate an accomplishment like a graduation, or mark a career or relationship transition. Ben Montgomery's *Grandma Gatewood's Walk* is an amazing story of Emma Gatewood's hike on the AT in the 1950s, done at least in part to escape the horrible restraints placed on women at the time. Anyone doing the hike has to confront their own fears—and doing so is a real confidence builder. But our society still places obstacles in women's way; it is wonderful to see female hikers of all ages tackling the tough AT and showing that they are up to any challenge.

My whole career, especially my political career, has been built with the support of strong women—colleagues, volunteers, campaign managers, cabinet secretaries, agency heads, Senate staffers, my wife and daughter, my mother and mother-in-law. I would never have been elected to anything without women voters. Like most Democrats, I narrowly lose the male vote in most of my elections but manage to win by taking a large share of the female vote.

It was one of the joys of my life to support Hillary Clinton, a strong woman by any definition, in the effort to elect the first woman president of the United States. Being on the ticket with her gave me the chance to offer something back to all the women who have supported me in such great ways. And how disappointing to fall short—the feeling of letting both Hillary and so many other women down has not completely gone away.

It was tough to see the double standard that was applied to Hillary—demeaned for foibles far less momentous than those overlooked in her opponent, sideswiped by a virtuous but self-absorbed FBI director who followed agency rules in keeping quiet about the serious investigation into her opponent's connections to foreign actors while seeking headlines about the more trivial investigation into her emails. Neither investigation led to any conclusion of criminal conduct, but one was repeatedly aired before the electorate, including in the pivotal days right before the election. The most revolting thing of all was the spectacle of Donald Trump leading big crowds in chants of "Lock her up"—something that's more at home in a dictatorship than in a leading democracy.

And it was sad to see Hillary's personality so misunderstood. She's tough because she's *had* to be to succeed in professions of law, politics, and diplomacy that have been so dominated by men. That toughness put off some who saw it as defensive, cold, or overly cautious. But I got to see the Hillary who would go out of her way to quiet the crew on the campaign bus at a rest stop so that the bus driver could complete a phone call with her teenage daughter back home. I witnessed the care she lavished on Tyrone, a young press staffer back at headquarters who was diagnosed with colon cancer during the campaign. (I officiated Tyrone's wedding in May 2018 and then spoke at his funeral six months later.) Why couldn't others see what I saw? Hillary was not a perfect person or perfect candidate—who is? But she was and is a caring woman, accomplished professional, devoted mother and grandmother, dutiful public servant, patriotic American. She would have been a superb president.

Still, who am I kidding? A sentient American can hardly profess surprise at an unqualified man being chosen over a qualified woman. It happens every day, both here in the US and all over the world. And while we are better than many societies in treatment of women, we are uniquely bad at electing women to national office. We haven't had a woman president. But let's look deeper—the US Congress, made up of 23.6 percent women as I write this, is seventy-sixth in the world in terms of the percentage of women in our national legislative body. We are tied with Afghanistan, but behind China, Iraq, Vietnam, Israel, the UK, Mexico, Canada—and far behind the global leader, Rwanda, which has a national legislative body that is 61 percent women. As a country, we have so much more to do.

I get to my water stop about 2:00 p.m. and am just about dry.

As if the long day isn't enough, a detour to veer around a power line reconstruction has added an extra mile to the hike. The shelter and water source are about six hundred yards off the trail so I drop my pack and take the empty water bottles in search of a refill. I finally see a tiny wooden sign with the word "Spring" carved next to an arrow. But when I arrive, the water source is a muddy trickle across the trail that seems completely inadequate in flow and too gritty to stomach. I am not sure what to do and I definitely need some water if I am to do another eight miles today.

As I stand there frustrated, I hear a faint gurgling sound and cut through brush and undergrowth on the left side of the small trail. A few yards uphill the spring emerges from underground and flows over a small rock waterfall, no more than six inches high. It takes a long time to fill two liters, but the water is cold and seems clean—it had better be because I need a drink now and can't wait three hours for my purification pills to work.

The cold water does wonders and I push on without any lunch. I am still having trouble eating in the middle of the day. The heat and effort make the thought of food unappealing even as I am vaguely aware that I lose energy as the afternoon wears on. But with Anne as my motivator I pick up the pace. I consider hitchhiking toward her at one road crossing but few cars are on the Drive, so I press on after five minutes of halfhearted attempts.

Now I get to the final four-mile stretch, where I expect to see her at any moment as I round a turn. The map shows the trail tracking the Drive; it is going steadily downhill. But the trail is routed on a ridge above the Drive—a rocky up-and-down section with bad footholds. Not the way I want to finish after having already done eighteen miles. At one point, a hornet flies down from above like a guided missile and stings the base of my right index finger. (For the first time, I understand the origin of the term "beeline.") I can't shake the hornet off and have to pull it out as the venom from the sting causes intense pain for five minutes and a lessening throb for the next hour.

Finally, I round a corner and Anne is there, climbing up to meet me. She is now two weeks into her new job as college president and has as many stories for me as I have for her. She spies my unshaven face, dirty clothes, leaner frame, and somewhat stooped shuffle and seems a bit worried. But when we reach her car, now 160 miles into the hike, and the pack comes off, my energy and gait improve markedly.

As we drive down into Waynesboro, I ask her, "When was the last time you picked up an unshaven hobo on a trail and took him to a motel?"

Her response? "I'll never tell."

14

In Waynesboro, I have a Sunday down while I wait for two friends from California to join me for the next few days. Anne leaves in the mid-morning to go visit her parents, and I avail myself of air-conditioning, hot water, and laundry at the motel. I also restock food for the next six days on the trail, a stretch of about eighty miles until I reach the James River near Lynchburg.

My friend Charles and his son Adam arrive at dinnertime and we grab barbecue as we plot the next three days. Charles is part of my second guys group—eight friends who connected when I was in law school at Harvard. Four of us were in law school; two were recent Yale business school grads working in Boston; one was a Mizzou college buddy working for a federal appellate judge after going to UVA School of Law. And Charles was a Midwesterner with a Harvard undergrad degree in film who was running the concessions operation for a local movie chain and planning a Hollywood future for himself.

The group of eight has stayed close over forty years even though we have spread to the winds. We started vacationing together early in our time in law school and have kept it up—first as guys, then guys with a shifting collection of girlfriends, then guys with wives, then guys with wives and kids. We have been all over the country and world together to hike, sail, kayak, bike, judge BBQ contests, listen to music. We refer to ourselves collectively as "Nightwing," a stupid name that we cribbed from an Air Force country-and-western band we heard repeatedly in 1996 when we cycled across Iowa on the annual RAGBRAI. We have celebrated professional and personal successes, commiserated over our challenges and failures, lived the powerful ups and downs that come with marriage and kids, grappled with health issues. One friend, Scott, has a family farm south of Charlottesville that has become a regular meeting place for us all.

Together with my Richmond friends, and my brothers and boyhood friends in Kansas City, the Nightwing crowd has been a real godsend— keeping me sane, inspiring and consoling me, making me laugh. And the two guys who have been the glue holding us together are Charles and Scott. They each have a gift for making and keeping connections as the rest of the group go through cycles of greater or lesser availability over the years. I am psyched to have Charles with me now. Scott is likely to join, too, but his plans are characteristically up in the air as to when he will pop up—maybe later this week, or at the end of the month, or in October as I finish.

After college, Charles amazed us all by ditching the popcorn concession in Boston, moving to LA, and actually succeeding in the business side of movies, network and cable television, live performance, and video gaming. He has brought his youngest son, Adam, a Harvard undergrad just about to begin his senior year, to hike with us. We make an interesting group. Charles might be in the best shape of any of my friends, but he is not a regular camper. I am a great camper but creaky in the joints. Adam helps run the outdoor orientation program at Harvard and he is young, super fit, and wilderness savvy—and a bit of a snob about trail comforts that the old-guy hikers enjoy.

We get a ride to the trailhead from a local shuttle driver who tells us how cell phones have completely altered the AT experience. Most of this change is good—phones mean better maps and they make it easier to summon help or connect with family. It's always good to access a weather report online or arrange to meet a friend or find a shuttle driver. But some of the change is not great—a key part of the experience is to disconnect from the daily grind, something you cannot do completely while still tethered to your phone. It is hard to believe that people hiked the trail for decades without phones.

We start our three-day walk under a blazing sun. The day—and many of the days during August—is notable for the massive presence of butterflies. Again and again we come across swarms of multicolored enchanters, monarchs, zebra swallowtails, and black butterflies with bright-blue wing tips predominating. I have never seen this before, but I soon remember that I almost never hike in these mountains during August.

Our goal is to hike thirteen miles to a picnic area on the Blue Ridge Parkway called Humpback Rocks that will have bathrooms, potable water, and picnic tables. There's no camping allowed at the picnic area, but the side trail leading to the AT is supposed to have some good spots to pitch a tent.

Charles is prepping to give a talk at his Harvard fortieth class reunion about language transitions in modern life—changes driven by new ways of seeing race, gender identity, feminism, masculinity. We offer him advice as we walk.

The trail is eerily quiet. Aside from one hiker we pass at the start of the day, we see no one on the AT—no one at the beautiful triple-deck shelter where we stop for lunch; no one at the tent campsites abutting a big cliff overlook where we are tempted to stop for the day due to the sheer beauty of the view. Even when we hit the picnic area, we are late enough in the day that most day visitors are gone. We claim a picnic table for cooking dinner, make liberal use of the running water in the bathrooms, and enjoy a pleasant evening sampling a collection of freeze-dried dinners.

After we hang all our food high in nearby trees—Humpback Rocks is notably beset with bears—we set up camp for the night in the woods, about two hundred yards away from the picnic tables. Charles and Adam's gear looks familiar—it is my son Nat's. Charles and Adam flew in from California empty-handed and then visited Nat, a Marine living in DC whose basement is like a makeshift outfitter with all the gear he has accumulated over the years. I'm glad Nat was able to help them out, but I'm mostly just happy that—on the fourteenth day of the hike—I finally get a night in the bivy without any rain.

15

Though our camping spot is near an area well-known for bear activity, we neither see nor hear any action in the night and sleep soundly. We have enough cell reception when we wake to check the weather forecast and see that rain is expected during the hike today, so we get back on the trail quickly.

The rain starts almost immediately—a steady drizzle that lasts for about three hours. Every foothold is slanted and slippery, and the heat makes wearing a rain jacket uncomfortable. We slog on.

Adam has accepted a full-time job with a management consulting firm he worked with in DC this summer. To pass the time, Charles and I give him advice along the lines of what we wish we had known when we started our first jobs. Things like: never bring a problem only—always have a proposed solution too; don't ever burn a bridge unless absolutely necessary; think long-term; take care with written communication—especially emails; pick a place to make a difference—geography matters; the team you work with will be just as if not more important than the work itself. Adam encourages and humors us by listening and asking questions.

We cross the Blue Ridge Parkway at an overlook. As we stop to rest, a couple from Connecticut pulls up and asks us about our hike. They have decided to move south and are cruising down the parkway, pulling off every so often to explore places where they might consider living. They want a farm near a nice-sized town or city in Virginia or North Carolina. We go into Virginia sales mode—Charles even more enthusiastically than me. (I'm in politics but he's in showbiz.) We tell them to visit Roanoke, the town where Anne grew up. In return, they give us cherries and cashews as they drive off.

Nearly nine miles later, we reach the Maupin Field Shelter at lunchtime, and now the sun is out. Boots off, socks drying, restocking water at a barely trickling spring—all by ourselves. The trail log in the shelter describes an active timber rattler near the fire pit, so we stay alert.

We have a choice to make after lunch. Our preferred ending is at the Harpers Creek Shelter; the AT winds about seven miles south to that point, but I have done this stretch of the trail—known as Three Ridges—many times in both directions. There is an alternate trail—the Mau-Har Trail—that follows a stream that promises waterfalls and good views. I have seen it before but never hiked it. The Mau-Har Trail connects with the AT very near the Harpers Creek Shelter. This alternate route is two miles shorter. The trail app warns that it isn't really a shortcut because it's so challenging, but the thought of waterfalls on a hot day wins out and we veer off onto the Mau-Har Trail.

This is a choice that comes up often on the trail: stay on white-blazed AT only or consider alternate routes, normally marked by blue blazes painted on pathside trees. The first time I faced this dilemma was on the very first day of this hike, when I was at Harpers Ferry. I had exited the AT and hiked half a mile down to the Blackburn Trail Center. After getting water and visiting with the manager, I asked him to point me the way back to the trail. He asked, "Are you a purist?" I didn't know what he meant, so he explained that I could walk directly back up the trail that I had just walked down, get to the AT crossing, and turn south—but there was another trail up the hill that put me on the AT south of the turnoff I had taken. It was a shortcut, although the extra walking down and back from Blackburn was easily more than the small stretch of the AT I would miss if I took the shortcut—which I did end up taking, my first compromise away from AT white-blaze purism. My rationale? Alternate routes are okay so long as they do not shorten miles.

As I hiked, I made slight variations to a pure southbound Virginia AT hike. I would exit the AT and walk to a road or town for provisions or an overlook or milkshake. I hiked two stretches south to north because it facilitated meeting up with folks who were connecting with me on the trail. For four days I slackpacked—hiking with an eight-pound daypack but not the full thirty-plus pound backpack. A plan is good; so is being flexible. One of the great bits of hiker wisdom is "Hike your own hike." Not someone else's hike, but your own. A life lesson as well.

The Mau-Har with Charles and Adam is the only time I take an alternate route that saves miles. It is both worth it and a royal pain. The trail descends from the Maupin Field Shelter at a steep clip and then starts to follow a rushing stream with cool waterfalls as promised. Because water is in short supply today, it is good to be close to a full water source. But the trail is tough because it keeps dropping down to the creek banks and then back up to the bluffs above the creek. With the trail still wet from morning rain, it is slow going.

Eventually, the alternate trail veers away from the creek and climbs steadily up to the intersection with the AT. Hot and sweaty work. It doesn't help that to puncture the strain of the climb, Charles keeps breaking into the chorus of "The Happy Wanderer": "Fol de ri, fol de ra, fol de ri, fol de ra ha ha ha ha ha." His sarcastic delivery of "ha ha ha ha ha" is funny—the first time.

But we eventually make it to the AT, mock-curse the founder of the Mau-Har alternate, and hike another mile to Harpers Creek Shelter, a wooden-framed Forest Service shelter just like the others along the way. The setting is magnificent, with the shelter perched on a ledge about fifty feet above a small gorge cut by Harpers Creek with tent sites and a picnic area on the other side.

The gorge gives evidence that Harpers Creek can be a torrent, but now there is barely enough water to use for cleaning and cooking. No trickles or waterfalls where you can fill a bottle. Adam finds one promising pool, but the surface is skimmed with water bugs and more than a little algae. But he's an ace camper and uses a slowly swirling bandanna to clear a small section of the pool of all bugs and visible plant life. We refill and pray for the potency of our water purification tablets.

We'll part ways the next day, though I'm reluctant to say goodbye to my friends. The trail drops down to the Tye River, a low spot on the trail where Charles and Adam will catch a ride back to their car. The AT then commences the longest climb I will experience, three-thousand-plus feet of elevation gain up The Priest mountain in a little over four miles. Daunted by the hot climb and not looking forward to being alone once again, I pass a restless night.

16

As we head down the trail, finishing the Three Ridges section at a mid-morning pickup spot where the AT crosses the Tye River and Route 56, Charles makes a good observation about the hike. He came expecting the AT experience to be fundamentally about the trail. But even after three days where we only saw a few people, he departs knowing that the AT is at its core a community. He's right—and his observation captures Benton MacKaye's intent.

The trail itself is the organizing principle, to be sure—it's the reason why people are here in the first place. But at the same time, it exists *because of* that vast and unending stream of people who care for it to this day. Who conceived of the trail? Who created the route? Who labored for decades over various reroutings to create the AT of today? Who built the shelters? Who lugged in the picnic tables? Who maintains the trail? This community did.

The AT also exists because of the thousands upon thousands who have walked it—in thru-hikes and section and day hikes—and taken the pictures and told the stories that shared the AT experience with the world. And it has created trail towns and shuttle drivers and hiker hostels and outdoor outfitters and trail angels who otherwise would not be where they are. The AT calls up a collective image that is a creation of this entire AT community. It exists in space but because of this continuous collaboration it has a broader existence—a mystique, really—in the minds of millions, many of whom may never even see it. Much of human activity is simply an effort to structure ways for people to spend memorable time together—and by that standard, the AT has to be one of the best projects ever undertaken.

At midmorning we hit the Tye River, a gorgeous stream I have canoed a few times. Charles and Adam find the shuttle driver to take them back to Waynesboro where they will retrieve their car and head to Dulles Airport. Through the miracles of modern travel, they awake on the wooden deck of the Harpers Creek Shelter deep in Virginia's Blue Ridge Mountains and will go to bed later the same day in their own home a few blocks from the Pacific Ocean.

Partly to avoid goodbyes for a few more minutes and partly to delay the big climb facing me, I hop in the shuttle and have the driver drop me off a few miles away at a country store. After I salute my intrepid friends as they drive off, I get a cold Dr Pepper and a deli sandwich out of the fridge. Even though I am not all that hungry yet, I know that I will need some extra energy today.

I hitchhike back to the trailhead, getting a lift easily, and start the long climb up The Priest, five miles and three thousand feet of elevation gain. It is a steady climb up with endless switchbacks, but not horribly steep except in a few sections. The heat is a factor. I have no companion but there are many day hikers—this is an exceptionally beautiful section of the trail where there are numerous day hikes, including Crabtree Falls, arguably the highest waterfall east of the Mississippi. The views along this stretch can be fantastic, although the full leafy-green cover of summer obscures what you might see from late fall through spring.

I take my walking slow, grateful that I had a midmorning sandwich to add extra fuel for the climb, and get to The Priest Shelter about 2:00 p.m. I had originally thought I might stop here for the night, but after twenty minutes of rest, I get my second wind and decide to keep walking, hoping to do another six miles to the Seeley-Woodworth Shelter.

Every shelter has a trail log—a simple spiral notebook like that purchased by every elementary schooler—and hikers make notes as they pass through. My second wind is at least in part from reading the trail log at The Priest Shelter—perhaps the most famous on the trail because hikers use it to "confess to The Priest" their mostly comic transgressions. The confessions cover an astonishingly wide and funny range of topics, but there are two predominant themes: many are about violating trail rules—illegal fires, tearing out pages from a Bible found in a shelter when there was no toilet paper, sneaking food away from a hiking companion, etc.—while others are about sexual indiscretions, which I will discreetly avoid repeating, mindful of the secrecy of the confessional. Let's just say that weeks of solitude on the trail are an inducement to an exaggerated sexual imagination.

The best single confession in the sexual indiscretion category wasn't even at The Priest Shelter, however. When Charles, Adam, and I passed through the Maupin Field Shelter at lunch yesterday, some guy had written a comical account of indelicate fantasies concerning his fiancée's sister. It stuck out like a sore thumb because confessions are not the norm in that shelter's log. But the last line explained the incongruity: "There are some things you just can't tell a priest."

Laughing as I depart the shelter, I climb farther toward the turnoff to Spy Rock, a bald overlook with a nearly 360-degree view of the area. On a memorable hike many years ago, my kids and I scaled this peak with my friend Scott and both his parents and children. A great memory, both dimmed and made more special because Scott's father Jim, a vigorous outdoorsman who really enjoyed our hike that day, passed away a few years ago.

I keep pushing on all afternoon, passing the two-hundred-mile mark of my hike and gradually losing my second wind before finally arriving at Seeley-Woodworth Shelter around 6:00 p.m., as tired as I can remember ever being on the trail—and yet I have only done fourteen miles today, far from my longest day hiking. But the elevation gain and heat have done me in.

One surefire test of how beat I am at day's end is how hard I endeavor to hang my food out of bears' reach. More and more shelters are starting to have bear boxes: solid metal cabinets with bear-proof doors where you can store food safely. But at the shelters without bear boxes, like this one, you tie a rope to your food bag and throw it over a high tree branch so it's out of reach of the bear. The recommendation is that you should hoist the bag about fifteen to twenty feet off the ground, positioned fifteen feet or so away from the tree trunk so a bear cannot climb up to get it. I can never seem to fully meet the standard, but today I am particularly lame and barely get the bag six feet off the ground before just saying "Screw this" and trudging back to the shelter. If a bear wants freeze-dried food so badly, she can have it.

I am close to sleep in the shelter when, just as the last daylight is fading, a northbound hiker trudges in. He is moving very slowly. We strike up a conversation—he's called Boxcar Willie—and he is out of fuel for his stove. I use my Jetboil to make hot water for his dinner. As he tells his story, I am glad he woke me up.

Willie is a retired wildlife biologist from Utah. He grew up in the Midwest and graduated from the University of Missouri a few years before me. After a life outdoors in the West, what was on his retiree bucket list? Hike the AT. He started in 2018 and did six hundred miles or so, hiking north from Springer Mountain with his wife trailing him in an RV. He is hoping to do another six hundred miles or so this year and will repeat until he finishes the trail.

I ask Willie—with so many great trails out west, why the AT? He has heard about it all his life and always wanted to experience it for himself.

Willie is a good example of the trail community Charles talked about. He has spent his whole life outdoors far away but had the dream of one day hiking the AT. And as he nears seventy, he is finally doing it.

17

Part of the fun of this trip is visiting places that I've been before and recalling highlights from earlier trips. Today, my goal is to hike about fifteen miles to Route 60 and get a shuttle into the nearby trail town of Buena Vista (pronounced in these parts as "Byoo-na Vista"). It's an old industrial town, with many closed factories, and the site of an annual Labor Day parade that marks the start of the fall campaign season every year.

I say so long to Boxcar Willie as he heads north and I head south. My hike today is four long ups and four long downs—up and down to Salt Log Gap, Hog Camp Gap, and Cow Camp Gap before a last climb and descent to the highway. It rained a bit last night and is misty as I start. Before too long, it feels like I'm walking through a steam bath.

This stretch of the trail is really beautiful—especially a long traverse of a breezy high meadow on Cole Mountain—and as I see new views, it strikes me that I actually haven't done as much of the Virginia AT as I thought. When I started the hike, I had the mind frame—"Of course, I've done much of the Virginia AT already." Turns out this wasn't true. What was true is that I had hiked a few stretches of the Virginia AT multiple times. Three Ridges and The Priest, the central and southern Shenandoah National Park, a stretch I will do tomorrow just north of the James River, the area around Mount Rogers. I had logged a lot of AT miles during my thirty-five years in Virginia. But I am reminded today as I pass through northern Amherst County that I have actually seen little of the trail—probably 80 percent of my hike is brand-new to me.

The trail is quiet today and my first encounter with any creature after leaving the shelter is a midmorning sighting of an enormous black snake sunning on the trail. He slithers off, and within one hundred yards I pass some northbound hikers and tell them to watch their feet. They tell me that there is a big timber rattler up ahead, but they are vague about where and I walk eyes down for most of the next five miles. No rattler sighting, thank God.

I make good time, except for one extended side-trail jaunt to find water at a spring far off the trail, and get to my highway pickup spot at about 3:45 p.m. Route 60 is a beautiful, old, mostly two-lane east-west highway through Virginia that predates Interstate 64. It will always be special to me because it's a road Anne and I love to travel, as it climbs over the Blue Ridge and then the Allegheny ranges. We drove our old Ford Escort over this stretch after our wedding as we went to an inn in Lexington to start our honeymoon.

Derek the shuttle driver picks me up and drops me off eight miles away at the Buena Vista Motel, where there is a fifty-four-dollar special rate for hikers. Nothing fancy—hasn't been updated since I first stayed here in 2001—but there is hot water, air-conditioning, an ice machine, and a local restaurant that delivers baked spaghetti and Greek salad right to my door. This is living!

I came here in 2001 as a candidate in my first statewide election. After four terms as a city councilman and mayor in Richmond, I won a primary to become the Democratic nominee for lieutenant governor. I was on a ticket with our gubernatorial candidate Mark Warner, a law-school buddy, and our attorney general nominee, longtime Richmond friend Donald McEachin. Our whole entourage checked into this motel the Sunday night before Labor Day to participate in the annual kickoff of the state campaign homestretch. And now, eighteen years later, I serve with Mark in the Senate and Donald is my congressman.

I don't know how the Buena Vista parade became the big kickoff event, but it was back then and still is today. When the tradition started, the factories were open and the town was a blue dot in the red western half of the state. Now the factories are closed and the area is very

Republican. I've done the event nearly fifteen times over the years—a Monday-morning breakfast at the local high school for Democratic candidates and supporters, mustering for the parade with good-natured banter between the Republican and Democratic marchers, the actual parade along a two-mile route through town crossing back and forth across the road to shake hands and give out candy, and the culmination at a local park where the candidates on the ballot deliver their stem-winding speeches to partisan audiences inside a massive picnic pavilion. Each side tries to blanket the town with campaign posters, which then have to be taken down within twenty-four hours of the parade's ending. Because Virginia has an election every year—federal in the even years and state elections in the odd years—this parade is a real ritual.

I still remember my nerves as I stayed at this motel in 2001—all the Virginia political traditions outside of my home city were new to me. The parade is covered by all the state press, and I was hoping to make a good impression on this Western Virginia audience. Democrats had been through a decade with virtually no wins in Virginia and we were hungry for victory. Anne and the kids and I were abuzz with the sense of adventure as we moved from the familiarity of politics in our city to the unknown of state politics.

How different it feels now—after five of my own statewide campaigns and innumerable visits to campaign for others, Buena Vista is a comfortable known rather than an adventurous unknown. And the restless night I passed here before the big parade in 2001 is now the sound sleep of an exhausted hiker.

Places carry enormous emotional significance for me. I have a good memory for people and faces, but a near-photographic memory of places where I have been. And the reason places stick so well in my memory is that they carry their own emotional tone. How I felt when I was there becomes embedded in my sense memory of the place. And Buena Vista, even on a quiet midweek evening a few weeks before Labor Day, still provokes a rush of memories and emotions.

18

Of course, the problem with taking a night off in an air-conditioned motel is stepping into the heat the next morning. But I am motivated to get a lift back to the trail on a muggy day because I am about to walk a stretch of the AT that is one of my favorite hikes.

At the trailhead, there are flyers seeking information about someone who came hiking here a few months back and then just disappeared. The national forest seems endless—it's not hard to imagine someone getting lost or using the vast wilderness to escape someone or something.

The plan is for this to be a shorter day—eleven or twelve miles from US 60 to a shelter called Punchbowl near the Blue Ridge Parkway. I have done this stretch a number of times. It is a pretty hike that skirts the edge of a reservoir deep in the Blue Ridge that serves as a source of drinking water for the city of Lynchburg, twenty-five miles to the southeast of here.

The reservoir was created by damming up Brown Mountain Creek, a small tributary of the Pedlar River that snakes through the valleys of Amherst County. And as the trail descends from Route 60 to the creek and then follows it miles downstream to the reservoir, the ghost of an old community comes to life.

Enslaved families lived along the creek for decades, and at the close of the Civil War, many of the newly freed peoples decided to stay. Every few hundred yards there are stone ruins of cabins or old mills or animal enclosures. A few interpretive signs along the trail describe life in the tiny valley. The sides of the hollow are so steep that it is amazing to think that people could have farmed here—sunlight would only reach the valley a few hours a day except in the peak of summer.

In the 1920s, the government bought out the families, and the land became part of the national forest and reservoir. Most of the families relocated down to Buena Vista or other small communities in Amherst. But their ancestors lived for years and gave extensive oral histories about life in this small enclave of freed people.

Not surprisingly, Old Guide describes this part of the AT with no reference to the history of slavery: "There are many stone chimneys and walls to show that once the Blue Ridge Creek valleys were lived in and farmed." Even the deepest wilderness in Virginia has profound layers of human history. Like the mostly white families relocated from their mountain ridge homes to create the Shenandoah National Park, these formerly enslaved families had deep roots in this valley stretching back decades when they were forced to leave. It is hard to imagine the heartbreak and anxiety about what new life elsewhere would be like.

If we are wise, we don't think about our own accomplishments without thinking about those parents, teachers, coaches, and friends who helped us to a place where achievement was possible. But our own opportunities and experiences are also so often built in spaces—physical and virtual—where others were pushed aside or cleared out and forgotten. We don't think about them much. Brown Mountain Creek exists as a silent reminder. I cannot think of a more moving section of trail anywhere.

The trail skirts the eastern edge of the reservoir for a few miles. I cross a bridge over the Pedlar River downstream from the dam and face a long climb up to the Blue Ridge Parkway. I am making good progress today and realize that I will finish far earlier than I want to. I carry no book or electronic entertainment with me. (Not reading anything is very unusual for me—I am always reading multiple books, but I usually leave them behind while I am doing outdoor adventures so as to not divert my attention from nature's story.) I have a harmonica to play, but when I get to my stopping point for the day, there is not much to do. Finishing too early is not ideal. Plus, I notice that the trail notes on my app emphasize the presence of very aggressive raccoons who want to ransack backpacks looking for food. I don't want to spend hours fending them off.

Instead, I do something that would have been almost impossible without a cell phone. When I get in a place where there is good reception, I devise an alternative route that will add some extra miles before I meet my wife's cousin Roger near Lynchburg tomorrow. It seems overly complicated now, but as I cross the road near Punchbowl, a shuttle picks me up and drives me about twenty miles south to Petites Gap Road. And I then start walking back north, determined to cover the miles I have skipped before the end of the day tomorrow.

The extra miles I do are in the James River Face Wilderness and I am really out by myself—mile after mile with fantastic views west as the James River cuts through the Blue Ridge. There is no one on the trail. It's a Friday in the summer—you would think that's a good day for hiking, but it's just too hot for most people.

I have done nearly twenty miles instead of my planned eleven or twelve by the time I have finished for the day. It is dark as I limp downhill into Matts Creek Shelter, a standard shelter next to a stream in a deep hollow with little light. (Song lyric fragment that occurs to me often on this walk: "I'd rather be/in some dark hollow/where the sun/refuses to shine/than to stay/here in Missouri/with your memory/haunting my mind.") The hollow is so steep that I see something I rarely see—signs prominent at the shelter, warning that you must be ready to climb to high ground if it starts raining. But it is dry as can be, just enough water in Matts Creek to wash, cook, and fill my bottles.

I eat dinner—all alone at the shelter as usual—and am about to turn in when two guys in camo carrying bow-hunting rigs and heavy packs stroll up. I tell them there is room in the shelter but they are determined to keep hiking in the dark and eventually find a place to set up their tent. Having seen *Deliverance*, I casually ask about the bows. They are in training for an elk hunt in Colorado and want to do a practice hike with all their gear even though they are unlikely to use their bows on this trip. They look at me for a while and say,

"Aren't you Senator Kaine?" Yep. "Aren't you staying in Lynchburg tomorrow night with our friend Roger?" Yep. My reputation—I mean Roger's reputation—precedes me!

Animals are active at this shelter, but now that I am trail-broken, they fascinate rather than scare me. First the bats. Once it's dark, they start flying around in front of the shelter. I can't see them, but the sound is unmistakable: complete silence until they are directly in front of the shelter opening, and the furious beating of wings seems loud enough to be a whole squadron. The sound immediately cuts as they move past the opening. Again and again they swoop by—thirty seconds of silence, a split-second racket, more silence. Repeat ad nauseam.

Just when I am tiring of this, the coyotes start. I was startled the first night I heard "yip, yip, yip, howl," but when I realized that I could chase a coyote off by waving a flashlight around, I lost any fear. So tonight, when a coyote starts up within fifty yards of my shelter, I just decide to be still and listen for a while. So glad I did.

After my nearby coyote howls, another coyote, maybe five hundred yards off, responds in kind. And then faintly—maybe one thousand yards out—a third coyote. There may have been others, too, even farther away. As I lie there and start to drift off, these night stalkers are having an amazing conversation with each other. Their animated talk morphs into my own dreams and I fall asleep believing I am Dr. Dolittle conversing with all manner of creatures.

19

I start early to hike two miles north to the James River and cross the beautiful footbridge—longest on the AT—over our state's signature river around sunrise. This bridge is not just a footbridge—for hikers only—but also the Foot Bridge, named for Bill Foot, the AT enthusiast who led the conversion of an abandoned rail bridge into the current pedestrian walkway. The James River—glistening in the morning light—is named for King James, who chartered the Virginia Company that settled Jamestown Island, about 180 miles downriver, in 1607. That humble settlement became the seed of the entire English colonization of America. If my plan holds, in about two years, I will paddle a canoe under this bridge and later paddle right by Jamestown Island.

Old Guide references a "dirt road to Bedford County Snow Creek Recreation Area for Negroes" on the south bank of the James River. That is long gone, but the creek near Snowden is still thought to be a good fishing spot.

I get a shuttle driver to take me north from the bridge to the Punchbowl shelter, right off the Blue Ridge Parkway where I exited the trail yesterday. Then I hike south for nine miles to get to Johns Hollow. I thought I might be beat after the twenty-mile day yesterday, but I am doing just fine. A common hiking phenomenon is getting your "trail legs" after you have been on the trail for a while. You get used to the exertion and get fitter as you go, absent any accident or fall. I'm definitely getting my trail legs as I approach the midpoint of my hike.

As your body adjusts, the walking gets better because you are more able to focus on your thoughts or surroundings and not be troubled by aches and pains. That's probably why so many over time have found walking to be so healthy, pleasant, and conducive to reflection. Thomas Jefferson loved to walk and wrote: "The object of walking is to relax the mind. You should therefore not permit yourself even to think while you walk. But divert your attention to the objects surrounding you. Walking is the best possible exercise." Henry David Thoreau saw walking much as Jefferson did, a mental escape as much as physical exercise: "In my afternoon walk I would fain forget all my morning occupations and my obligations to society." The poet Samuel Taylor Coleridge walked incessantly and composed "Kubla Khan" from a vision he dreamed following a long walk. Robert Frost was also a walker and built walking into many of his poems: "I have been one acquainted with the night / I have walked out in rain / and back in rain / I've outwalked the furthest city light." Walt Whitman equated walking with independence: "Freedom—to walk free and own no superior." Emily Dickinson filled her poems with observations from her walks or imagined walks: "I started Early—Took my Dog—And visited the Sea." And I've already recited Roethke: "God bless the Ground! I shall walk softly there. And learn by going where I have to go." Abraham Lincoln connected walking with determination: "I am a slow walker, but I never walk back." Martin Luther King analogized walking to moral choice: "Every man must decide whether he will walk in the light of creative altruism or in the darkness of destructive selfishness."

My favorite piece of advice, however, comes from George Fox, the founder of the Religious Society of Friends, more commonly called the Quakers. Fox was an itinerant preacher who walked everywhere in seventeenth-century England. He composed an injunction about living based on his walking: "Walk cheerfully over the earth, answering that of God in everyone."

What beauty—seven distinct thoughts in eleven words!

"**Walk**"—Be vigorous and get moving.
"**Cheerfully**"—Be a pleasant presence to those you encounter
    (a tough thing for the famously disputatious Fox).

"Over the earth"—Get outside your own neighborhood, your own comfort zone.

"Answering"—Two thoughts in one word because you cannot *answer* unless you first *listen.*

"That of God"—the divine spark.

"In everyone"—and remember that the divine spark exists within every person.

Of course, the New Testament stories about Jesus and his disciples have them walking everywhere—sometimes Jesus is alone, sometimes with a small group, sometimes with the multitudes. There's a beautiful old spiritual—"I Want Jesus to Walk with Me."

Powerful things happen on walks: the mercy of the Good Samaritan toward a man beaten while walking to Jericho; the conversion of Saul while walking to Damascus from Jerusalem; the appearance of Jesus to disciples walking on the road to Emmaus a few days after Easter.

And it is not just Christianity that sees the sacred in walking. This is from the Jewish prophet Micah: "And what does the LORD require of you? To act justly and to love mercy and to walk humbly with your God." And Buddha: "No one saves us but ourselves. No one can and no one may. We ourselves must walk the path." Thich Nhat Hanh builds up a whole spiritual practice around the "walking meditation." When I worked with Jesuit missionaries in Honduras forty years ago, one of the highest compliments that could be paid a person, especially a leader, was to note that they were *andando con la gente*"—walking with the people.

As I sit on a picnic table in the sun at Johns Hollow Shelter, where I once took my middle child, Woody, and his high school buddies camping as they approached high school graduation, Roger rounds a corner. We embrace and then finish the hike back to his truck. A cooler with cold beer awaits us, along with a ride into town where I can restock food and fuel for my stove.

We go out for dinner at a local restaurant after getting cleaned up.

But I am sunburned, wearing the only marginally clean clothes left in my backpack. I haven't shaved in nearly two weeks. People keep looking our way, no doubt thinking that I look a little like someone they might have seen before. They definitely recognize Roger.

20

Roger—my wife's first cousin—is a few years older than me. When Anne and I married and decided to live in Virginia, rather than my native Kansas City, I became part of her extended Virginia family with close friends and relatives in Richmond, McLean, Lynchburg, Roanoke, Abingdon, Big Stone Gap, and over the state line in Beckley, West Virginia. I only knew one person in Virginia when I moved here in 1984, but Anne's big family helped me feel at home immediately.

Roger is scaling back his work life and filling the time with outdoor activities—especially road biking and hiking with groups of friends in the mountains of Central and Western Virginia. In addition to being a great host for a bedraggled hiker, he knows the AT sections near Lynchburg and Roanoke well and gives me some tips as he drives me back to Petites Gap after lunch.

Today is a short day—I don't start until late and my hike is straight uphill for five miles, climbing two thousand feet to reach the Thunder Ridge Shelter. This shelter—at about four thousand feet elevation—is the highest overnight spot that I have stayed at, and the coolness is much appreciated after sweating through the ninety-five-plus-degree climb. I am by myself with the exception of a toad who sits right by the pooling spring where I get water. Every time I go to fill up, the toad hops into the spring, making the water seem a little less appealing, but what to do? I hope boiling and purification tablets filter out essence of toad. (I do develop a sizable wart on my left elbow during the hike. Haven't had a wart in decades. Coincidence?)

Spending a night and morning in Lynchburg gave me time to clear through emails, talk to my chief of staff about news of the day and some decisions I need to make on personnel matters, and have a long chat with Anne. I have been in a social media and information blackout on the trail and love getting my fix of info. But now at Thunder Ridge, with no cell reception, I am back in the blackout. This hike has convinced me that I am a social media junkie and need to kick the habit or drastically reduce it. Like virtually everyone in my profession—or maybe all professions these days—I carry an iPhone and iPad with me everywhere. I not only feel naked without my electronic lifeline, but I constantly check it all day long. Much of the checking is even done subconsciously—while walking somewhere on the Hill, in the middle of a hearing, even while on the phone with someone. It is not uncommon to walk into a room for a meeting and see everyone in the room looking at their screens instead of at each other.

I am a member of the Senate committee dealing with health issues, and we do a lot of work these days on youth vaping. I start to notice a parallel between vaping and iPhone addiction—you do it without even thinking about it. If you are around someone who vapes, count how often they puff in fifteen minutes. If you tell them, "Do you know you have puffed on that thing ten times in the last fifteen minutes?" they won't believe you. They're addicted by the supercharged nicotine hit that the manufacturers devilishly engineer to ensure a maximum flow of dollars from your pockets to theirs.

Social media addiction is like that. And while this wasn't one of the reasons for my hike, I am seeing what it's like to go nearly cold turkey and finding that I enjoy it.

I carry an iPhone with my Guthook trail app installed. I also carry a small solar-chargeable battery. But I keep the phone off during the day, stashed in a small dry bag in my backpack. I use the phone sparingly to save the battery. If I see a great view, I turn on the phone and take a picture. If I feel like I am lost or not sure how long it is until the next water source or overnight stop, I turn the phone on and check the trail app. Maybe twice a day, when I get reception, I turn the phone on and send a message to Anne and my staff, letting them know where I am and maybe forwarding a picture. I will check emails once a day just to see if there is any emergency needing my attention—staff knows to keep emails to pressing priorities while I am hiking. Finally, I type a few trail notes at the end of the day about the miles I have covered and any events of note. All told, the iPhone may be on about thirty minutes a day. The rest of the day I am unplugged. I don't even check news, unless it is so important that staff has put it in a priority email for me to see.

My news blackout can lead to some comedy whenever I reach civilization. Somewhere in this stretch, I hit a town and the TV is discussing President Trump wanting to buy Greenland. I clearly missed something! Or is it a surreal dream? Mostly, I realize how little I am really missing by keeping the phone off and stashed in my pack. (The thing I most regret missing was pictures of my bear interactions. Had I had my phone on and accessible, I would certainly have gotten two great shots. But there was no way that I was going to take off my pack, fumble through it, find the dry bag, extract my phone, turn it on, wait for it to power up, and then take a pic while I was face-to-face with a black bear—you'll have to take my word for it!)

One benefit of the blackout is time like this—the lull between arriving at a shelter and needing to make dinner. There is still a good bit of daylight left, as is often the case, so I find a shady spot and sit for an hour or two. I might play the harmonica a little, but mostly I just *listen*. I eventually get good at something that has been generally absent in my life for many years—being still.

21

Today the plan is to hike about fifteen miles from Thunder Ridge up through the Guillotine—an amazing rock formation that has a massive boulder dangling over your head as you squeeze through a narrow passage—over Apple Orchard Mountain and then up and down to Jennings Creek. Where the AT hits the creek and adjacent road, you can get a ride to a nearby campground that promises a store known for cheeseburgers and milkshakes. I am dropping pounds at an alarming rate on this hike and will be glad to splurge at the end of a hot day. Amazing how the promise of a simple meal is such a good motivator during a long hike.

I have been hiking alone on the trail for many miles now—five days by myself, with the exception of Roger joining me for two miles a couple of days ago. But at least I usually see a few other hikers on the trail each day. Now I hit a stretch that is truly barren. I saw no one yesterday. I will see no one today—until I hit the campground where there are a few employees and some families in RVs. As it turns out, I will see no one on the trail tomorrow. Not until midday the day after tomorrow will I see anyone on the trail. It is a little eerie to be hiking by myself for three and a half days without seeing anyone else on the trail.

The heat is keeping people away. Virginia is smashing records this summer for the most days with temperatures above ninety degrees. Temps in this range persist all the way into October. Rainfall is low and the combination of intense heat with limited water availability is convincing sane people that there are better things to do right now than backpacking.

I am an introvert as measured by the Myers-Briggs personality test. I actually like being with folks but need alone time to recharge my battery. But this hike, by many orders of magnitude, is the most solitude I have ever experienced in my life. I find myself thinking, *You wanted some alone time, but this is ridiculous!*

Of the many challenges—physical exertion, pain in my knees and shoulders, fear of all kinds of things, exiting social media, inadequate water, heat—the sheer amount of alone time might be the most notable. Again, not what I would have expected or planned, but there it is.

It is hard to be alone—really alone—with no television, radio, book, or other entertainment to distract you. And to be alone in a strange place—not the comfort of your home but on an unknown trail or in a shelter all by yourself—is a real test. Extended alone time is the soul's equivalent of staring at your own face uncomfortably close in a brightly lit mirror without blinking for hours at a time. No face looks beautiful too close to a mirror, at least when you first glimpse it.

My mood lightens as I think I might soon run into someone. At Apple Orchard Mountain (elevation 4,244 feet—from here going north on the AT you don't hit a mountain this high until Vermont), the trail skirts through a meadow and goes by a weather radar station—no one is there. At Cornelius Creek Shelter, where I stop to rest, no one is there. Someone has left a six-pack of beer chilling in the creek with a note for hikers to enjoy. (Thanks—even though it was only 10:30 a.m., I drank one!) At Bryant Ridge Shelter, advertised as one of the largest on the AT—a double-decker with space for twenty people and two bucolic streams meeting fifty yards away—no one is there. The longer you go without seeing anyone, the more your sense of anticipation rises as you round a bend.

But there is no one today save three deer—a doe and two fawns—who startle and skitter as I approach. I then see a multipoint buck a half mile later. His look conveys a surprised "What are you doing here?"

Finally I get to Jennings Creek and have enough cell reception to call Middle Creek Campground, along a mountain trout stream in Botetourt County. The campground has been here for a long time—Old Guide has notes about it from 1959. It's a few miles from the AT, and after calling for a ride and getting no answer, I walk it. My accommodation—a "hikers cabin"—is actually a large room-sized box made of plywood with windows, electricity, a fridge, and a window-unit air conditioner. Sparsely furnished with two chairs, a queen bed, and two bunk beds. No running water—walk two hundred yards to the camp bathroom for toilet, sink, and shower. But the camp store is as advertised, so I indulge. A fresh-made cheeseburger and chocolate shake for dinner. Dessert? A cold beer. My time away from civilization has scrambled my recollection of dinner chronology.

The electricity in my cabin comes in handy as I recharge phone and battery and spend the evening under real lights plotting out the next two weeks of the hike. I had a plan as far as Daleville, where I will arrive the day after tomorrow. But I will still have about 260 miles to go. For the first time, I now believe I will finish the whole hike. No guarantees on when, but I have done enough now that it would be foolish not to finish. Of course, in one sense the whole thing seems foolish . . .

22

I get a lift back to Jennings Creek and have a hot and solitary sixteen miles, a lot of up and down, to Wilson Creek Shelter. A lunch stop at Bobblets Gap Shelter is my only rest today, and the tiny box spring there may be the slowest-filling water source on the whole trail: four minutes to get a liter of water.

I'm all alone and find myself thinking back on other times of solitude in my life, like when I worked in Macon, Georgia, as a law clerk for a federal judge the year after I graduated from law school. Our office wasn't solitary—there was Judge Anderson, longtime staff Sharon and Sylvia, my co-clerks Tim and Bruce—but I lived by myself, and every once in a while, I would go from the end of the day Friday until Monday morning with no face-to-face human interaction. Reading, going on a hike, studying for the Virginia bar exam, listening to music. Sometimes, during one of those weekends, I would go on an unnecessary shopping trip just to hear a cashier's voice.

A few years earlier, after my first year at Harvard Law School, I took a year off to volunteer with Jesuit missionaries in Honduras. My mentor Hermano Jaime sized me up, learned that I grew up working in my dad's ironworking shop, and put me in charge of a technical school he had just started where I taught basic carpentry and welding skills to teenage boys. I was never alone, but for the first few months, my lack of proficiency in Spanish made me very lonely.

There is a difference between "alone" and "lonely." In those early months in Honduras, especially in a new environment seeing horrible poverty firsthand for the first time, my heart and mind were overflowing with thoughts that I could not express in words to those around me. That struck me then as the essence of loneliness—when there is so much you want to share but are unable to do so. (And not just loneliness—this inability to express oneself might even be an essential experience of childhood when you are filled with feelings and nascent thoughts but unable to put them into a form that those around you can understand.)

It's clear to me that you can be alone and not lonely, or you can be lonely while surrounded by people. I am testing these limits as I walk. Can I be alone and not lonely?

This green mountain trail reminds me a bit of being outdoors in Honduras when I was twenty-two, where there are two valleys of note and the rest of the country is a rippling quilt of mountains running to both the Atlantic and Pacific. An old joke there is to ask someone if they want to see a map of Honduras. If they say yes, you just crumple up a piece of paper, point to the balled-up wad, and say, "¡Aqui hay!"

We would walk on trails like the one I'm on now to nearby villages to say Mass and visit with folks in their tiny huts, thin walls, and thatched roofs. We would ride bikes on occasion if the roads and trails were a little more passable. The *really* magical trips were by mule— we'd drive a four-wheel-drive truck as far as we could and then go by mule to visit other villages way off any road.

One Christmas, I visited villages with Father Patricio. We handed out Christmas candy, offered Mass, shared a simple meal, then went onto the next village. When we reached the farthest village the children danced around Patricio's mule, knowing that he had peppermints— maybe their only Christmas gift. We visited a family he had befriended: a father, mother, and two small and clearly malnourished children. After we visited, as we left to go and set up the service in a tiny one-room school, the father gave a gift to Patricio, a small bag filled with food. Patricio graciously accepted, and as we walked away, I felt my sanctimonious mood darkening. How could this well-fed priest accept a bag of food from a family so poor, whose children clearly needed food more than he did?

Patricio was a good mind reader, and we walked together in silence for a few minutes before he put his hand on my shoulder, looked at me, and said, "Tim, you have to be very humble to accept a gift of food from a family so very poor." I have never forgotten those words—tears come to my eyes thinking about them and my now-deceased friend forty years later. Patricio taught me two things: First, you must be humble because you don't have it all. You have been helped—are being helped, will be helped—by others throughout your life. This help comes from obvious sources but also from completely surprising sources. Some of your help comes from sources you never even know to acknowledge. You'd better be open to receiving help and acknowledging that you stand in need of help. And second, everyone has something to give to another. That, indeed, is the essence of humanity. Denying someone else's gift—or their giftedness—for any reason is to deny the one thing that most makes us human. I think of these two lessons every day of my life.

As I walk, I remember—after Christmas Mass in the dirt-floored school, the evening sky now December dark—how we silently rode sure-footed mules on a steep mountain trail to Victoria, the night lit only by stars as if we were on our way to Bethlehem itself.

Where am I? Honduras forty years ago or Virginia now? The hazy swoon of solo summer hiking is narcotic. I pass a wooden sign on the trail, assuring that trail maintenance from this point on is now within the hands of the Roanoke Appalachian Trail Club. The well-crafted sign seems a subtle rebuke to the Natural Bridge Appalachian Trail Club that has been responsible for the perfectly fine stretch I have just passed through, although they didn't advertise their stewardship with a sign.

I climb up a ridge to the shelter to spend the night. Alone again, naturally. I cannot find the advertised water source. And it is breezy—hard to light the stove. After dinner, I fall asleep in the heat with loud, hot winds swirling about.

I wake in the middle of the night to pee and am witness to an invasion. The shelter was clear when I drifted off. But now, over my pack, my sleeping bag, my hiking pole, my boots, my other gear, seven or eight wolf spiders have emerged and are poised for . . . I don't know what. I grab the shelter broom and chase all spiders away. But as I lie back down, it is hard to come by rest.

23

I awake at Wilson Creek Shelter with a half liter of water and a ten-mile walk to Daleville, where the AT crosses beneath Interstate 81. I will grab dinner with Senate staffers who work in my nearby Roanoke office, spend the night in a local motel, and take a long weekend off the trail. I will attend a commemoration at Fort Monroe in Hampton of the four-hundredth anniversary of African presence in the English colonies, then return to Daleville at the end of the weekend and keep hiking south.

The Fort Monroe event is special for many reasons. It is a small point of land, originally called Point Comfort, that was surveyed by the first English settlers in 1607 before they moved further upriver to build the Jamestown community. "Twenty and odd" Africans, taken from a slavery ship, were traded to the colonists here in 1619 for supplies and provisions. They were enslaved because they had been stolen by Portuguese traders from Africa against their will. But once ashore in Virginia, where there was no law providing for slavery, their status was uncertain.

By the 1640s, the Virginia General Assembly and our courts began to erect the legal architecture of modern American slavery. The "twenty and odd" were followed by multitudes, and Virginia became, for a long period of time, the epicenter of America's monstrous institution.

I am personally invested in being part of the commemoration. I practiced law as a civil rights lawyer for eighteen years, fighting against housing discrimination, and have always been motivated by the tremendous strength of our African American communities in overcoming the pain of bigotry. When I was governor, Fort Monroe was closed as an army base and reverted to ownership by Virginia. I worked with President Obama—a friend ever since we realized that our mothers and maternal grandparents were from the same Kansas town—to designate the historic core of the fort as a national park dedicated to the freedom struggle that defines our nation. And as a senator, I wrote and passed legislation to establish a federal commission charged with planning events to fully and fairly honor the legacy of 1619—the enduring consequences of slavery and the bounteous African American contribution to America. I will have an official role in the weekend program and am excited to attend and learn.

And if I finish my entire quest sometime two years from now, I will pull my canoe up at Fort Monroe, where the James River empties into the Chesapeake Bay. Having started my Virginia journey on foot at Harpers Ferry where a bloody moral spark led to the Civil War, I hope to end it by stepping ashore at Fort Monroe, where American slavery began.

But I have to get to Daleville first with almost no water. I skip my oatmeal and coffee so I can drink my meager half liter on the trail. The Wilson Creek for which the shelter is named is dry for miles. Eventually I reach the Fullhardt Knob Shelter. No creek or spring there, but the shelter has a cistern, where water collects in rain gutters and runs into an underground storage tank. You stand on the downhill side of the shelter, turn a spigot, and wait to see whether the tank has any water left. It hasn't rained in a long time, so I am doubtful.

I'm pleasantly surprised. Cool water flows out and I fill two liters for the last few downhill miles. As I leave the shelter, a married couple hikes up together. They are northbound thru-hikers and have just returned today after a five-week break from the hike. They just couldn't handle the heat in Virginia from mid-July to late August and are just starting back with a long way to go.

I hurry to Daleville, the sound of traffic on I-81 pleasant for a change—it signifies approaching civilization where in two hours I can drink two ice-cold twenty-four-ounce Dr Peppers. Gwen and Mitchell from my Roanoke office come meet me and we go to Three Li'l Pigs—a popular local barbecue spot. Gwen's dad was a tough federal judge before whom I tried many a civil rights case.

I have lost fifteen pounds in my sixteen-day stretch and haven't shaved for more than two weeks. No one but my staff recognizes me in the restaurant.

24

Back on the trail after a three-day hiatus for the inspiring Fort Monroe commemoration. Twelve days' hiking ahead of me before I head back to DC for Senate sessions.

The AT has crossed to the west of I-81 for the first time, a massive relocation from the original route that was carried out by the Roanoke Appalachian Trail Club from 1951 to 1955 to move it away from the busy Blue Ridge Parkway.

This is the third time during the hike where I have stopped for a few days or weeks before coming back to pick up where I left off. Each time it's the same. I finish a stretch, get home, throw my accursed pack in the basement, and vow not to think about hiking ever again! But sure enough, within a day or two, after a shower and some laundry, I start to plan the next segment.

The next twelve days will be pleasant for two reasons. Now that I am in late August, rather than the peak heat of mid-July to mid-August, the temperatures are not so extreme. And I will start to get to higher and higher elevations, making it even more comfortable. Water is still short, however, as there hasn't been much rain.

But the real improvement is company. I lose Old Guide for much of the remainder of the hike due to extensive reroutes of the southern portion of the Virginia trail since 1959. But my son Nat, the Marine infantry officer, is joining me for two and a half days with a plan to cover forty-plus miles through a beautiful section neither of us has hiked before. And I will have other friends—plus my wife and daughter—joining me later during this stretch.

Nat and I start in Daleville under inauspicious conditions. It is cool and rainy. I lamely suggest that we wait a while before we start hiking but my commanding officer points out that the weather forecast says rain all day. Indeed, this will be one of just two days on the AT where it rains nonstop.

Hiking with a twenty-nine-year-old Marine who is used to carrying one hundred pounds on his back is humbling, but we hump our gear up and down mountains, talking all the while. Nat is not a big guy—maybe five feet eight and 140 pounds—but he's always pushed the envelope physically. Winter hiking, rock climbing, extreme whitewater kayaking, bicycle racing, piloting gliders. He tells me once, "Dad, in the Marines, I am not the fastest. And I can't carry the most weight on my back. But if you need someone to carry a lot of weight for a very long time, I will always be the best." He is also an expert with a compass and can find his way anywhere. In training exercises at Twentynine Palms in desert California, he usually drew tough water duty, carrying heavy water containers for his unit, along with his own pack. But it was at least a little strategic—the guys carrying the water were the most popular, and unlike the guys carrying big weapons, the watercoolers got lighter as they went along.

We are trying to do sixteen miles to Campbell Shelter. We stop at one empty shelter along the way where we have lunch and struggle with how to deal with the rain. We see some hikers swathed in ponchos but we are hiking with no rain gear on because, though cool, you just get very hot hiking. So we deal with being wet instead of overheating.

We hit a famous overlook called Tinker Cliffs—part of a local trio of beautiful peaks along the AT west of Roanoke. But fog is so heavy that we cannot see anything. We press on.

We finally near the Campbell Shelter around 5:00 p.m. I am hoping for a dry shelter with no one else there. Fat chance. A freshman orientation group from Washington and Lee University, about forty miles north, has completely claimed the shelter, and the rain is still pouring down. But the first-year students are very polite and offer to make room for us when they hear how many miles we've done. I take them up on the offer and they move closer to let me have a narrow space along one wall of the shelter. Nat doesn't like crowds and chooses to set up his bivy in the rain nearby. Space is so limited that most of us put our packs underneath the raised shelter to keep them dry—no room inside.

The kids—seven first-year students from all over the country and three upper-level students who are leading the trip—are doing icebreaker exercises while Nat and I have our dinner and talk about what's up in our lives. While the leaders are all skilled outdoors, it is clear that some of the frosh have never camped. The privy, with its stench and spiders, is particularly daunting for them. At one point, some of the kids realize who I am and we get a round of late-night selfies, drenched but smiling. I turn in early and the kids are not that far behind. Eleven of us are packed in a shelter for eight while the rain pours steadily down.

In the middle of the night, I awake to a strange sound. It is always disorienting waking up in a shelter on the AT but this time especially so. What is that noise? It takes me a moment, but then my dad sense kicks in. One of the first-year students, a young girl, is crying softly, trying to keep others from hearing her. Far from home, soaked, tired and dirty, embarking on college life in a new place with new people—it is just too much. I would like to say something to comfort her but she is clearly trying to avoid being heard and there is no way to speak to her without waking up a lot of people. I think about how young eighteen is and send a silent prayer to my wife, in her first weeks as a college president, that she never forgets this. College presidents deal with boards, alums, donors, faculty, staff, legislators. But the critical population is teenage students starting their independent lives. It can be a scary time—just as scary as being in the wild outdoors on a cold and rainy night.

25

The Washington and Lee kids are awake and out before sunup, hiking uphill two miles to McAfee Knob to watch the sunrise and make breakfast there. It is still raining and we let them go, hanging around for a more leisurely breakfast and start to a long, hard seventeen-mile day to Pickle Branch Shelter.

We start the climb to McAfee Knob. Neither of us have ever been there. But if you've seen pictures of the AT, you've probably seen McAfee Knob. It is a sharp cliff jutting out into space, with mountains extending forever into the distance. It is known as the most-photographed spot on the AT.

Just before we arrive at the 3,200-foot peak, we climb through the top of the rain cloud that has been drenching us for twenty-four hours. The view from McAfee Knob is magnificent, clear blue skies above with an endless blanket of clouds spread out below us.

The college kids are there having a leisurely breakfast. They seem happy, and it makes me glad to see them enjoying themselves and drying out after a hard day yesterday. One volunteers to take a picture of Nat and me at the edge of the cliff—it will be the best photo of my hike.

We stay a few minutes but then keep walking south. Today is a day of many long climbs and long descents. The last climb is up Dragon's Tooth, a really hard scramble with high fall danger. After that peak, we follow a ridge and then have a long descent to the shelter.

Nat is a real gearhead and we spend a lot of the day—now clearing and hot—talking about the stuff we rely on and the stuff we can do without. My old pack, much-used boots, new stove, and bivy have all performed well. Other items—a small folding knife, spork, walking stick, beat-up coffee cup—get used every day. A seasoned Timex camping watch lights up at night to tell me what time it is. Even when the band breaks, I just rig it to my pack. Bug/tick lotion—I slather it on and it works. Blues harp in the key of D—worth its weight in gold. I wear nondescript running shorts and a T-shirt on the trail, but good wool socks are a luxurious necessity.

But the top three—my star performers—are my Guthook trail app, my Nemo insulated sleeping pad, and my collapsible bowl. I've talked about the app already—so helpful to know where you are and, better yet, how far to the next water source, killer view, camping spot, town. And the Nemo is amazing—it sets up easy, is comfortable, and the insulation really blocks cold and damp. But my real genius hiking hack is the collapsible bowl. I dip it into a creek or spring at the end of the day, fill with cold water, add a little biodegradable soap, and wash enough to feel semi-human—which is somewhat ironic, given that it's a dog bowl.

There is also the gear you don't need. I've hardly ever used my sunscreen or sunglasses—the trail is mostly a green tunnel of shady trees. Plus, it is so hot and humid that the sunglasses fog up immediately. I've only used my rain jacket a handful of times—rainfall has been at a minimum, and when it has rained, it's almost always been too hot to wear the jacket. I've used it more often as a pack cover than as a jacket. I carry a heavy-duty first aid kit and it gets virtually no use—aside from ibuprofen (or "vitamin I," in backpacker speak) and one small bandage, I hardly open it. If I had left it behind, no doubt I would have needed it!

One kind of gear that I typically have with me but which I'm not carrying for this trip—fire supplies. One of the best parts of backpacking is making a fire. But the heat of the hike, combined with dangerously dry conditions, makes a fire unnecessary and unwise. So aside from a few books of matches in case the stove's self-ignition feature malfunctions, nothing to use for fire starting or tending.

As we are hiking along, we keep hearing a loud buzzing sound.

Could it be a factory? A sawmill? The sound goes in and out but we hear it for many miles. As the AT crosses a one-hundred-yard swath cleared for a powerline, we see the cause of the buzz. A helicopter dangling a massive chainsaw is flying low, cutting branches too close to the power line. The branches fall with a thud all around. We are not sure the pilots can see us, and we wave with broad exaggeration so they won't drop limbs on our heads as we hurry by. I imagine this chainsaw-wielding helicopter being used for a stunt in the next Bond movie. (Note to self: trademark this idea upon return to society.)

Finally—well after lunch—we cross State Route 624 and start the climb to Dragon's Tooth. How hard can this be? It is 2.2 miles with an elevation gain of 1,100 feet. I've climbed steeper grades. But I have not read the map closely enough. The mileage is right and the elevation gain from start to peak is correct. But . . .

The trail is steep on the way up and the way down. As soon as you climb five hundred feet, you drop four hundred, meaning you still have one thousand to climb. And this repeats—steep uphill and then a steep drop where you lose most of your progress. After a long set of these reps, we descend into a hollow where there is a sign—unique on the Virginia AT—announcing "Steep Climb for Next .7 Miles." Wait—I thought it was already steep! Apparently not.

This last .7 miles to Dragon's Tooth is thigh-busting, fate-cursing, lung-burning, fall-defying, hand-over-hand climbing. We are already tired so scrambling up uneven slopes with thirty-pound packs is very dicey. As bad as going up is, I cannot imagine climbing down this stretch. (Two friends of mine—hiking here a few years ago—got blocked on the climb by someone who had fallen coming down, broken a bone, and was waiting for a rescue team to carry him out.)

Thank God Nat is leading the way. At one point near the top, he reaches to a ledge, pulls himself up, then grabs a stick and starts pounding the rock. I pull myself up and see a copperhead slithering away, a few feet from where he planted his hand a few seconds earlier.

We finally reach Dragon's Tooth, a serrated set of rock spires that offer 360-degree late-afternoon views of the surrounding mountains and valleys. We rest and celebrate, but we are still miles from stopping. The app shows a gentle ridge walk and then a long, gradual descent to our shelter. But even a close read of the topography on a map can be deceiving. The ridge walk isn't steep, but it is truly on the ridge, with uneven footholds the norm. The one flat part of the day turns into slow going as we avoid falls and twisted ankles. Nat gives me a pep talk to keep me trudging on.

Finally, a long, pleasant downhill to the shelter. We spy a shadowy figure across a valley hiking away from us. In the late-day gloaming, it looks a little like a grainy Bigfoot photo I saw in my youth. We hit the shelter with one question on our mind: Will there be any water in Pickle Branch? Nat takes the bottles two hundred yards down to the stream and returns with all filled, cold and clear!

As we eat, we visit with the other occupant, Paul from Newport News, who did a group bike ride across America last summer and is hiking the Virginia AT this summer. He says the hike is harder because it is solitary. Paul has set up a covered hammock between two trees and sleeps there, swaying in the breeze while Nat and I claim the shelter. For the first time, I need socks at night to keep my feet warm. Fall must be coming.

26

Today will be an easy day—just ten miles from Pickle Branch Shelter to Niday Shelter—but I am not looking forward to it. When we get to a road crossing at the 8.5-mile mark, Nat will meet a shuttle driver to take him to Daleville so he can hop in his truck and get back to his wife and work. I will continue on by myself for two days until I meet up with Anne and some friends over Labor Day weekend.

It has been so nice having one of my kids with me. Anne and I continually marvel at how two public-interest lawyers ended up with three super-independent kids who grew up to be a Marine, a visual artist, and an actress. Not only have we not done these things, we don't even know enough about their paths to give any of them meaningful career advice. Hopefully our advice on life and values has been enough.

I do remember an epiphany I had once, following a parent-teacher conference for one of my boys when he was in middle school. (It was either Nat or Woody—while they are quite different, they are the same in this particular way.) "Your son is so smart! He should have the best grades in the class. But if he's not interested in the subject, he just zones out." I heard this, and variations on the theme, many times as a dad of two boys. (It was different with Annella, whose parent-teacher conferences usually included the word "perfectionist.")

After one such session, Anne and I were commiserating and I said, "You know, our kids have shown us that when they pick something they like they can be really dedicated and master it. So the key isn't their discipline or ability. It's whether they can pick something they care about. And when they do, they'll be fine." And they did exactly that. Our children have each picked something they are passionate about. And while sometimes we feel that the only thing we can do is stand on the sidelines and root for them, they are each diligent in pursuing their own happiness.

I do like that Nat's Marine path has taken our meager outdoor skills and amped them up many levels. We have a great morning and hit an interesting spot on the trail about five miles into the walk. Audie Murphy was one of the most decorated combat soldiers in American history. A Texan who lied about his age to enlist early in the army after Pearl Harbor, he was awarded the Congressional Medal of Honor for valor in France at age nineteen—*after* he had already earned the Distinguished Service Cross, Purple Heart, Silver Star, and Bronze Star. He had a successful postwar acting career doing war movies and Westerns, even as he suffered from PTSD, unable to sleep without a loaded pistol nearby. In 1971, he was killed in a plane crash right here on Brushy Mountain, where the AT passes above the town of Catawba. A memorial to him was built on the spot by a local VFW chapter.

Nat and I stop to pay our respects. The memorial is adorned with flowers, military pins, flags, and dog tags left by hikers passing by, or veterans who climb up on Memorial or Veterans Day. But there is nothing to reference the AT that brings people to Murphy's memorial. I take the AT pin off my pack that Shenandoah Park Superintendent Jennifer Flynn gave me a few hundred miles ago and leave it on the stones with the other tributes.

We descend to the place where Nat will drop off, and within a few minutes, an amazing shuttle driver/trail maintainer/hiker named Homer is there to pick him up. Homer asks us where we stayed last night and when we tell him Pickle Branch, he says, "Did you see anyone weird up there?" To which the only accurate answer is: "Anyone out here is weird, you and us included."

Homer laughs and tells us why he asked: He and a local park ranger had just been called in yesterday by hikers complaining of being harassed at Pickle Branch Shelter by an aggressive man. They walked to the shelter but no one was there. The shelter had been trashed, with empty beer and wine bottles and drug paraphernalia and other junk lying here and there. Whoever did it left a one-dollar bill on the picnic table as if to say, "Sorry I wrecked the place, but here's a buck for your trouble." They packed all the trash up and hiked out with it.

Nat, Paul, and I passed a good night at the clean shelter and saw no one, although I couldn't help but wonder if the Bigfoot type we saw hiking away from us yesterday might have been the culprit. Nat and I hug and off they go—leaving me alone once again for a steep but short climb to Niday.

I arrive by midafternoon and take my time setting up. The water source is dry as a bone and my heart sinks—but then I hear a trickling sound. I walk farther down the empty streambed and find a cold rivulet tumbling down the mountain, hidden by a screen of mountain laurel.

Two hikers eventually join me. Cotton is a northbound section hiker from Tennessee. He does three weeks solo on the trail every year. "I get six weeks' vacation and I do three with my wife and three on the AT." Each year, he returns and picks up where he stopped the year before. Very cool.

Later, just at dark, a small wiry guy arrives with a massive backpack. He is also carrying a big plastic bag in his arms. Cotton says, "Oh no—I thought I had given him the slip when I passed him while he was chopping down a tree a few miles back." Chopping down a tree?

The guy—call him Lumberjack—sets up a tent nearby and immediately takes out a big machete and starts chopping down trees and cutting up fallen branches. He needs a headlamp in the dark. Is this the "Bigfoot" I saw earlier? But he is too small and wiry.

"Is he going to make a big fire?" I ask Cotton.

"No—just watch," he says.

I now notice that Cotton—set up in the shelter with me—carries a large sheathed knife attached to his pack. He sees me looking and says, "You can't be too careful, especially after that guy got killed near here a few months ago."

I find myself increasingly concerned. The man Cotton was talking about had been killed by a machete. But they had arrested that guy, hadn't they? My four-inch folding knife will be no match for these two if it comes to that.

Lumberjack just keeps chopping and stacking branches—no fire—and Cotton and I turn in, talking softly in the darkening shelter about our respective trips.

I realize that he must have been just as wary of me as I was of him. After thirty or forty minutes, Cotton allows a freighted silence and then says, "Are you a churchgoer?" When I tell him yes, he apparently decides he needn't fear me. I imagine his hand loosening on the knife, and we both fall asleep.

27

Up early. Cotton is already packed and ready to hike north, hoping to put some miles between him and Lumberjack, who is also hiking north. Thank God I am hiking south and take my normal ninety minutes to pack, eat, stretch, and get hiking. I pass Lumberjack's campsite as I start, and all is silent. A massive stack of branches, logs, and sticks sits right outside the tent. Unclear what the woodpile is for. (I later find a note in a shelter log written by Lumberjack a few days before as he hiked north: "Why do people fear me?")

A fairly short hike today—ten miles from Niday Shelter to Route 42—before a splurge. I will call a shuttle and get a lift to a lake resort high in the Alleghenies, where I will spend one night and recall memories of a vacation there with Anne and the kids twenty-five years ago.

Growing up, the Kaine family were not originally campers. Picnickers and outdoor people, yes—campers, no. But I joined the Cub Scouts and then Boy Scouts in Troop 395 at Curé of Ars Catholic Church and went camping for the first time at a farm south of Kansas City. I was hooked. Though a lackluster Scout, I would get really active before any weekend camping trip or the summer camping week at Camp Naish. Something about sleeping in a tent and cooking over a fire was just magical. The worse the weather, the better the memories.

This was back in elementary and middle school. My introduction to life outdoors came from my Boy Scout experience and two shop teachers—Joe McKenzie and Bob Clark—who would take large groups of kids on camping trips. I remember once urging my parents that they should take me and my two younger brothers camping. My parents were always game to try anything to harness the energy of three rambunctious sons. Dad dutifully rented a big Coleman tent for a weekend. We loaded up the Buick Skylark station wagon and drove to a campground at Tuttle Creek Lake near Manhattan, Kansas. It was *National Lampoon's Vacation* but before anybody knew who Chevy Chase was.

Arriving at sundown on Friday, we struggled with the tent and could not get it set up. Eventually we just laid our sleeping bags on top of the flattened and spread-out tent canvas. All fine until it started to rain in the middle of the night. We all eventually found our way back into the Buick to sleep.

Saturday started clear and sunny and we figured out how to get the tent up. Then we went fishing. Brother Steve caught a fish, but then stepped on a piece of broken glass and cut his foot. We drove into the tiny town nearby, found an elderly doctor with trembling hands and a practice in his front parlor, and Steve got stitches, a bandage, and a tetanus shot. (I'm sure the traumatic experience was pivotal in his decision to become a caring pediatrician.) Then it was back to the campsite where Mom prepared a nice dinner on a Coleman stove resting on the tailgate of the station wagon. Brother Pat slammed the door of the car, giving the tailgate just enough bounce that the skillet flew off the Coleman and all our hash browns landed in the dirt. We ate our hotdogs grumpily.

As we made plans to turn in after that drama-filled day, the car radio blared out a tornado warning. Dad made a game-time call: break camp and head back to Kansas City. Our first family camping trip had been a twenty-four-hour disaster.

But you can probably guess what came next. We were hardly home for two days before we started clamoring to go on another trip. Over the years, we did multiple camping and canoeing trips, both as a family and with neighbors. My parents even got into camping trips with their friends. Today at our Kaine family gatherings in Kansas City, the stories of our outdoor adventures are the ones we really cherish.

This set the stage for excursions all through high school, college, and law school. At Mizzou, it was hiking, rock climbing, caving around Columbia, and canoe trips in the Ozarks over spring break while the kids with more folding money went to Florida, New Orleans, or Padre Island. At Harvard, it was biking out to Walden Pond and hiking and camping in the Berkshires, Whites, Greens, and Adirondacks. I joke about my Harvard Law School years—"I may not have been on law review but I set the record for most time spent camping while I was there." When I met Anne and discovered that she liked outdoor activity as much as I did, I knew I had found someone special.

I will always remember a law school hike with Anne and friends up the New Hampshire peak Mount Monadnock on a snowy winter day. We could see the Boston skyline at the edge of the horizon and I accomplished a rare poetry double—reading aloud Galway Kinnell's "Flower Herding on Mount Monadnock" at the summit and swinging a birch in homage to Robert Frost as we walked downhill to our car.

As a young couple and then later with kids, Anne and I hiked, camped, canoed, bicycled, and backpacked all over Virginia. We had some notable near-disasters, just like my first family camping trip as a kid. But those are the ones we all laugh about now.

The hike today takes me through a wooded stretch dotted with stone cairns—big stacks of stones, eight to ten feet high—spread every few hundred yards for a little over a mile along the crest of Sinking Creek Mountain. I've never seen them before—they are called the Bruisers Knob cairns and they were built by early farmers a long time ago. Some say they mark graves; others say they are just piles left as farmers tried to clear the land here. But why clear the land? The ridge is narrow, rocky, and covered in trees. What could grow up here? No matter how deep in the wilderness, people have tried to make a go everywhere.

When I start a long downhill stretch to Route 42, I call my buddy Shawn, who runs an outdoor outfitter in the nearby town of Pembroke. He comes to pick me up—cold beer in a cooler for me—and drives me a few miles to Mountain Lake. He is a consummate outdoors guy who used to help shuttle us around on annual canoe trips in Western Virginia. When I was governor, I nominated him for the state's tourism board because we didn't have enough folks pushing Virginia's outdoor opportunities. I am not sure he has ever forgiven me for making him dress up and go to so many meetings! We compare notes on our kids and on a controversial interstate pipeline project bisecting the area. He refuses to let me pay him for the shuttle when he drops me off.

Mountain Lake Lodge is a resort dating back to the 1850s, built on a lake at an elevation of nearly four thousand feet. *Dirty Dancing* was filmed here. Anne and I visited for a summer vacation in 1995, right after our youngest child was born. The boys were five and three and loved hiking the hills and swimming and fishing in the lake. We stayed in a cabin, and I remember Anne getting up in the middle of the night to breastfeed our two-month-old daughter when a curious baby mouse emerged from a hiding place to watch our nocturnal stirrings.

The lodge today is much as I remember it—homey and welcoming— but the lake is dramatically different. It fills and empties on irregular cycles as rocks underlying the lake bed shift and move. A few years ago, it had shrunk to nearly nothing. Now it is coming back slowly, not yet full enough for all previous water activities. But it is still striking— beautiful marsh grasses and fog hanging low over the lake in the cool mountain air.

As I walk by the lake after dinner, my immediate senses and the memories from long ago combine into one vivid impression and the quarter century collapses in upon itself. I will be with Anne tomorrow and then my twenty-four-year-old daughter, Annella, will join me in a few days. Who knows where the time goes?

28

Today is my earliest start, and I am motivated. After a cushy night in a comfortable bed at the lodge, I get an early lift back to the trailhead. Following two days of only ten or eleven miles each, I will hike eighteen miles today: two long climbs gaining two thousand or so feet with a final long downhill to Stony Creek Road. Then Anne, my friend Ned, and his wife, Patty, will meet me. The plan is for us all to hike two more miles to Peters Mountain Trailhead before driving into the nearby town of Pearisburg where we will all stay the next two nights in a cabin. Ned and I will hike tomorrow—a nineteen-mile slackpack between Peters Mountain and Pearisburg. I won't be by myself!

It is amazing how fast I can walk if I know I will see Anne at the end of the day. On a normal day, with short breaks and a lunch stop, I can comfortably make two miles per hour. If I am meeting Anne, I take fewer and shorter breaks, skip the lunch stop, and make two and a half to three miles per hour. Today, I am walking by 6:30 a.m. and really cruise.

It is the Saturday of Labor Day weekend. Surprisingly, for the first eighteen miles—until I meet Anne, Ned, and Patty—I am all alone. I pass two shelters, expecting to see somebody each time—they are completely empty. I would think this weekend would be busier but for some reason it is quiet. There are so many ferns overgrowing the trail today, I often have a hard time seeing where it's heading. This stretch has not been traveled much recently—northbound thru-hikers came through weeks or months ago and southbound thru-hikers are still a week to ten days north of here.

I have picked up some hiker chatter along the trail about a decline in trail usage—not just due to this summer's heat, but part of a gradual disconnection of people, especially children, from the natural world. The phenomenon has a name—"nature deficit disorder"—coined by American writer Richard Louv in his 2005 book *Last Child in the Woods*. The basic concept, subject to spirited critique, is that fewer and fewer kids spend time outdoors due to competition from electronic devices and social media, reduction in school physical education programs, and overwrought parental fears about unsupervised outdoor time. A Richmond friend raised not far from here in the town of Richlands once told me that, when she returns home, the change she notices most is how few children are outside—riding bikes, playing sports, walking around town—compared to when she grew up. The consequences of this are troubling—obesity, depression, worse cardiovascular and joint health. Plus, since loving the outdoors can translate into passionate stewardship later in life, there is concern that we will face an advocacy deficit as well, just as a growing population should be more focused on preserving our natural bounty.

The phenomenon is not just about children, though the overall evidence is mixed. The percentage of American adults who hunt has fallen from 10 to 5 percent in the last fifty years and shows every sign of continuing decline as a huge proportion of hunters hits sixty-five, the age when many stop purchasing weapons and hunting. While the *total* number of people fishing increases with the growth in American population, the *percentage* of people who fish has been on a slow decline. However, visitation to national parks has steadily increased in the last decade—even though 2018 saw a significant decrease from the previous year—and the AT is seeing a big increase in thru-hikers. The number of Americans hiking at all rose from thirty to forty-five million between 2007 and 2017. There has also been an uptick in activities like bird- and wildlife-watching.

While the statistics are arguable, there is a troubling and understandable logic to the concept of nature deficit disorder. I only have to scrutinize my own behavior and that of those close to me to see that general busyness and the addictive appeal of digital devices and media can subtly work to keep us inside more. This makes me thankful for a longtime sitter we had work for us when the kids were growing up. Shirley was a grandmotherly type who came in right as the kids got home from school and stayed until Anne or I got home from work. Her all-purpose directive to our three kids was "Go outside and play." "But it's cold/snowing/raining/hailing!" "It will do you kids good!" I need to give Shirley's memory some credit for our kids all enjoying outdoor life today.

The intensity of this outdoor sensory experience—wind, sun, shade, sweat, silence, rain on your skin, birdsong, vistas—reminds me that I should get outdoors more as part of my daily life.

I hit Stony Creek Road in the midafternoon and sit to wait at a small National Forest Service fishing area along a beautiful trout stream. The Forest Service has built a raised boardwalk winding its way down to the stream, and I realize that it is specifically designed to allow someone to access the creek and fish while using a wheelchair. Silent and empty today, but I am impressed with the thoughtfulness of the design.

Before long, Anne, Ned, and Patty pull up in my car. Ned and Patty were our first friends in Richmond, living around the corner from Anne when she worked for a federal judge the year before we got married. They are godparents to our son Woody and have three adult children close in age to ours. I throw my pack in the car and we prep for a simple two-mile hike—only carrying water bottles—to the Peters Mountain Trailhead. But Ned, the ace hiker, has pulled a calf muscle playing basketball earlier in the week, so he explores by car while Patty, Anne, and I walk together for about an hour. Hiking with no pack feels like cheating.

We reconnect with Ned and drive fifteen minutes to the town of Pearisburg, a nice trail town on the New River in Giles County. We've heard about a hostel called Angels Rest Hiker Haven where they have a small house for rent on the property. We have booked it for two nights. After getting cleaned up, we go to a nearby Mexican restaurant that is completely authentic, inexpensive, and packed. La Barranca is known by locals, visitors, and AT hikers alike. A good example of how immigrants come to a town and, whatever the initial reaction, so often quickly become integral to the life of the community.

Back at the Haven, it is a simple creature comfort to catch up and laugh together as the UVA football game plays in the background. Ned and Patty vacationed with Anne and me at Mountain Lake on our long-ago trip, and they are all interested in the details of my stay last night. So good to be with old friends.

29

I really must be deranged to get up early and hike today when Anne and my friends are here. Why not sleep in, take a zero day, eat more Mexican food, laugh with my wife and companions? I guess I am a hiker on a mission.

The original plan was for Ned and me to hike about fifteen miles and then meet our wives for the last four miles into Pearisburg. Anne and Patty—best friends and members of a neighborhood book club that is now nearly thirty years strong—would get most of the day together before inspiring us on the last miles.

But Ned's calf injury scrambles the plan. He drives me to the trail-head after breakfast and I hop out to do the fifteen miles alone before meeting the women for the last stretch. Ned heads back to spend the day with Anne and Patty, exploring the area and finding a few supplies to restock me.

After an hour-plus climb in which I pick up 1,400 feet in three miles, I stay on a ridge with easy foot placements for ten miles before a sharp downhill two-mile stretch to the spot where Anne and Patty will meet me. Today I am carrying a daypack only—water and snacks. What a luxury after weeks of struggling under the weight of a full pack.

It is Sunday, and the first folks I see are volunteers from a Virginia Tech trail club doing trail maintenance. The trail clubs really are the front line on the AT. I thank them but don't even break stride as I keep the uphill momentum going. I pass three other couples day hiking during my trip today; we exchange quick pleasantries and then move on.

For most of my life, Sunday has started with church. My mom and dad are devout Catholics and would never miss Sunday Mass at Curé of

Ars parish. If we returned from a family vacation at 7:00 p.m. Sunday night, they would know the one church in Kansas City that had an 8:00 p.m. Mass we could still make. We boys hated that at the time, but years later, my brain is a massive storehouse of Scripture and church songs that I absorbed during weekly Mass. (I remember few, if any, sermons.)

The Roman Catholic Church then became more personal for me as I attended Rockhurst, a Jesuit boys high school with the motto "Men for Others." As I found then, and in the years since, the Jesuits hold onto an appealing mix of intellectual rigor and passion for social justice. After my parents, the influence of the Jesuits I knew in high school and in Honduras were the key to my spiritual formation.

I slowly fell away from churchgoing when I left home to go to the University of Missouri. For the first time in my life, I met a lot of evangelical Christians. Most were admirable people, but I didn't agree with the certainty some expressed that people who wouldn't worship Jesus were due for eternal punishment. What about all the wonderful non-Christians I had met in life? I had a hard time imagining a just God considering them as anything but good.

It was my time in Honduras that reconnected me with the person of Jesus. I came to see that his life and message are transformative: perfect and so profound that one will always find new dimensions to it. The two linked promises that will always make Jesus relevant to mankind are the continuous availability of forgiveness plus the promise that worldly success is not the guarantor of happiness or salvation.

We all make mistakes, but Jesus's second-chance message—expressed so vividly in his forgiveness of the woman about to be stoned for adultery, his choice of Peter to lead his church even though he knew Peter would curse and deny him, and his pardon of the thief hanging next to him on the cross—is so comforting. This message is underscored by the prayer we say as we prepare for Communion: "Lord, I am not worthy that you should enter under my roof, but only say the word and my soul shall be healed." How personally liberating it is to believe that past failures do not consign you to a future of failure.

And the truly revolutionary message—that worldly success matters little—is all through Scripture. *The last shall come first and the first shall come last. He who exalts himself shall be humbled and he who humbles himself shall be exalted. The wisdom of the world is foolishness in the eyes of God. Blessed are the poor. Blessed are the persecuted.* People throughout time, suffering under injustice and oppression, have always found such hope in this message of social liberation. And people riding high with status or wealth should always be challenged by this dichotomy, forced to ask, "Am I really focused on the most important things?"

In Honduras, I came to understand that even our mammoth human capacity to screw up the message of Jesus, so often using it as a divider of people rather than an elevator of people, cannot subtract from its power.

Honduras also convinced me of the joy of communal worship. Personal prayer and reflection are so important. But immersing yourself in the life of a church community assumed great importance to me as I saw how poor Hondurans helped each other deal with adversity that seemed unimaginable to me. Church provides a place to share burdens and joys, welcome life, and mourn death. And it is not only a community, but a community with a Leader who has wisdom to offer at every turn in life.

My challenge coming home from Honduras was finding a communal worship experience that matched what I felt when I was there. The suburban parish of my youth and the hundreds like it no longer fully satisfied. It was during my year as a law clerk in Macon, Georgia, that I found a small segment of American Catholicism providing the soul satisfaction I first knew in Honduras. I happened upon St. Peter Claver parish, a mission church set up in a low-income African American neighborhood, not too far from the more ornate St. Joseph Catholic Church where white Catholics primarily worshipped. In the traditions of this church, born out of deep faith but also born into the same pain and discrimination felt by my Honduran friends, I felt spiritually at home.

And that is how we have worshipped since. For thirty-five years, we have attended St. Elizabeth's parish in Richmond, a broadly diverse inner-city parish whose core has been the experience of African American Catholics. It is a small but mighty parish with a welcoming spirit and an inspirational gospel choir. Within the Roman Catholic Church, it has often felt like an uneasy fit. As one who believes that the greatest human-rights issue on the planet is the near-universal and continuing second-class status accorded women, worshipping in a church that will not ordain women remains a persistent point of discomfort. I believe that so many of the Roman Catholic Church's faults and scandals proceed from a fundamental misunderstanding of human sexuality that is linked to its exclusion of women from full spiritual participation.

But the Roman Catholic Church's multiple virtues in carrying forward the message of Jesus, my prayerful confidence of how much greater the Roman Catholic Church will be when we do fully embrace the equality of women, and my own innate stubbornness keep me part of the broader family. Plus, my spiritual heroes are mostly Catholic—my parents, the Jesuits at Rockhurst and in Honduras, Óscar Romero, Dorothy Day, the matriarchs and patriarchs at St. Elizabeth's. Like many Catholics all over the world, I think of myself as much a "parish Catholic" as a "Roman Catholic," with my sense of Christian responsibility directed toward my Creator and fellow man rather than toward any hierarchy.

As I entered public life, I began to attend many other churches, synagogues, temples, and mosques to be with my constituents at important moments or celebrations. These experiences have educated me more deeply about other faith traditions and also given me a real appreciation for America's tradition of religious freedom, our still-rare status as a society where you can worship or not as you please without being preferred or punished for your choice.

In my work both in state government and the Senate, I have been a weekly participant in spiritual discussion groups where colleagues share their own faith journeys and trials. These have added much to my life and work and also given me better understanding of what makes my colleagues tick. And as one of my Senate friends Roy Blunt famously joked, "It is hard to go to a weekly prayer breakfast with someone and then stab them in the back. It's not impossible, but it's hard!"

But the personal demands of faith and representing a broad electorate of numerous faith traditions is a constant struggle—as it should be. My personal opposition to the death penalty was a major obstacle to becoming governor of what was then a solidly pro-capital-punishment state. And my position on abortion—personally opposed and living that value but accepting that others may resolve the issue differently—has put me in an uneasy place, with both pro-life and pro-choice activists (and my church and party) often unhappy with my votes. The only consolation here is that so many people occupy the same place—living their lives pro-life and supporting policies that reduce unwanted pregnancy but opposing use of the criminal law to stigmatize and punish women and their doctors for their decisions about contraception and abortion. I grapple with the difference between church doctrine—which a religion has a right to set and then expect its followers to accept—and civil law that is applicable to all regardless of their faith backgrounds.

The long, solitary walk today is like church, with the beauty of the ridge views north into West Virginia reminding me of the line from Gerard Manley Hopkins: "The world is charged with the grandeur of God." I eventually hit my meeting point in midafternoon and am barely there ten minutes before Ned arrives to drop Anne and Patty off for the last four miles. We get a few steep climbs to test our wind, but the conversation makes the miles pass quickly. When we meet Ned, I find that the three have shopped for chicken, fresh vegetables, and ice cream to do a proper Labor Day BBQ meal. We eat outside, watching the clear night fill with stars and a crescent moon rise over the surrounding mountains. I am not looking forward to their departure tomorrow morning.

30

We make a good breakfast and then Anne, Patty, and Ned drop me off at the trailhead so I can keep trucking south. I am sad watching them drive off but my melancholy is reduced because I will meet three of my neighborhood hiking friends at a trailside hostel tonight. They will be with me for the next five days. As an added treat, my daughter, Annella, will join our group for the last three of these days. I have company to look forward to after today's solo hike.

The hike starts with an awesome climb up Angels Rest, a peak with a jutting cliff looking out over Pearisburg and the New River Valley near the West Virginia border. The 1,800-foot climb in a little less than two miles is a struggle, but I am rewarded by magnificent views and then hike the rest of the day with only modest elevation changes. I did the hike to Angels Rest with my kids and neighbors nearly fifteen years ago but remember nearly nothing about it until I get to the overlook. That view was burned into my memory and comes back immediately.

You've probably noticed that I meet some folks along the way and refer to them by trail names. This is an Appalachian Trail tradition. You leave your own name behind and simply go by a trail name that you use to introduce yourself to others or to sign in at shelters. Together with wearing the same hiking clothes day after day, hardly showering, and not shaving, the trail name thing is an egalitarian leveler out in the wild. Those who do this for a long time set aside their normal personas, along with any status indicators, and just become hikers.

How do you pick a trail name? I learn that you do not pick your own name but instead have to wait until a name is bestowed upon you, usually after some comedic event or quirky trait you display. One thru-hiker I know who hiked the trail years ago used to annoy her companions by her overly talkative demeanor first thing in the morning, so they took to calling her Pop Tart in honor of a favorite hikers' breakfast that seemed to capture her ubiquitous cheerfulness. I have spent time with Boomer, Magic, Tracker, Underdog, Redbush, Choo Choo, Cotton, Boxcar Willie, Lumberjack, Pacman, and others along the way—intrigued by their names but never asking, "How did you come by your trail name?"

(I did meet a guy who introduced himself as "Achilles" and I said, "Great trail name." He looked puzzled and said, "What do you mean? Achilles is my real name." I wondered if perhaps his trail name was something like "Bill" or "Hank.")

I don't have a trail name yet and just introduce myself as TK. (I did contemplate choosing the name Spiderface after my propensity for breaking early morning spiderwebs spun across the trail, but you are not supposed to pick your own name.) My friend Ned, having now been with me twice and seen my quirky and enthusiastic use of a collapsible dog bowl as a sink, started calling me Dogbowl yesterday. It seems to fit—my Chinese zodiac sign is Earth Dog, and our family dog Gina died not long ago, her empty dog bowl still sitting next to our kitchen table. So, in Gina's honor, Dogbowl it is.

Today's hike, after the first tough climb, is pretty straightforward, with two notable events—one annoying and one memorable. The first is swarming gnats that surround me for what seems like miles—not biting or stinging but just bugging the hell out of me. No matter how fast I walk or how much I swing my baseball cap back and forth to clear them away, they just hang with me until suddenly they are gone. One notable aspect of this is that it only occurs once on my hike. An hour of swarming gnats plus my hornet sting weeks ago—that is the extent of any flying-insect woes.

The second memorable thing about today is rhododendron tunnels. Rhododendrons are beautiful flowering shrubs, common in the

Virginia mountains, that bloom in every possible shade of red/purple/ pink/white in the late spring and early summer. By now the blooms are long gone. But these slick-barked shrubs have formed a canopy over this stretch of the trail for miles and miles. The canopy is thick and fairly short—eight to ten feet high. It is so thick that it blocks out most light even at midday and you feel like you are walking at night. The canopy deadens sound as well, and the dark, solitary quiet is unnerving.

I hit a dirt road in midafternoon after about twelve miles and walk down it for fifteen minutes to the Woods Hole Hostel, a beautiful old chestnut cabin and surrounding outbuildings that was turned into an AT hikers' haven many years ago. It is far off the grid, with a big outdoor woodstove that heats water for the owner and hikers passing through. The owner, Neville (not a trail name), used to visit her grand-parents here as they offered hospitality to hikers. Years later, she came and took over the operation, running it with a no-nonsense spirit of welcome that has made it a real favorite along the AT. A highlight of the place is a cooked communal dinner and breakfast, available for a nominal price so long as you help prepare the food and clean up after.

Three buddies from my neighborhood hiking group—John, Mark, and Tom—arrive just before dinner to join the hike. We herd into the kitchen and are each given chores—mine is dredging fresh green tomatoes from the garden in seasoned flour and then frying them up for the group of about eight hikers who will be eating together. We take all the food out to a table behind the cabin and sit down to eat. Neville tells us to hold hands and go around the table introducing ourselves and saying something we are thankful for.

What am I thankful for? So many thoughts crowd into my head. In fact, of all the thoughts filling my head day after day on the AT, the most common has been, *What am I thankful for?* A wonderful marriage, three independent and adventurous adult children plus an amazing daughter-in-law, parents and in-laws who have lived long lives together, a broad and supportive extended family, a network of lifelong friends, an uplifting church community, a memory full of vivid experiences, the many opportunities I have had throughout my life to help, advocate, and fight for people I care about.

In the seconds before I speak, I realize that I'm literally counting my blessings and that this period of reflection has been facilitated by this hike. It has been the longest vacation I have ever taken. It has also been the most time I have ever spent by myself. I have taken this extended time alone to really grasp how lucky I am.

When it's my turn, I say, "I am Dogbowl, and I am thankful that I have taken the time to do this walk."

My buddies—who haven't been with me yet on this trip and didn't know my recently bestowed trail name—look at me strangely. Dogbowl? But I don't care. I'm a blessed man.

31

We help Neville with the communal breakfast of curried potatoes, eggs, and fresh-baked bread. Afterward, we get a lift up the hill to the trailhead on a Gator—an ATV with an open flatbed where we crowd with our backpacks. Today's hike will take us into Bland County where we will stay at a newly opened hostel with the alluring name Weary Feet.

Hiking as a group of four is very different than what I've been used to so far. The trail seems lively, even though we only see one person all day long. The three friends with me are good companions. John and Mark are the best outdoorsmen in our neighborhood hiking group. John was in the Virginia National Guard for many years and has spent plenty of time camping in the outdoors. He also worked as my Senate state director for six years after a career in management and government relations with our telephone utility. Mark worked a full career in the parks department of Chesterfield County and knows how to do everything and fix anything outdoors. The two of them inspired me on my hike by committing to do the whole Virginia section a few years ago. In the five days they will be with me, they will very nearly finish the entire trail after tackling it a week or two at a time.

Tom is six years older than me and in great shape due to a twice-weekly basketball game that is his passion. He and his wife, Carol, are godparents to my oldest son, Nat, and we used to practice law together. But unlike John and Mark, Tom is less likely to be found schlepping along with a backpack out in the wild.

I have camped many times with John and Mark and our children. They were part of our yearly spring break on the AT tradition and our neighborhood Memorial Day group camping experience at Douthat State Park in the Allegheny Highlands. For a number of years, we would take our kids canoeing on a different river each summer, carrying our gear in dry bags in the boats and camping along the way.

Tom and I have done a lot of outdoor trips over the years. We both like walking in and around the neighborhood where we live. We went camping a few years ago in Fort Valley, an obscure valley hidden inside Massanutten Mountain in the northern Shenandoah Valley, and we once almost drowned together on a reckless float trip on the flooded South Anna River.

All of us are part of a weekly group that crowds into a corner booth at a local diner every Tuesday at 7:30 a.m. for breakfast. I usually miss it because I am in DC, but they don't give me too much grief about that. And all of us have been together on hut-to-hut hikes in Europe.

Today is the flattest day of the entire hike. We start high on a ridge and stay there almost all day. It is a hot fifteen miles with water sources mostly dry but the lack of big climbs makes the day pass quickly as we catch up on family news and the latest neighborhood gossip. Our wives and children are friends and spend time together, so there is a lot to talk about.

Hiking in a group is pleasant because you sometimes hike together, sometimes hike alone, and sometimes break up in differing groups of two during the day for one-on-one conversation. Knowing that you will be together for a few days makes the conversation unrushed. In the informal rules of hiking with a group, those ahead pause every hour or so to make sure everyone catches up and all are doing okay.

One pause is de rigueur with Tom—he will always go for a swim au naturel if there is even a marginally acceptable body of water. And there is a stagnant pond high up in a wilderness area we pass through where the three of us relax in the shade as Tom goes for a dip. We notice snapping turtles in the water and cross our fingers for our friend's safety. Tom is tough and no water is too cold for him—even when high in the Alps or Dolomites with snowmelt in streams and lakes, the temperature doesn't bother him. This water is lukewarm but he swears by it. I stay out of the water because I don't carry a towel and I don't like hiking while wet if I can avoid it.

Toward day's end we descend a slight hill and then walk about six hundred yards down a road to the Weary Feet Hostel. It's an old farmhouse near the AT, just open to hikers about a month ago, and the four of us are the only guests tonight. The owner, Julie, who lives on a nearby farm with her family, kept seeing this house right near the trail and developed the dream to open it as a hostel. The dream percolated for years, and finally she just did it. A friend who moved to the area is helping her—they seem intrigued by the random people the AT delivers to their door.

I see this a lot along the trail—sometimes the hostels are run by people who have done the AT and it changed their lives—Angels Rest and Mountain Home are like that. But other hostels—like Woods Hole and Weary Feet—are started by longtime residents who live near the trail and develop a fascination for the characters who tackle the challenge.

Julie and crew are still renovating the house and working out the kinks when we visit, but they make a hearty dinner—with a vegetarian option for Tom—and we relax with lemonade on the big front porch after our meal, looking downhill toward Kimberling Creek, which is more like a river in size. Some of the family work at a nearby state prison farm, and we hear stories about the crops they grow there and famous escape attempts. The prison is known for the homemade pizzas that they make and sell to other prisons and institutions. We are in Virginia but feel very far from the hustle and bustle of Richmond or Washington.

Our overnight accommodation—four of us in an upstairs bedroom with the only bathroom on the first floor—is a little comical. But the four of us have shared accommodations many times over the years and know each other's quirks very well.

32

Up early, a great breakfast, and off walking. Our sixteen miles to Helvey Mill Shelter will be long today—both hot and up and down the entire way. (I have slept in a real bed the last five nights but am back to shelter/bivy now.) Mark is limping a bit—he hurt his knee a few weeks ago playing soccer, and when he jumped from the flatbed of the Gator yesterday morning, he twisted it further. We take our time today.

These neighbors—all living within a few blocks—have been part of my career in politics from its first days. I was happily practicing law with Tom in the early 1990s right after my oldest son, Nat, was born. I found myself increasingly frustrated by local leadership, especially around issues of racial polarization. As a naive civil rights lawyer, still somewhat new to Richmond, I thought I might be able to be a bridge builder in a city that needed more unity.

I still remember kicking off my first campaign—for the second district seat on Richmond City Council in early 1994—with a tiny event in my backyard. By then, Anne and I had two boys, ages four and two, so I got a local juggler to entertain all the neighborhood kids. Tom, John, Ned, and Mark were there along with maybe forty people max. It was an inauspicious beginning, but we ended up beating an incumbent with the vote total being 1,300 to 1,200, as I remember. The total votes cast in my first election were fewer than in some large high school student council elections! Having also been on a campaign where we got 66 million votes and lost, I will observe that the psychic gulf between not being a candidate and running in a city council ward race is bigger than the difference between running in a small ward race and being on a national ticket. Being the candidate is hard no matter the scale of the race. The supersmart political pundits and bloggers who haven't run for office have no idea how massively different it is to be the one with your name on the ballot. It's a little like fantasy football experts—they may know a lot about football, but playing it is radically different from analyzing it.

My neighbors have been with me every step of the way through ten elections now. They've contributed and helped me campaign, sure—but more important, they've given me encouragement, getting me outdoors so I could get my mind off work, tolerating my lower standard of yard and home maintenance that comes with being in public office where so much work happens at night and on weekends. They know enough to minimize too much political talk when we are together since they read my mind and know that I consider my friends one of my few respites from work.

John and his wife, Fay, even went way above the call of duty and friendship when I was on the ticket in 2016. They live across the street from us and allowed the Secret Service to set up a trailer in their driveway and use a small apartment attached to their garage to provide security during my 105-day Magical Mystery Tour. For that period, they had the safest house in the entire state.

When you are in public life—especially in our polarized politics—you expose your family and friends to some level of hassle. I wish it were otherwise, but along the way people close to me have lost or strained friendships because of their connection with me. They find themselves in the middle of a conversation with someone who doesn't like me, or hates the Democratic party or Barack Obama or Hillary Clinton, and it just gets uncomfortable. I've even had friends and family who have lost job opportunities because of their support for me—usually because their support for their friend Tim was not appreciated by a potential employer who disagreed with my political views or some action I had taken.

I have done things or taken votes that not all family and friends have agreed with. I try never to do anything to embarrass anyone, but there is no way to make everyone happy. You just do your best and count on your real friends to hang in there with you even when they disagree.

Certainly for our kids, being in the spotlight has often been hard—with normal mistakes while growing up being magnified, and merited achievements sometimes dismissed as "You only got that because of your mom and dad." Kids also have to get thick skin when they hear criticism of their parents in politics. My kids have always been good at this—I once walked into the three of them in front of the TV watching a JibJab-style attack ad being run against me in my gubernatorial campaign. No need to comfort them or explain politics is tough—they were all laughing their heads off!

But the challenges for family and friends also have compensations. It has been fun to introduce those close to us to people none of us ever would have met otherwise—Michelle and Barack Obama, Queen Elizabeth, Tom Hanks, Tommy Stinson, Hillary Clinton, Sandra Day O'Connor, Elvis Costello, Charles Barkley—or bring them along to events around Virginia, in DC, and sometimes around the country or even overseas. Especially when I was governor, living in the Governor's Mansion on Capitol Square—a mere three miles from my house—we shifted the venue for a lot of traditional neighborhood events like Christmas and birthday parties, a Passover Seder, and Super Bowl and March Madness watch parties to the Big House and had a lot of fun doing them together.

I also still remember the big party that the neighbors threw for us when we moved back into our house the day my gubernatorial term ended in January 2010. It was a welcome-home party and it felt so good to be back in the neighborhood. I knew the kids felt particularly good to be out of the fishbowl and back with their buddies. And at the pivotal moment of the party, the neighbors presented me with a gift to clarify my new status—a sign made by the Virginia Department of Transportation, commonly seen on unpaved roads around the state, saying "End State Maintenance." True, humbling, and funny.

I will say that these friendships help me keep going in public life after twenty-five years. While it would be much easier to be a Virginia senator living in Northern Virginia a few miles from the US Capitol, Anne and I purposefully keep our home base one hundred miles south in Richmond so that we can maintain the relationships with friends whose lives don't revolve around politics and who knew and accepted us long before either of us got into public life. In Richmond, everyone calls me "Tim," and if someone calls me "Senator," it's like my mom calling me "Timothy"—reserved only for times when I have done something wrong!

I'm brought out of my reverie and back to the trail. Will we ever get to Helveys Mill Shelter? Mark and John are well ahead of Tom and me when we finally reach the turnoff to the shelter. Sadly, it is far off the trail, so we hike down the side trail until we find it. The water source is even farther away. We descend a long way down a hollow until we come to a tiny trickle as the nearly dry stream pours over a rock. We wedge our bottles in the four-inch gap and slowly fill them up for our evening cooking. The long climb back up to the shelter seems to take forever.

33

I get to see my daughter today! The four of us are set to hike about four miles downhill to a spot where the AT crosses I-77 near a tiny grocery/deli called the Brushy Mountain Outpost. This place has meager restocking options but is well known for its homemade sandwiches. Tom will drop off here but my daughter, Annella, will take his place, getting a few days off from her actor life in New York. Once we connect, she will hike about eleven miles with Mark, John, and me to the Jenkins Shelter.

Tom and I start about twenty minutes after John and Mark, and actually get lost walking the side trail from the shelter back to the AT. Then we nearly blunder into a bunch of poison ivy. But after an otherwise pleasant ninety minutes we hit the Outpost and Annella is there waiting for us. John and Mark are eating breakfast biscuits and I splurge for a cheeseburger and Dr Pepper at ten in the morning. All of these guys have known my twenty-four-year-old daughter since she was born. We sit there snacking until Tom's shuttle driver arrives to take him back to Woods Hole to get his car. For a sixty-five-year-old guy who has not backpacked for many years, Tom has done very well indeed.

As John, Mark, Nelly, and I get ready to hike south, we ask the Outpost manager where we can leave my car that Annella has driven down from Richmond. He points to a small gravel lot next to the trailhead with a stone picnic table, and we park there. As we walk away, I look back and wonder whether my car will suffer vandalism in the three days before we get back. It has three bumper stickers: "Kaine 2018" from my Senate reelection, an AT decal, and a bright blue "No Hate" sticker. Bland County is a Republican stronghold that was my worst performance in 134 cities and counties in Virginia when I was up for reelection last year. Oh well—it's only a vehicle!

We climb a long stretch and then hit a set of rises and falls with some great views of the valleys west of Brushy Mountain. I get to catch up with Nelly. It's a tumultuous time for her—she's broken up with a longtime partner and just moved into a new apartment with two friends. She and her writing partner have written a short film script that they like enough to have hired a film crew to shoot in New York when she gets back after the hike. She is still finalizing a few shoot details whenever she can get cell reception on the hike.

Anne and I are both public-interest lawyers, but our children are all so different from us. They are all adventurers in their own way. Nat has been deployed in Africa and on NATO's eastern border with Russia. Woody and Annella are pursuing their artistic dreams, cobbling together odd jobs in and out of the arts to pay the bills so they can do what they love. They are kind and caring people, very focused on their own passions. There were many wonderful events growing up with a politician dad and visible public servant mom but many sacrifices as well.

Annella is a match for the guys as we climb and drop mile after mile. (John says, "Your daughter has grown into Wonder Woman!") Water is short—again—and we hit some streams where we hoped to get water but find none. We finally get to Jenkins Creek and there is water in pools that seem a little stagnant but are at least deep enough to fill our bottles. The shelter is uphill, with signs warning ominously of bear activity.

At the shelter, I make dinner and then Annella and I opt to sleep inside while John and Mark set up their tents. These guys are a hoot. They each sleep in near-identical tents. They have backpacks that look the same. They wear the same kind of hiking clothes, and morning usually starts with "Are you wearing shorts or long pants today?" followed by "I don't know, what about you?" They specialize in hiker hacks that reduce the weight of what they carry by an ounce here or an ounce there and compare notes incessantly about the latest innovation. But they really entertain at the end of the day when we all hang food out of bears' reach.

This is an evening ritual. John chooses a branch where the food bags are to be hung—high enough off the ground that a bear cannot reach it and far enough away from the trunk that a bear cannot climb up and grab it. Mark is then charged with throwing a rope, attached to a stone or stick, over the chosen branch to attach the bag and haul it up to hang. Watching these guys pace around the shelter area discussing each tree and branch until they find the perfect one, and then observing Mark's repeated efforts to get the rope over the branch— punctuated with the inevitable back and forth of "That was a weak throw!" "Well, do you want to try?" "No; I chose the branch, it's your job to get the rope up there!"—is like watching, and then rewatching, a Laurel and Hardy routine.

But we finally get the food hung and turn in. It is cooler tonight and I burrow into the Marine poncho liner Nat has loaned me to replace the fleece sleeping bag liner I was using in the hot weather. Annella and I have no sooner turned off our headlamps when acorns blown by the mountain breeze land on the tin roof with a sound like gunshots. I wonder whether Mark and John are throwing rocks on the roof to spook us. Who knows what Annella thinks—this shelter in the middle of nowhere is a world away from the East Harlem apartment she was in less than forty-eight hours ago.

34

Today we will climb to a bucket-list vista—one I've never seen but have always wanted to during my thirty-five years in Virginia.

Burke's Garden is an obscure geologic feature in Tazewell and Bland Counties, a massive collapsed limestone sinkhole named after an Irish immigrant who was part of a team that first surveyed the area in the 1740s. The collapse formed an elliptical valley, a few thousand feet deep, about eight miles north to south, and three or four miles across at its widest point. The valley floor is fertile farmland, with many Mennonite farmers who came here after discovering how cut off it was from civilization. One paved road comes in from the west, and a winding gravel road enters from the east.

I have seen Burke's Garden from the air while flying but have never been here. Our thirteen-mile hike today ascends to the eastern ridge of the valley and then follows it all the way to its southern tip, where we will stay at Chestnut Knob Shelter, an enclosed stone shelter that used to be the hut for a fire warden who manned a long-ago-destroyed fire tower looking out over the valley.

Getting there will be a challenge due to acute water shortages. We have water at Jenkins Creek, but hikers posting on Guthook note that there is no water between here and eight miles past the Chestnut Knob Shelter. We have to plan for twenty-three miles—about two days—without a water refill. Each of us is carrying three one-liter bottles.

As we fill up at Jenkins Creek, Annella and I hatch our plan. We will try to do the hike on one liter of water each. The second one-liter bottle will be for cooking our dinner and breakfast. The third and final liter will have to last us through tomorrow, until we finally hit a refill spot.

But hiking in the heat immediately challenges the plan. It is very hard to carry a thirty-pound pack for thirteen miles, climbing and descending in ninety-degree heat, on one measly liter of water. Wisely avoiding dehydration, we don't pace ourselves and each drink at a more rapid clip.

God, how we take ample clean water for granted. So many in the world cannot, and they spend an enormous amount of time planning their days and lives around getting water. Now, climate change is driving water shortages in the US, and the incompetence of some government leaders means that even communities with apparent access to water—Flint, Michigan, is near the largest set of freshwater lakes in the world—find themselves cut off from a healthy supply of life's essential necessity.

But we catch a break. About two-thirds of the way to our end point, we reach the winding gravel road that crosses the eastern ridge before descending into Burke's Garden. Someone has left an entire case of bottled water just sitting next to the trail. It is trail magic—a nearby resident noticing the dry conditions and deciding to take pity on bedraggled hikers. We refill our own bottles—probably one and a half liters each—and now have confidence that we will make it through the day and tomorrow morning.

We reach a last climb: one final mile that gains eight hundred feet in elevation to the open ridge where the shelter sits. John and Annella hike ahead but Mark and I move slowly. He is feeling his knee getting more and more painful. I am trying an experiment—trying to walk so slowly that I stop sweating. I am the last to reach the peak—a beautiful meadow with the hut sitting two hundred yards ahead, out in the sun with an amazing view north across the length of Burke's Garden. I arrive to see Annella flat on her back in the meadow, beat after the long day. The quilt of tiny farms in the valley below looks like an oil painting. I see why folks call this place "God's Thumbprint."

The hut itself is simple—enclosed stone with a boarded-up fireplace, six bunks, and a picnic table. It is clear and breezy, the highest shelter I have stayed at yet—two thousand feet higher than our shelter last night—and something suggests it will get cold tonight. We make our dinner at the picnic table inside and spend time outside watching the sun set and stars fill the dark sky, so far from any manmade light.

Two guys hiking from the opposite direction of our group arrive after dark, South Carolina college friends who live in different cities but meet every year for an AT hiking weekend. They wonder about water and are disappointed to hear that there is none near. They are hopeful after we tell them about the trail magic they will experience tomorrow, although they confirm that *we* will need to walk about eight miles first thing tomorrow before we reach a creek to refill.

The six of us have a restful night, the howling wind outside making us grateful that this shelter—unlike any other during my hike—is fully enclosed. Nocturnal trips outside the hut reveal bright stars and fall temperatures. I am happy to finally be at Burke's Garden, sharing it with Annella and my friends.

35

Today will be the last day of my twenty-eight-day stretch of hiking during our summer recess. It is a Saturday. When we finish our mostly downhill twelve-mile walk to Route 42, Annella and I will have some friends pick us up for a ride back to the parking area in Bland where we left my car two days ago. John and Mark are trying to decide whether they will hike on for another day before coming home. I have come a long way and will still have about seven days of walking to Tennessee, but I relish the thought of doing those miles in early October rather than the dead of summer.

I walk with a definite spring in my step, proud of the twenty-eight days I have been out in the wild. I wear long hiking pants for the first time as the temperature is at least fifteen degrees cooler than yesterday. As we descend a long stretch, we hear two hounds baying in the distance. They get closer and closer until they encounter the four of us on the trail. Each dog is wearing a bizarre contraption around its collar with antennae sprouting on both sides of its neck. I have never seen this before, but it must be some form of transmitter that their owner is using to track the dogs as they head deeper and deeper into the woods. The dogs follow us for miles, bolting into the woods to our right and left every so often, baying loudly when they think they detect an animal worth chasing. We worry that we are taking them far away from their home, but at some point they just turn around and start running back the way they came.

We finally hit an ample creek with water and visit with two hikers who are there going northbound. One hiked the entire Pacific Crest Trail this year and is already itching for more. The other wears earbuds, listening to music along the way. As much as I love music, that seems sacrilegious to me.

Having John and Mark with me for five days has been great. They truly are consummate backpackers with a solution to any problem faced in the wild. We talk about neighborhood stuff with Annella as we walk this morning. The current controversy is whether the name of our street—Confederate Avenue—should be changed.

Our street was built around 1915, right on the spot where the Confederate Army erected an intermediate line of defense—raised earthworks—to protect the heart of Richmond, about four miles away. The name was designed to commemorate that feature. While most, though not all, neighbors think the name should be changed, there are widely varying views over what the new name should be. John and his wife, Fay, do what they always do: volunteer to be good neighbors and solicit opinions of everyone on our block. Now John realizes that he is in a thankless position, trying to harmonize the many different points of view.

In Richmond, I have dealt with such issues—erecting or removing statues and naming of public streets, parks, bridges, buildings, etc.— throughout my time in public life. When we put a statue of Richmond legend Arthur Ashe up on Monument Avenue, previously reserved for monumental statues of Confederate generals, complaints from the Sons of Confederate Veterans, David Duke and his nutty followers, and African Americans arguing that the street wasn't good enough for Ashe rippled through the city for weeks.

Virginia is so drenched with history, good and bad, that these controversies are destined to occur again and again. I generally follow two rules when they come up: (1) the quality of your listening has a direct relationship to the public acceptance of your resolution, and (2) the issue is not just subtraction (what to take down) but also addition (what to put up). Kehinde Wiley's monumental statue *Rumors of War*, soon to be installed at the Virginia Museum of Fine Arts on the newly renamed Arthur Ashe Boulevard, is a great proof of the second principle.

Mark is slowing down a good bit because of his knee, and when we reach a shelter around lunchtime, he and John decide to rest there a while as they decide how much they want to keep hiking today and tomorrow. Annella and I say goodbye to them and press on down the mountain.

We reach the road near the tiny community of Ceres, and Annella gives me a big hug to celebrate our accomplishment together. She has done about thirty-six miles in three days and handled it like a trooper. I have now finished nearly 470 miles. We've arranged for two local friends of mine, John and Linda, to come pick us up and take us back up the road to our car parked near I-77. There is a Dairy Queen along the way, and we stop for ice cream.

John and Linda are stalwart Democrats from the nearby town of Wytheville. They are wonderful examples of the giving, energetic, fun friends I have made in every corner of Virginia during my time in public life. Linda used to work for a congressman, back when this part of the state was willing to elect a Democrat, and she is always up for helping candidates, no matter their chances of victory. John is a baseball fanatic like me and we always have sports news to catch up on, especially the ongoing comeback of the Washington Nationals after their horrendous start to the 2019 season.

I make a deal with John and Linda—when I come back to complete the hike in about a month, I will be the special guest at an event for their favorite local candidate. This year, the entire Virginia state legislature is up for election, and Linda has a young doctor who has really impressed her. We check our calendars over ice cream and choose the first Saturday in October as the date of the event.

As we leave the Dairy Queen to drive to our car, I recall my trepidation as we left it a few days ago. Would I find my car vandalized because of the sympathies evidenced by my bumper stickers? I felt guilty thinking about it, but I nevertheless am anxious as we round the curve to my vehicle. As it turns out, there was no need to worry—my car is just as I left it. I should not be surprised. People may be intense about politics on the air or online, but in my quarter century in Virginia politics, I have had fewer than ten unpleasant interactions with anybody in person.

Annella and I pile in, wave goodbye to John and Linda, and start the five-hour drive back to Richmond, where we will arrive in time for a late dinner with Anne. We talk about the hike and about Annella's plan to shoot her script in New York starting Monday. As we head north on I-81, I keep looking up at the mountain ridges with a shocked feeling of "I've actually walked all of this." It doesn't seem possible.

36

I return to the trail after a month back in the Senate. I have seven days of hiking ahead and ninety-one miles to the Virginia-Tennessee border just south of the town of Damascus.

A lot has happened in the month back in DC. First, my colleagues all looked amazed when they saw me, with many asking, "What happened to you?" In the twenty-eight-day hiking stretch in August and September, I lost twenty-six pounds and have a hard time tightening my belt enough to keep my pants on. My friends' reactions run from jealousy to doubts about my sanity.

The House of Representatives has started an impeachment inquiry into Donald Trump's efforts to strong-arm Ukraine to help him dig up dirt on Joe Biden. That we would be at this point is unsurprising to anyone who has paid attention to the character Trump has demonstrated so plainly throughout his life. The outcome seems clear—there will never be enough Republican votes to convict this president for anything he does—but the specter of an impeachment trial, thankfully so rare in our history, is casting a dark shadow on the Capitol.

Anne is now full speed ahead as president of George Mason and is back and forth between Fairfax and Richmond, working to help her school attain equity in the way it is treated by state government. As the first woman president of the school, she is everywhere with students. I love going with her to events and being introduced as "the First Man of George Mason." It makes me proud to see how women faculty, employees, and students are particularly excited to see her and inspired by her leadership to go after their own big dreams.

I fly to Seattle to officiate at Heath's wedding, a great former staffer. It is the eighteenth wedding I have performed. One of the best parts of my job is being surrounded by young and altruistic people, who often meet their life partners while they work for me.

Virginia is in the midst of a big campaign season. I did a lot of campaigning from spring until August and then have been heavy on the campaign trail since I got off the AT a month ago. Democrats stand on the verge of taking control of both Houses of the state legislature, completing an eighteen-year effort to turn Virginia politics around.

When I ran my first race in partisan politics—for lieutenant governor—in 2001, Virginia Democrats had nothing. We held no statewide offices, no Senate seats, and hadn't won electoral votes for a Democratic presidential nominee for nearly forty years. Both our state legislative Houses and our congressional delegation were overwhelmingly Republican.

But 2001 started our comeback. Mark Warner had a big win for governor and I won my race for lieutenant governor. Slowly, we have returned from the wilderness—flipping both Senate seats; gaining a majority of the Congressional delegation; winning electoral votes in 2008, 2012, and 2016 for Democratic nominees; taking three out of four governor's races since Warner's breakthrough win in 2001; and frequently winning other statewide offices. The most elusive piece of the puzzle has been winning our two state Houses—gerrymandered in 2011 to benefit Republicans—so that we can finally address issues like gun safety, empowering voters, increasing the minimum wage, ratifying the Equal Rights Amendment, immigration reform, and other priorities that a Republican legislature has long stymied. I have been heartened by the energy I have seen as I have been out helping our state candidates, and—after one week finishing my hike—I will throw myself back into campaigning in the home stretch before early November.

I often tell my colleagues that Virginia is the best example of how to turn a red state blue. Democrats nominate practical progressives instead of ideologues, while Republicans normally nominate ideologues instead of practical conservatives. (And the practical conservatives are actually being chased out of the Republican Party in Virginia and across the nation.) Democrats appeal to a diversifying state—with outreach to young people, racial minorities, and our fast-growing immigrant populations—while Republicans push voters away by denying the reality of climate change, opposing immigration reform, and pushing an agenda seen by young voters, women, minorities, LGBTQ+ folks, and others as anti-equality. We started to really switch the suburban vote from Republican to Democratic during my 2005 governor's race, and that trend has only accelerated in Northern Virginia, the Richmond area, and Hampton Roads. Perhaps most important—when Democrats win races, we show we can run things competently. We had to convince voters to take a chance and vote Democratic. We then govern in ways that don't disappoint. Voters do like competence.

I get frustrated that national Democrats don't seem to pay much attention to how we've done it in Virginia—as pro-growth, pro-equality progressives. At the national level, the Democratic economic message is muddy, and Republicans tend to have the polling edge on management of the economy, the biggest issue for most people. We still win races by making it up on other issues—health care, support for education, belief in science, support for safety-net programs, commitment to equality, and women's rights. But we shouldn't cede the economy to Republicans.

Okay, enough politics. It's not just campaign season, it's finally fall! I started my hike in the cool, rainy spring, did the bulk of the trip in a record-smashing hot summer, and am striving now to finish in Virginia's highest mountains as temperatures drop, hours of daylight shrink, and our massive tree cover starts its dramatic change in color. Spring and fall in Virginia are truly magical.

I start at Route 42 and have thirteen miles from Ceres to Groseclose, a small crossroads town where the AT crosses back to the east side of I-81. It is a cool, breezy, overcast day. I hike in a long-sleeve shirt for the first time. At my first extended stop, I check my phone and see a text from John and Linda reminding me that today is the opening of the season to bowhunt deer. I notice the drab colors I am wearing and decide, even though it's not raining, to put on my bright-blue rain jacket. I have come too far to get shot by a bowhunter who sees motion in the woods and fires an arrow my way.

Literally fifteen minutes after donning the jacket, I round the corner and see two camouflaged guys standing over a buck they have just killed. I see four more pairs of hunters during the remainder of my hike today. I haven't thought much about dangers on the trail for weeks, but today and tomorrow I am hiking in the area where a disturbed guy attacked two hikers with a machete in May, killing one and badly injuring the other. The injured hiker played dead and then, bleeding, hiked six miles to a place where she could call 911. This stretch of trail was shut down so local law enforcement could make an arrest. (The shelter logs have some tense trail notes from during the search, when people were awoken by law enforcement in the middle of the night.) The attacker has been in custody, charged with murder and assault, and as of this writing is under evaluation for mental illness.

One of the many sad things about the case was that the attacker, known by the trail name Sovereign, had been harassing hikers for weeks up and down the AT. I find out long afterward that he had been hassling folks very near to where I was during my first weekend hiking in Northern Virginia in early May. He had even been arrested and then released by law enforcement in Tennessee a few weeks before his rampage. Everyone who encountered him knew he was very disturbed. The massive undertreatment of people with mental illness in this country claims so many lives, especially among those with mental illness who harm themselves or are victimized by others.

I get to Groseclose in the early afternoon and John picks me up for a ride back to his house in Wytheville. He and Linda have helped organize a campaign event for Starla, the talented young doctor running for the legislature in a very Republican district nearby. The crowd is enthusiastic and glad that I am there to help. Starla does very well in telling us why she moved home to Appalachia after going to Harvard Medical School and why her experiences with her patients motivate her to run for office.

One of my favorite things in politics is helping first-time candidates. Starla reminds me of a more talented version of myself from twenty-five years ago. But there is also a cold reality to any campaign that is unrelated to the talent of the candidate. I ran my first race as an upstart underdog—but in a Democratic district where I definitely had a real path to win. Starla is running as a Democratic underdog in a gerrymandered district in the most Republican part of the state. Her race is very tough. She knows that and is going for it despite the numbers. God bless her and all like her.

37

Linda and John make me a great breakfast and then Linda drops me off at the Groseclose trailhead where John picked me up yesterday. I will try to hike about sixteen miles today and then will get a shuttle driver to meet me at a road crossing so I can go in and stay at a historic hotel in Marion, one of my favorite small towns in Virginia.

Of the many things I have enjoyed in politics, getting to know our very diverse regions—Appalachia, Southside, Tidewater, the New River Valley, the Shenandoah Valley, the Northern Neck, the Middle Peninsula, the Eastern Shore, Central Virginia, Northern Virginia—has been the best. I love my hometown of Richmond, but the small towns around Virginia remind me of the farm towns where my grandparents lived—El Dorado and Wamego, Kansas. We spent many a summer and holiday in small towns growing up.

The Appalachian part of Southwest Virginia is a particular favorite. Anne grew up in Roanoke and had family in Big Stone Gap, St. Paul, and Abingdon, along with some relatives in Beckley, West Virginia. Long before I even got into local politics, we would come here together to visit friends and relatives, enjoy a vigorous arts and culture scene, and spend time camping and hiking.

Anne has her own amazing political pedigree. Her dad, Linwood Holton—raised in Big Stone Gap right on the Kentucky border—was the first Republican governor in Virginia since Reconstruction, serving from 1970 to 1974. He absorbed as a Depression-era child that discrimination was wrong as he saw how some folks looked down on people from Appalachia. He went to Washington and Lee, served as a submariner in the Pacific during World War II, went to Harvard Law

School on the G.I. Bill when he returned home, and started his law practice in Roanoke.

At the time Lin began his career, Virginia politics was dominated by a Democratic Party committed to segregation and keeping voter participation low. Republicans were few and far between, and strategies like poll taxes and literacy tests were used to disenfranchise virtually all African Americans and many poor whites as well. Lin vowed to create a two-party democracy in Virginia to bust up one-party rule and the discrimination that he had hated ever since he was a kid.

Lin and his wife, Jinks, the daughter of a prominent Roanoke lawyer and unique person in her own right (having worked for the CIA in Brussels and Washington after she graduated from Wellesley in the late 1940s), worked so hard to change Virginia into the state it is today. They labored with others to build a true competitive democracy, and after three unsuccessful runs for office, Lin was elected governor in 1969.

He did many great things—created the cabinet system, expanded state parks, cleaned up polluted rivers, formed the unified port in Hampton Roads that is a key global gateway for Virginia—but is best known for striking the death blow to school segregation. Within a year of assuming office, Lin abandoned the previous state policy of fighting integration and escorted his own children into Richmond's predominantly African American public schools. One photo of him walking Anne's sister, Tayloe, into her high school—at a time when other Southern governors were photographed standing in schoolhouse doors to block students of color from attending—was a *New York Times* front-page shot now reprinted in many Virginia history books.

Sadly, Lin's work to promote integration made him a political pariah in the years after his term ended. He tried to run for the Senate in 1978, but even as a founder of the modern Republican Party, finished a distant third out of four in a Republican nominating convention. That was the end of his role as a candidate or party leader, and it was very hard for him at the time. But he got to see his dreams for a better Commonwealth and country coming true. (I took him as my guest to President Obama's inauguration in January 2009; when it was over, he said, "This is everything that I worked for my whole life.") Today, people see Lin and Jinks—in their mid-nineties and still going strong—as real heroes for what they did at a critical time to turn Virginia from the past to the present and future. He is my political hero—both for standing for racial justice when it was tough and for busting up one-party rule in Virginia.

In my own state campaigns, it was fun to get Lin back on the trail after a twenty-five-year absence, especially as we toured Appalachia. He would often begin addressing a crowd of local Democrats in towns like Marion with "I sorta feel like a skunk wandering into the family picnic," but the affection for this heroic Republican former governor—who never forgot where he came from—always made me feel really good. When I was governor—with Anne serving as First Lady in the same place where she had spent her teenage years—it was a certain kind of poetic justice to welcome Lin and Jinks back home to the Governor's Mansion again.

I am sure that this family tie is why I love Appalachia so much—despite having never been able to win races here. My vote percentage—like all Democrats—really dropped after the Obama 2008 election, but my supporters here are probably my most loyal. It's relatively easy to be a Kaine backer when your neighbors are too—much harder when 65–75 percent of your neighbors are going the other way. But supporters or not, folks here are unfailingly welcoming and fun to be with. And when you are done with a meeting or an event, they say something that I only hear in Appalachia: "'Preciate ya." They mean it too. No wonder my own Senate staff always fights to accompany me on trips to Southwest Virginia.

Back to the task at hand. After a fairly easy twelve-mile hike, I reach a national forest visitor center that is open and surprisingly busy on this fall Sunday afternoon. There is a phone for hikers to use and I call a shuttle in Marion—seven miles away—to arrange a pickup in two

Start of Appalachian Trail trip at Harpers Ferry—the Bloody Stone Steps.

Be it ever so humble . . .

Balance is everything . . .

Whiskey Hollow shelter.

Atop Mount Marshall.

Early morning visitor at Lewis
Mountain cabins.

Tentsite A-20 at Loft Mountain in the Shenandoah National Park.

Charles and Adam.

Breakfast of
champions.

Crossing the Foot Bridge over the James River.

Does this meet Senate dress code? Maybe.

The Guillotine.

Bruiser Cairns.

Crescent moon over Pearisburg.

Neighborhood gang at Woods Hole Hostel.

Neighborhood gang plus Annella climbing near Burke's Garden.

Chestnut Knob shelter.

Near Mount Rogers.

At the Virginia/
Tennessee line!

Playing with the Cary
Street Ramblers in
Richmond.

Nightwingnuts.

Morning fog near the Parkway.

My first bike.

Trying out the repaired canoe at Great Dismal Swamp.

Day 1 on the James River.

Annella, Fern, and Anne on the Upper James.

My normal riverside set up.

Above Balcony Falls.

Standard canoe
sunburn.

Rassawek.

Old Raggedy beached at east end of Jamestown Island.

Arriving at Fort Monroe during a small craft warning.

Birthplace of the James River in Iron Gate—dark water from the Jackson and clear water from the Cowpasture forming Virginia's mighty stream.

Picked up a hitchhiker along the river.
Photo credit Tom Wolf.

My twenty-seven-hour drive to DC in an ice storm.

My favorite picture of the whole journey: Nat and me on McAfee Knob.

hours at another road crossing four miles south. The shuttle works like a charm, and within a half hour of finishing, I check into the General Francis Marion Hotel, a classic old hotel recently renovated on Main Street, next door to the Lincoln Theatre, a great old venue for live events, especially bluegrass music.

I am no sooner in the lobby than some folks arriving for a small conference with independent pharmacies in the region recognize me and press me into attending a reception with them, hiking clothes notwithstanding. We talk about some state and federal regulatory issues, catch up on the local political races (two Republican legislators are also in attendance), and then I wander across the street to grab some food to bring back to the room so I can watch the Chiefs and Colts play on Sunday Night Football. (My pro sports loyalties are with the Royals and Chiefs—as befits a Kansas City native—and now the Nats.) I luxuriate at the small hotel, knowing that tomorrow I will be far from creature comforts in Virginia's highest mountains with cold and rainy weather on the way.

38

The town of Marion is quiet as I leave early in the morning and pass right by the historic Smyth County Courthouse. Back during my days practicing law, I was one of a handful of lawyers in Virginia willing to take on habeas corpus cases for Virginia death row inmates who lacked attorneys. No one should face execution without an attorney. When I was appointed to represent an inmate who had committed two murders here, I spent a lot of time in the surrounding area, investigating the case and interviewing witnesses and the attorneys who had handled the trial. Even though the case was notorious, I will always remember how cooperative all the Smyth County court personnel were. And when I ran for governor and was attacked by my opponent for representing death row inmates, a local legislator used to remind audiences that John Adams had the courage to represent the English soldiers tried after the Boston Massacre.

I catch a ride to the AT road crossing where I dropped off yesterday, and start a twenty-mile walk to Old Orchard Shelter. For the next three days, I will be hiking in the wilderness areas near Virginia's two highest peaks: Mount Rogers and Whitetop Mountain.

The trail today is steadily climbing and will get to nearly 5,500 feet elevation tomorrow. It is also very winding—the twenty miles of walking looks like it would be about five miles as the crow flies, but that is due to steep mountains and some rerouted sections of the AT. All day long it is foggy and occasionally drizzly, with a weather forecast promising a cold front and torrential rain starting mid- to late afternoon. I do not dawdle.

This stretch—from here all the way to Tennessee—is one of the three parts of the AT that I have done many times: Thornton Gap to Rockfish Gap, the section between the Tye and James Rivers, and this section. They have always been my favorites. And now that I have seen it all, including many new stretches I really like, I still put this finishing stretch at the top of the list.

I first stayed at the Old Orchard Shelter in May 1987. Anne and I came out to the area to backpack for four days the weekend after I left a job to find one that would be a better fit for the civil rights work I wanted to do. We had been married less than three years, and the weekend was so memorable because it felt like I was embarking on a new chapter, one that seemed open, uncertain, and exciting. Anne, working hard as a legal-aid lawyer and glad for a long weekend off, had climbed Mount Rogers once before with her sister and talked often about that trip. This would be my first journey up Virginia's highest peak—named after William Barton Rogers, a professor of geology at William and Mary and UVA who did pioneering studies of how the Appalachian Mountains were formed. He went on to become the founding president of MIT. I remember many aspects of that hike in 1987 but two stand out: soaking our sore feet in an ice-cold stream at the end of the trip, and driving a sick thru-hiker to the Roanoke airport on our way back to Richmond so he could head home.

Nearly twenty years later, in my first year as governor, my Richmond neighbors (John, Mark, and some others) and I brought our kids out here for spring break in early April. The night we arrived, we had to set up tents in the midst of a swirling snowstorm. After watching our group of about eight struggle to get set, my security detail wisely chose to sleep in a nearby cabin! But we hit the trail the next morning together in steadily improving weather and camped back at Old Orchard one night. That time, the meadow downhill from the shelter was used for a cutthroat Wiffle ball game.

I wonder how the area will look now after the passage of another fifteen years. As the sky looks more and more ominous, I pick up the pace to get there before the promised rain starts. I see no one on the trail for most of the day, pass two empty shelters and a pretty waterfall on Comers Creek, and eventually reach a small road that signals there are fewer than two miles to go. Filling up on water in a swift-running stream, I race up the mountain and get to the shelter just ahead of the raindrops. The shelter looks the same, but the meadow where I camped before has now been overgrown, not as much clear space as I remember from 1987 and 2006.

I set up first in the shelter and am soon joined by a group of students from Duke who are part of an outdoor club hiking in the area during fall break. They set up tents and a cook tarp in the meadow, and the heavy rain does not dampen their spirits. Just as dark sets, four guys come up the trail after a long drive from Ohio, starting their own multiday trip. They also set up tents, but by now the rain and cold are serious enough that they come sit in the shelter to visit and make dinner until they are ready to turn in. They travel well fortified—wine, whiskey, beer, pot brownies, and at least one handgun in case of trouble. They are clearly frequent outdoor companions by the stories they are telling. They are generous with their whiskey to the solo hiker in the corner, and I'm grateful. It is the first really cold night of my hike, but the shelter is dry, and I drift off to the sound of drenching rain, sleeping soundly until just before dawn, when I hear the howl of a lonely coyote.

39

Today is not a long day—just twelve miles to the Thomas Knob Shelter—but it is foggy and raining, making the trail slippery. I leave early and notice that the Dukies and Ohio guys are still asleep in their tents.

It's slow going as the trail climbs through a steep forest. The only sounds are water dripping on leaves and my own labored breathing. Although I have been able to keep my mind off work for most of the hike, today I find myself unable to shake my thoughts about the Senate—and, indeed, what is happening in the country. The start of the House impeachment inquiry has made the moment even more extraordinary, and I naturally grapple with the question: What does it mean for America?

After 9/11, when some Virginia preachers suggested that the attack might be a punishment America suffered because of moral transgression, I found myself thinking of the various explanations for why societies go through trials and tribulations. I was drawn to the Book of Job. Whatever one thinks about the Bible, the stories contained there, read by people around the world for millennia, have a profound appeal based on their lessons about human nature. The Book of Job tackles one of the most universal questions—how to understand suffering. And while most consider the story as one about the suffering of individuals, you can also apply its lessons to gain insight into why societies go through rough times.

Job was a good person who had it all and then started to lose his wealth, health, family, and reputation. He raged against the injustice of it—after all, he was a good person. Was his goodness irrelevant and pointless in a random universe where people suffer despite all their efforts to be faithful and do right?

Those around Job saw his suffering and had a different reaction. Because Job was suffering, he must have done bad things. These bad things—whatever they were—were not known by his neighbors but were visible to God. His losses were a divine punishment.

These are two basic approaches to understanding suffering: it is either random and pointless, or it is a punishment for sin. But neither was the reason for Job's predicament. The reader knows that Job suffered because *he was being tested*. The book opens with God and Satan engaging in a wager. Job is a good and faithful man. Satan posits that Job is only good because he has everything. God says Job would be good and faithful regardless. The two of them decide (cruelly—if we are to be honest) to progressively strip Job of all human comforts and see whether he still holds to his faith. Job isn't happy and argues with God about the way he is being treated. But even in his anger he refuses to abandon his principles. As the book ends, all that was lost is restored. Job is sadder and wiser, but his steadfast hold on his principles carried him to a better day.

Job helps us understand that tough times need not be either pointless or a punishment. Instead, they can be viewed as a test—in times of trouble, will you hold to your principles or abandon them? Over the course of my walk, and in the months since as I seek to understand the moment we live in, this is the answer that comes to me: We are being tested. Will we remain true to—or abandon—our principles?

So many American principles seem under stress these days. Will we respect the religious beliefs of all, or kick Muslims around and allow antisemitism to fester and grow? Do we believe in a vigorous and free press, or should we demean journalists and turn a blind eye to authoritarian thugs who imprison or murder them? Are we all equal under the law, or are some above it? Are public servants to be respected or viewed with suspicion as part of some deep state? Do we recognize science and facts, or demean competence and knowledge and just allow the one with the loudest microphone to win? Are we proud of our status as a nation of immigrants, or do we pull up the drawbridge now to refuse others entry?

I have no doubt that if we hold to principles, we will get through our challenges. And—while I admit to a few more doubts about this next proposition—I do believe enough of us are still dedicated to basic American principles that we will come through all current and future storms. Sadder and wiser, perhaps, and certainly recognizing our own capacity for error, but moving forward to be the great nation we are meant to be.

I can think of some friends—especially Mark Warner, my friend of forty years and Senate colleague—who would call that observation a classic overly optimistic Kaine perspective. "Keep calm and carry on, eh?" he'd say. But my simple epiphany—hold fast to your values and there are better times ahead—is no panacea or guarantee. It depends on two things: a critical assessment of the values we proclaim and an honest examination of whether we truly act consistently with them.

I think the values that Americans proclaim—the equality of each person; the notion of democratic rule combined with legal protection of minorities who might have much to fear from majoritarianism; wide tolerance of free speech, thought, assembly, belief, and expression; the ability of all to participate—are sound and eternal. In fact, they are not even American values but universal human values. We can claim pride in the fact that our imperfect founders wisely chose values like the equality principle, but they are not our exclusive intellectual property.

Still, while America proclaims the right values, it has always been fair to question whether we fully appreciate and live by them, and whether we remain willing to sacrifice to maintain them. This has been the continual tension in American life—the gap between high-minded ideals and our actual practice. We are struggling with it today in an epic manner.

Speaking of struggles, I emerge now in a grassy meadow called The Scales, a large meadow on top of a ridge. This area is known for wild horses and ponies and was once used as a place to gather and take them to market for sale. Normally the views here are magnificent but the fog is intense—more like clouds blowing through the slight gap—so I press on. Higher I climb, and horses appear and vanish silently in the fog, paying me little attention as I walk by.

The trail briefly enters one of my favorite places to camp—the Little Wilson Creek Wilderness—and then approaches another gorgeous spot, Grayson Highlands State Park. I keep rising, eventually climbing up Wilburn Ridge, requiring a scramble up some cliffs and a comical push through the Fat Man's Squeeze, a narrow rock passage made harder by the backpack I am wearing.

I keep thinking I will round the corner and find Thomas Knob Shelter, 5,400 feet in elevation and about a quarter mile from the summit of Mount Rogers. I am soaked, tired, and cold. It has not been one of my longest days, but it has felt like it.

Finally, there it is—a double-decker shelter with the second floor fully enclosed, like an attic on top of the open three-sided first level of the shelter. One southbound thru-hiker who I saw briefly yesterday is set up downstairs. I wrestle my pack up the ladder and into the attic. It is much dryer and warmer there. I cook dinner down on the first level and visit a little before heading up the ladder to turn in.

But where are the Ohio guys? They told me their plan was to stay here tonight. Once again, right at dark—hours after I arrive—they stumble in, soaked to the bone. I hear one of them say, "I know what the map says, but that was at least twenty miles."

They all make dinner downstairs, but two want to get out of the cold and climb the ladder up to the attic to spread out their sleeping bags on the wooden floor while their friends set up below. Under the influence of the liquor and brownies, and assuming I am asleep, they converse in whispers with real vulnerability about their romantic relationships. One is divorced and regrets it, now missing his ex-wife. The other is in a long-term relationship but thinking of breaking up, yet finding the decision agonizingly hard. Just like trying to fathom the reason for suffering, the desire to love and be loved is a unifying eternal for all humankind.

40

Day forty. If I were really calculating, I would have pushed harder earlier in the trip so that today would be my finish. Forty days in the wilderness has a poetic, scriptural ring. But alas, I will have a medium hike today, a long hike tomorrow, and should finish the following day with a short mountain climb from the trail town of Damascus, Virginia, to the Tennessee border. I'm still not counting my chickens, though, because I remember the woman I met weeks ago who got within two hundred miles of finishing her 2,200-mile thru-hike only to break an ankle. But it feels good to be close.

First, I ditch my pack and race up the blue-blazed side trail to the Mount Rogers summit, the highest in Virginia at 5,729 feet. The summit is covered with pine trees and affords no view, but it is good to return there for a few minutes. I have stood in this spot with my wife and then again with my children and neighbors at very different times in my life. Today I am alone. The trees drip with last night's rain, and fog blankets everything.

Back down to the AT where I don my pack and begin today's thirteen-mile hike to Lost Mountain Shelter. My law-school buddy Scott is flying down from New Hampshire to finish the hike with me. He just decided a few days ago, right around the time when I lost cell service. I hope my directions for the meeting spot went through.

The hike today is mostly downhill to a beautiful valley called Elk Garden, then a climb up the side of Whitetop Mountain, rounding the mountain to Buzzard Rock and then a long downhill to Route 58, where Scott is supposed to meet me. We will then climb a mile or so up Lost Mountain to the shelter.

Because of nearly forty hours of straight rain, the streams are finally flowing again! So much of the trip has been about water scarcity, and it feels good to see abundance. By the time I hit Elk Garden at midmorning, the clouds have moved out and the bright sun warms things up. The views of mountains and valleys in every direction—Virginia, North Carolina, and Tennessee—are magnificent. On this trip, I have hiked when it's been ninety degrees and sunny, when it's been ninety degrees and rainy, and when it's been fifty degrees and rainy. But finally, on day forty, I've hit my favorite hiking weather—sixty degrees and sunny.

This part of Virginia is known for many things, but for me, music is the standout. Bluegrass or mountain or old-time bands—with a guitar, bass, banjo, fiddle, mandolin—are everywhere in Southwest Virginia. The Carter Family popularized this music at a revolutionary recording session in nearby Bristol in the 1920s. Ralph Stanley built a decades-long career from his base near Coeburn, Virginia, and today you can hear music any night of the week in virtually any community near here. World-famous guitar maker Wayne Henderson lives just a few miles from Whitetop.

The real heart of Virginia music is The Crooked Road, an assemblage of music venues and music history sites connected by the winding backroads in these mountain counties. From the Ralph Stanley Museum in Clintwood and the Carter Family Fold in Hiltons to the Birthplace of Country Music in Bristol and the Floyd Country Store in the mountain county south of Roanoke, the local talent, and the national talent and visitors they draw, put this area on the map with music aficionados from around the world.

When I was a kid, I envied my friends who had music lessons, so I decided to teach myself to play the harmonica one summer when I was thirteen. By summer's end, after painfully dissonant practice every day, I had taught myself to play ten songs or so. But more importantly, I now had the instinctive knowledge about how the instrument worked so I could play by ear—listening to a song and then figuring out what would sound good if I played along.

I played with small groups from high school through young adulthood, even occasionally with the gospel choir at my church. But other than family and church friends, no one really knew that I played harmonica until I ran for governor in 2005. Anne and I were campaigning at a wonderful event—the Galax Old Time Fiddler's Convention, an annual music festival and competition near here that has been going since the 1930s—when she heard some music she liked and started flatfooting, a style of dance very popular with mountain music. The press following the campaign gathered around to watch and film her dancing, and when she finished, she threw a challenge at me: "Now it's time for you to make a fool of yourself." So I said, "Anyone have a harmonica?" and the marital competition was on. I was known as the Richmond mayor and lieutenant governor and definitely thought of as a "big-city" guy. So when I joined the band, got handed a D harmonica, and they asked me, "What can you play?" I earned real cred when I said, "Play anything you want in D or A and I'll be fine." They started on a Carter Family tune and I picked it up before the first verse was half done.

That one impromptu performance, spurred by Anne's challenge at an Appalachian music festival, opened up a whole new part of my life—playing music with bands all over Virginia and the United States. I'm no pro, but I am an enthusiastic amateur and can play virtually any kind of music—jazz, blues, bluegrass, country, folk, gospel, rock, Irish, Hawaiian—by ear. I have a passable voice, too, after years of church singing. I've even done special events—weddings, funerals, one bar mitzvah!—for people I care about. (Anne—to puncture any pretense I may develop about being really good—always says when I am invited to the stage: "Always say yes when you are asked to play, because once you are not in office anymore, you won't be asked up to play anymore!") By far the most common kind of performance, and the most common place to perform over the years, has been playing at multiple venues here in Southwest Virginia with bands both famous and obscure. It's a blast. I learn new songs every time I come out here, and it is a wonderful icebreaker during our polarized politics. People walk away thinking, *That Tim Kaine is all right—I may not vote for him, but I kinda like the guy.*

I circle one side of Whitetop and there is a piped spring with cold water gushing out of it. Nirvana! I get to Buzzard Rock—a jumbled set of cliffs on Whitetop's western flank with postcard-quality views— and the breeze nearly knocks me off. Then down the mountain I go. I round a corner about ten minutes before the designated meeting spot and Scott is hiking toward me. I am so glad to see him. He had flown into Bristol and gotten a confused Uber driver to drop him off in the middle of the national forest at Lost Mountain.

We walk up the trail and have a good visit as we set up in the shelter and make dinner. At some point a lanky twentysomething guy in running shorts arrives, too, and tells us about his southbound thru-hike. He will finish Virginia tomorrow and keep trucking until the trail ends in Georgia. I ask him how many days it has taken him to do the entire Virginia stretch. He tells me forty. At forty years his senior, it makes me feel good that I will likely finish just two days after he will.

41

Scott is a talented guy in so many ways, a father of four, a pioneer in the solar industry, and now a successful alternative-energy investor. But his real gift is maintaining friendships. We met our first day in law school and he got me to join an intramural football team he was forming. When I took a year off from law school to go to Honduras, he took charge of finding me a place to live when I came back and even registered me for classes while I was away. When I started dating Anne the year after I came back, she was already in Scott's network because he was a close friend of her sister, Tayloe, ever since they'd attended Dartmouth together.

It is very like Scott to fly down to finish the hike with me. When he finally arrives, we pack up after a good night's sleep—it's much warmer at Lost Mountain Shelter now that the cold front has cleared out and the rainfall is over. It's also two thousand feet lower in elevation than the Thomas Knob Shelter. Breaking camp, we each hit the state-of-the-art privy and have a good laugh. Someone with perhaps too much time on their hands has carefully written Dr. Seuss's *The Lorax* on all four interior walls of the privy in clear, even script. The entire story—with illustrations! You have to see it to believe it.

Our sixteen-mile hike to Damascus is up and down and completely in the green tunnel of the national forest until the trail intersects with the Virginia Creeper Trail, a converted rail-to-trail path running from the town of Abingdon through Damascus and then climbing up Whitetop. "Creeper" refers to the slow pace of the train climbing up the steep mountain grade. It stopped running in the 1960s, and the crushed gravel trail is now a wonderful place for walking and biking, with much of the section near Damascus following Whitetop Laurel Creek, a beautiful trout stream.

We catch up on work and politics but talk mostly about our kids. Scott is as intentional about fatherhood as anyone I know. He and Mary are fun and loving parents, and their four kids match up in age pretty well with our three. He even wrote a book many years ago about negotiating with your kids.

I've shared about my own kids and my understanding that public life has required certain sacrifices of them. They have had some experiences that are certainly unique, but they've also had experiences along the way with Anne there for them while I am out at some endless meeting. I've said it before, but a lot of politics is done at nights and on weekends.

I wasn't a stranger to these sorts of sacrifices. After I had served seven years in local office, I announced in late 2000 that I was going to run for lieutenant governor. Anne and I were in the car driving to Scott's farm with our kids in the back seat. The law school crowd—seven couples and all our kids—were going to descend on him for the weekend. Since the others were coming from far away, Anne and I had camping gear so that we could sleep outside while the other families filled all the bedrooms. As we drove the ninety minutes from Richmond, I admitted to Anne that I was a little afraid of the race I had gotten myself into. She said: "Are you afraid you'll lose?" And I said, "No, I'm afraid I'll win."

I told her that I had looked into my future a little bit. (While many of my predictions don't come true, this one was dead-on.) I was in a one-year campaign to get an office that I would hold for four years. And if I won the lieutenant governor race, I would certainly run for governor in four years. Virginia is unique in not allowing a governor more than a single consecutive four-year term, so if I won that race, I realized that I was potentially on a nine-year ride. By the end, Nat would be off to college, Woody would be nearly gone, and Annella would be in high school. Would I miss too much in nine years of state politics?

Anne gave me good advice, and Scott underscored it when we talked during the family weekend: *Be a good dad.* In the unlikely event that striving to be a good dad meant that my political career was hampered a bit, that's fine. I could lose and still know I'd kept my priorities right—but I shouldn't assume that a life in politics meant that I had to be a bad or absent or inattentive father. Anne's own experience with a father in politics helped her see it this way—she missed him at times, experienced some amazing things, and ended up with a strong passion for public service because of his example. Not all positive, but the net was overwhelmingly good.

But I do wonder, now that my kids are all grown, whether I did fatherhood the right way. As Scott and I talk about our own children during the walk—their work lives, love lives, happiness levels, future plans, relationships with each other and with their parents—I come to see that my own questions are not unique. All caring parents have the same question: *Am I doing it right?* I once heard someone say that when your kids are growing up, you teach them all you can, and once they are grown, you simply love them all you can.

What Scott and I both realize, even amid our own questions or as we help our kids grapple with the ups and downs that they all face, is the deep soul satisfaction of parenthood. I once said that having kids was the emotional equivalent to discovering that you have a completely new wing in your house that you had never known existed before. In life, everyone experiences a wide range of emotions—but once you have kids, it's like you discover a whole new set of emotions buried within your soul that you had never felt before. At different phases of your children's lives, you keep entering new emotional rooms. Not all the emotions are positive—though most are—but they are all deep and rich.

We reach the Creeper Trail. Mountain bikers pass us as we near Damascus. It is a tiny community that is beloved by AT hikers with a raucous Trail Days celebration every May timed to match the peak of northbound thru-hikers reaching Virginia. Outfitters, ice-cream shops, hikers hostels, diners—the town has it all.

Scott and I have booked a room at an inn: a renovated barn and mill built right on the creek that we have followed as it tumbles down the mountain. We sit on the porch with a celebratory whiskey as the sun sets, the mountains around us awash in fall color, before grabbing dinner. Tomorrow is a 3.5-mile hike up a mountain to the Tennessee border, and then, because the border crossing is not near any road access, you turn around and walk back to town.

It doesn't seem possible that I am almost done with this part of my journey.

42

Day forty-two. Finish line in sight.

In Damascus, it is sunny and crisp. After a good breakfast, we throw our gear in the car and head to a small visitor center near the trailhead. We take a few water bottles and snacks in a daypack. Scott chivalrously takes the pack and we start climbing. I have bestowed on him the trail name Mr. Blue Sky because his three days are the only perfect-weather days during the entire trip. Damn him!

The trail just powers up Holston Mountain. We pass one northbound hiker who eagerly asks how far he has to go to reach town. Later, there's a tent off to the side with no apparent activity inside. Otherwise, there are no other signs of humanity on this beautiful fall Friday. My Guthook trail app cut off at Damascus, so I can't check to see how close we are to the endpoint. But a guy back in town said, "You'll know it once you get to the border."

And indeed we do. Even uphill, we make great time hiking without backpacks. By 9:15 a.m., we look up a long straightaway and see a sign approaching on the right: "Tennessee/Virginia State Line." We're 559 miles from Harpers Ferry! I kiss the sign and Scott takes a photo or two. We swig some water—still cold with the ice we filled up on at the inn before we started walking. Why didn't we bring champagne or moonshine or something more celebratory? We walk to a nearby overlook where we can look west toward Bristol from our spot high on the mountain.

After ten minutes or so, we turn around and start to slowly walk back down the trail—and I emphasize *slowly*. There's no need to rush or worry about making more miles. The feeling of accomplishment slowly comes over me as we descend, but suddenly I hurt all over. My knees ache, the bottoms of my feet feel sore, my shoulders throb even though I am carrying no pack. When I was pressing on with a purpose, I didn't feel these pains after the first week or so. But now that I am done, I notice them. This has been the hardest physical challenge of my life. It gives me great appreciation for those who do the entire trail.

We reach the car by 10:30, get gas and coffee, and then have a long drive north on I–81 to Staunton before we turn east toward Charlottesville. All along the route—as Scott and I keep up our steady chatter—I interrupt the flow of conversation to point out different mountain ridges along the way and tell stories from when I traversed them days or weeks ago. In Charlottesville, we turn south for twenty miles until we reach Scott's family farm, located on the James River just south of the town of Scottsville (no joke). His mother, Judy, comes out to greet us, glad to see me and especially excited to have Scott home for the weekend.

I would stay longer to visit, but Scott and Judy understand how anxious I am to get home. My son Woody and his partner arrived last night from the Midwest, home for a ten-day visit. I can't wait to catch up with them. We will all attend a favorite family event—the Richmond Folk Festival—this weekend. I will reenter polite society by playing a song or two with a wonderful group—Linda Lay and Springfield Exit—tomorrow afternoon during their set.

When I finally return home, Anne greets me when I walk in the kitchen door. "I am really proud of you."

As we get ready to head downtown to join the festival, I realize that I am too.

AFTERMATH

My knees remain sore for nearly a month. I'm unsteady when climbing stairs, and the soles of my feet are bruised and tender until Christmas, but that pain passes. Most of the twenty-six pounds I lost during the hike slowly come back on. But there are some changes that stick.

I find more ways to be outside. I walk more and move my morning gym workouts outdoors if the weather gets within shouting distance of passable. I even look for ways to do sedentary work—reading, paperwork, correspondence—in my backyard or on our screen porch in Richmond instead of indoors.

Having actually done the whole Virginia stretch, I start to think about the hike not as the first step in a three-stage "last hurrah" of wilderness adventures, but as the start of a long, new chapter of extended immersions in the wilderness. While I immediately start planning the cycling trip for the summer of 2020—and fantasizing a bit about canoeing the James River in 2021—I start creating a bigger bucket list of adventures for Anne and me—walking the Camino de Santiago, biking the C and O Towpath, canoeing the Boundary Waters, etc. I did the 559 miles of the AT just fine at sixty-one, so why can't I keep doing big adventures—alone and with others—for a long time? That thought is an exciting one.

I start to leave my iPhone at home or in the office more, instead of always carrying it on me.

But the most important change I notice is a sense of calm.

I take the brief trail notes I kept at the end of each day and slowly transform them into this diary of my trip—what you're reading right

163

now. Writing this journal takes about five months, and life resumes its rush. Virginia Democrats flip both Houses of our legislature from Republican to Democratic (sadly, the talented Appalachian doctor Starla is not successful) and use the new majority to pass progressive laws we have worked for years to achieve. The Nats win the World Series, and then my Chiefs win the Super Bowl. I work to raise the national age for using tobacco products from eighteen to twenty-one. We enter a new decade. More ominously, America gets close to an unnecessary war with Iran and goes through an impeachment trial and, just as I finish this journal of my hike, sees the beginning of a frightening pandemic. The Senate is in the midst of all of it. The nation's trials and tribulations that I pondered on the trail seem to multiply. But there is calm in me.

"Theoretically there is a perfect possibility of happiness: believing in the indestructible element in oneself and not striving towards it." This is from Franz Kafka—hardly a happiness expert. The aphorism has intrigued me for many years.

I get the meaning of it now. I am aging and my body is definitely not indestructible. I handled the physical challenge better than I thought I would, and Providence spared me any injuries or illness along the way. But it is much harder to do this than it would have been ten years ago, and easier than it will be ten years from now.

I certainly was striving toward something bigger than just the Tennessee state line by doing this walk. There wasn't one single question that motivated me, and there is not one single answer that I can point to that has changed everything. But the walk, and my thoughts along the way, teach me that "the indestructible element in oneself" is a fusion of will and faith.

The simple will to serve others, especially those in need—instilled by family, teachers, the life of Jesus, and my own experiences of what makes me happy—pushes me forward. That will was clarified after 2016 as lesser motivations—personal ambition, desire for popularity, unproductive competitiveness, petty concerns about getting credit or being appreciated for my work—were largely burned off. My faith—both spiritual faith and faith in the values of this country—has shaped that will and takes over when my will falters.

The combination of will and faith guarantees that I can meet the challenge—any challenge—even when I want to quit or turn back. Not that I will overcome or master each challenge. It is unrealistic and prideful to believe that. But I now know I can face any challenge head-on without fear or doubt.

And now that I understand that, I needn't strive toward it. It's there and it will be there whenever I need it.

RIDE
2020

About two months after I finish the AT, I attend a weekly prayer breakfast in the Senate. Chaplain Barry Black says, "Welcome to the last prayer breakfast of the decade." It is December 2019, and we will not reassemble until January.

Barry's words get me thinking about the decade we are just completing. And I quickly reach the conclusion that virtually nothing in the decade went the way I would have predicted.

If you had told me when the calendar switched to 2010 that I would be in the Senate and on a national ticket in the next decade, I would not have believed it. To think that Anne would be a cabinet secretary and college president—no way! That Nat would be a Marine infantry commander with two deployments and Woody a visual artist and pre-K teacher—*what*? (I would have believed that Annella would be a scuffling young actress—theater has been her passion since she was five years old.)

In 2010, we were entering the second year of the Obama administration, a high-water mark in America toward the realization of our equality principle. If you had told me that Donald Trump would be president as we closed the decade, I would have laughed out loud.

And Virginia—still an overwhelmingly Republican state as we started 2010 with all state offices held by the GOP and an overwhelming Republican majority in our congressional delegation and state legislature. If you had told me that Democrats would win every statewide race during the decade, electoral votes in 2012 and 2016, and flip control of our House delegation and both Houses of our general assembly, I would have said you were dreaming.

Bottom line: I would have been wrong about virtually everything. And so I wondered, *Will the next decade be equally wild and unpredictable?*

The beginning of 2020 is momentous yet predictable. I had never been a juror before I was sworn in as a juror in the impeachment trial of Donald J. Trump. The trial seemed destined to happen from the moment he narrowly escaped accountability for obstruction as revealed by the Mueller report but then chose to try to strong-arm Ukraine to help him beat Joe Biden. When you get stopped by a trooper for speeding and he's good enough to give you a warning, you don't burn rubber and speed away! But if you're Donald Trump, that's just what you do.

The unwillingness of any Republican—save Mitt Romney—to vote for any article of impeachment against the president is no surprise. The verdict is a foregone conclusion, especially once the Senate GOP majority blocked the effort to subpoena relevant documents and witnesses necessary to put the truth of what happened before the American public.

Following the impeachment trial, I speak on the Senate floor on February 4 and explain my vote in words that now seem scary and prescient: "Unchallenged evil spreads like a virus. We have allowed a toxic president to infect the Senate and warp its behavior. And now the Senate's refusal to allow a fair trial threatens to spread a broader public anxiety about whether 'impartial justice' is a hollow fiction.

An acquittal will lead to worse conduct. I will not be part of this continual degradation of public trust. Thus, I will vote to convict."

Within a month of the historic impeachment trial, the nation gets hit with three back-to-back shocks during the spring: the coronavirus pandemic, in which the anti-science and narcissistic traits of the president combine with other missteps to turn the US into the world's leader in deaths; the economic collapse, with a quadrupling of the unemployment rate driven by the health crisis, as other nations that manage the health crisis better see less economic damage; and the irrefutable video evidence of police brutality against African Americans in the vicious public execution of George Floyd.

These three shocks turn Americans out to street protests throughout the country. People are tired of racism, tired of violence, tired of unnecessary COVID-19 deaths, tired of diminishing opportunities, tired of repeated promises of leaders to undertake reforms that never come, tired of congressional gridlock, tired of the nation's continued glorification of slavery-defending Confederates, tired of a president who ordered federal officials to fire tear gas at peaceful protestors lawfully assembling, tired of massive job losses hitting minorities and young people the hardest. Young people—worried about student debt, a shaky economy, and the lack of progress toward racial equality—are particularly energized in demanding change. They cast off the complacency and apathy that saw so many sit on the couch in 2016 instead of taking seriously the threats to our nation's values and start to demand that those of us in office cast off politics as usual.

While the weight of these three shocks doesn't fall equally across society, it does affect everyone. I contract coronavirus in late March, likely in the Capitol as we work to pass the large stimulus package to help America through the crisis. I get hit with a bizarre set of symptoms, and not recognizing that these are signs of COVID-19, I give the virus to Anne as we quarantine at home during the month of April.

Two of our three children are laid off for months as their jobs close down. Annella, wondering whether the New York City theater community will ever return to normal, joins street protests and volunteers at the World Central Kitchen to provide meals to health workers and first responders. Woody's school closes for months and he escalates his activism for racial justice in the aftermath of George Floyd's murder. Nat retires from active duty after eight years, joins the Marine Reserves, and starts a job with the Biden campaign. Anne finishes her year as interim president of George Mason University, ending her time with four tough months as all classes switch to online in mid-March.

The stakes are high in the Senate as we battle the health and economic carnage, initially finding bipartisan agreement on sizable COVID-19 relief but falling into a predictable partisan standoff over police reform and then the follow-up measures to ease the COVID-19 crisis as the presidential election draws near. The intensity of the work makes me long for the sense of calm and connection I found on the AT last summer. I get books about Skyline Drive and Blue Ridge Parkway and spend time in the evenings planning leg two of my Virginia Nature Triathlon.

Planning a trip with a group of friends is more complicated than planning a solo hike. Just finding the window of time that works for everyone is challenging. The trip will be a reprise of a ride I took across Iowa with these law-school buddies in 1996. Iowa's RAGBRAI ride was the first big adventure we took together, and there have been many since—but we are twenty-four years older now and our route will be a lot hillier than what we did then.

On a Friday in late August, I pick up Charles at Dulles Airport and we reminisce about our days on the AT last summer with his son Adam. We drive about ninety minutes to Front Royal, where the Skyline Drive begins to meet up with the crew at the Mountain Home B and B, the inn I stayed at during my hike last year.

The group includes Charles and Scott, both of whom joined me on the AT last year. We meet up with Dave, the founder of an asset management firm based in Des Moines and organizer of our bike trip many years ago. He has driven out from Iowa, picking up Jim, a constitutional-law professor in Chicago, on the trip east. I've known Jim the longest because we went to Mizzou and then lived together when he clerked for a federal judge in Boston after finishing law school at UVA. The sixth member of the crew, Roger, is the longtime president of a music college in Boston. There was to be a seventh, another Jim who is a pioneer in the field of large-scale open space conservation, but an emergency surgery caused him to scrap his plans at the last minute. An eighth friend—David from San Francisco—is often part of our trips, but the timing was not good for him this summer.

We called ourselves the Ellery Gang because five of us (Scott, Dave, law professor Jim, Charles, and I) lived together in a row house on Ellery Street near Harvard Square, and the other three (David, conservationist Jim, and Roger) were friends drawn into that orbit during those years. Then we switched our name to Nightwing in honor of a country band we heard on RAGBRAI years ago.

We have wisely hired a guide, Phillip, to drive a van and trailer, provide support and bike repairs, and generally be nearby if/when things go wrong. We won't be camping this year, instead staying in local hotels and inns or with family along the way. Phillip helps us load all our gear as we prepare for a four-hour drive south to our starting point on the Virginia-North Carolina border. This being at the height of the pandemic, we are masked and well-stocked with the essentials: hand sanitizer and cold beer. In a bizarre coincidence, Lisa—one of the inn's owners—learns that Charles was a Harvard undergrad. She was, too, so they compare notes and realize that she used to date Charles's brother and even went on a cruise with Charles and his family nearly forty years ago. We grab barbeque for the road and head south, talking all the way until we check in to our hotel in Galax around midnight. I instantly recognize the familiar feeling I had the night before we started RAGBRAI. I am nervous about the physical challenge of the week ahead.

1

I should have figured I would wake to rain—just like my first day hiking the AT last year. The forecast calls for rain off and on all morning, and it's likely to get worse in the afternoon.

We gather in the Hampton Inn lobby for breakfast. It's unusual for a hotel lobby to be this packed so early. Fox News is loudly playing a story about the just-completed Democratic convention. The Republican convention will be happening as we are blissfully cycling during the week ahead. I was doing a full blitz of press during the DNC week and am glad to be disconnecting for a few days.

Folks look at us in our bike gear and note the weather. One member of a big group of motorcyclists says, "How far are you guys riding?"

When we tell him three-hundred-plus miles, he deadpans, "And you're doing this voluntarily?"

I deadpan back: "It's actually a work-release assignment." The group (unaware of who I am) takes a second to make sure I am joking before cracking up.

Into the van we go, cupping our hands around Styrofoam cups of hot coffee as we drive thirty minutes to our starting point. Streaks of rain line the windows. Cumberland Knob is just over the state line at BRP milepost 217.5, about a mile into North Carolina and the place where construction began on the Blue Ridge Parkway in September 1935. (The four hundred-plus-mile parkway, including the Carolina portion, was not fully complete until 1987.) The parking lot is empty on a rainy Saturday morning—partly due to weather and partly because many of the amenities along the parkway are closed due to COVID-19. We help Phillip unload the bikes from the trailer, fill water bottles and tires, and half listen to the safety lesson that is mandatory for Wilderness Voyageurs trips. Phillip refers to us as "Nightwingers" and we instantly correct him with "It's Nightwingnuts!" Then we coast downhill, turn north on the parkway, and start the journey to Mabry Mill, our first-day stopping spot. By now the rain has stopped.

The ride this week will go down the BRP to milepost zero at Rockfish Gap where it becomes Skyline Drive; from there, we will ride down the Drive from milepost 105 to milepost zero in Front Royal. We need no map—we will ride north on the same road for the entire eight days. Most days cover forty miles or so—with Phillip usually finding an overlook about a third of the way for a snack stop, then a lunch stop at the two-thirds mark before a final push to finish. We start the trip at about 2,800 feet of elevation and climb up and down all week—hitting a high of 3,900 feet at Apple Orchard Mountain near Lynchburg and dropping down to a low of six hundred feet at the James River crossing just thirteen miles later. Most days involve about four thousand feet of climbing and an equivalent amount of downhill.

While I have ridden a few times on Skyline Drive, I have never done a mile on a bike on the parkway. None of the Nightwingnuts have done any of it either. It is a narrow national park, just a ribbon of right-of-way cutting through farms and forests with frequent pullouts featuring magnificent mountain views. Many structures—log cabins, mills, farmsteads, old churches—are along the parkway. It's bordered by split rail fences lovingly maintained by the Park Service. It is a road built for the views—limited access, forty-five-miles-per-hour speed limit, no billboards or signage—so not used heavily by local traffic. And the folks touring along the parkway are generally very accommodating to cyclists. An article I recently read calls it one of the world's ten best bicycle road tours.

We make good time in cool, cloudy weather, talking and trying to accustom our butts to long stretches in the saddle. The hills are rolling today—we climb five hundred feet or so over a mile or two, followed by a similar downhill. We enter Virginia and soon pass the Blue

Ridge Music Center, a museum and outdoor concert venue devoted to the music of these mountains. While it would normally be open on Saturday, COVID-19 has closed it today.

The skies open up, drenching us for about thirty minutes before we make our lunch stop at Groundhog Mountain, an open picnic area on the top of a mountain with good views and shade for resting. We dry out while getting homemade sandwiches, chips, and fruit. Cold soda, Gatorade, water, and beer are available, but it must be a mark of age that no one drinks beer mid-ride out of worry that it will throw them off on the final stretch.

We finish the day at Mabry Mill, often called the most-photographed spot on the parkway. It is a beautiful mill with a classic millpond and general store/restaurant that is famous for its pancakes. Some of us are paying close attention to elevation changes—*Where is the next big climb?*—but others are scrupulously avoiding thinking about what's next and just taking the road as it comes. We do notice, though, that the names of our starting and ending spots tell us a lot about whether we'll be climbing or coasting. We started today at Cumberland Knob. Since *knob* means *mountain*, we knew that we'd be going downhill first. And we finish at Mabry Mill—mills are along streams, and that means they are usually in a gap or valley of some kind. Sure enough, the last two miles to the mill are a swerving, shady downhill that makes us seem like pros when we speed by the van at the bottom. But that also means that when we start here tomorrow, we start by climbing.

But first, we pile into the van for a twenty-minute drive to Floyd, a small mountain town known for its fantastic music scene. We check into our small hotel, grab pizza at Dogtown Roadhouse, and sit on an outdoor patio while vaguely listening both to the country blues band playing inside and an impromptu drum circle performing a random-sounding bongo concert in an outdoor amphitheater next to us. As we sit, we begin our tradition of putting each member of the crew under the microscope for intense discussion. By week's end, each of us will be the subject of an hour or two of analysis and advice. *Tell us how you are doing personally. Is your health okay? What's going on in your marriage? How are your kids?* (We have eighteen children between us, though only Dave has grandchildren.) *How are you doing professionally? What do you want to be doing ten years from now? How can we each help you?*

All of us are between sixty-two and sixty-four, and these discussions over the course of our lives have been a real touchstone. The tradition was initiated by Charles—he is a master of small talk but also knows that we might never *really* talk all week unless we make an intentional effort. Our discussions have covered all kinds of successes and failures, achievements and disappointments. Even though we are all people of professional accomplishment, the personal, marriage, and family discussions are always dominant in a way that shows where people's deepest priorities are.

A late-night walk by the county courthouse—home to a Confederate statue that is the subject of much local controversy—takes us back to our hotel. Charles and I are roommates and we turn in knowing that the hills today were the easiest we'll experience all week.

2

Today is Mabry Mill to Adkins Gap, a little over forty miles. We start the day by being first in line for pancakes at the Mill's first-come-first-served restaurant when they open the doors at 7:30 a.m. Anne and her family used to drive here from Roanoke for breakfast on special occasions when they were kids. When I point this out, the guys look around the restaurant—one other table of parents with small children is our only company—and comment that there has been nothing done to renovate the place since then. And the enormous pancakes—buttermilk, cornmeal, or buckwheat—have not changed much either, thank God.

We need the food to fuel us up a nine-mile climb to Rocky Knob. I start out strong to see if I can do the climb fastest in our group, and succeed. I usually challenge myself once a day to be first over a tough segment. And I can do it—once a day. Of the six of us, Jim, Charles, and Scott are frequent and solid riders. The other three—Roger, Dave, and me—are just good athletes who are competitive. I may be the weakest rider in the group. My bike is twenty years old—wonderfully built, for comfort in the flatland and not for mountains. Still, I am amazed how quickly I get used to the hills.

The feeling of struggling up a long hill—usually humming a song to keep me motivated (the Stones's "Soul Survivor" is a mantra this week)—and then zipping down long downhills is a physically and mentally freeing way to spend hours a day, especially if you are not trying to cram a ride in before doing other things. And I find myself thinking about how much joy cycling has brought me over the years. I find an old family photo as I start writing these notes—me at age five in pajamas sitting on my first bicycle (training wheels attached) in my grandmother Pauline's living room on Christmas morning. I'm so happy with myself in that photo, and the smile on my face looks remarkably like the one I have today while riding.

That bike shed its training wheels a few months after I got it; a few years later, I got a Raleigh three-speed that I used for a long time to ride around the neighborhood, to school, and summer jobs. I worked after school and Saturdays for a while in a bike shop doing odd jobs: I'd clean up and work the cash register when things got busy. I'd fantasize about the new bikes there but could never afford one, so I kept jerry-rigging my Raleigh, installing drop handlebars and building my own water-bottle holder at my dad's ironworking shop.

Late in high school, I bought my first ten-speed bike—a Magneet built in Holland with the lowest-end Campagnolo components. Volkswagen was having a promotion, and folks who bought VW Bugs got a bike too. So many Bug buyers said "No thanks" to the bike that our local dealer sold off the excess stock for seventy-five bucks each when the promotion ended. This bike lasted me through high school, college, law school, and into young adulthood—riding to and from school, around campus, in the country, to Walden Pond when I was at Harvard, occasionally to church or work in the years after Anne and I married, around town with friends. Eventually kids and work conspired and I stopped riding and sold the bike at a garage sale.

Dave invited the Nightwing guys to Iowa to experience the fun of RAGBRAI in 1996. Thousands of cyclists start in the west with their back tires in the Missouri River and then ride sixty to seventy miles a day across the state, camping in small towns along the way, until you arrive at the Mississippi River, where you dip your front tires to end the ride. It's a cross between summer camp for adults and a rolling state fair. But by then, I hadn't ridden in years and, perusing the weekly *Trader* paper (if you're under forty, ask your parents!), found a used Panasonic twelve-speed with a Tange steel frame and Shimano 105 drivetrain that I could buy from a guy in my neighborhood.

That Panasonic bike lasted across Iowa—even did the optional century ride (where you ride one hundred miles or more in one go) one day that week—and then became my companion for two Bike Virginia multiday tours, an inn-to-inn fortieth birthday trip with Anne in Vermont (with a broken collarbone as my souvenir!), and my initiation of the Mayor's Tour de Richmond, a fun Saturday ride for hundreds of cyclists through our city that I started when I was mayor. Anne had her own bike group with friends from the neighborhood—the MotherBikers—who did annual trips together.

Our kids all loved biking growing up—each spent time on a bike attachment hooked to the back of my Panasonic before graduating to bikes of their own. Once, on the Mount Vernon Trail, I was pulling Woody when he was about six and I could tell from his long silences that he was getting sleepy. Suddenly, the whole bike wobbled and I realized he had fallen asleep and toppled from the bike. I slowed, turned, and saw him sitting up in the middle of the trail with a "Where am I?" look on his face as other bikes whizzed past him. As an adult, he bikes everywhere, even in the dead of winter.

My oldest son, Nat, started racing road bikes in high school. I once left the house for work and got a call five minutes later from Anne: "Meet me at the emergency room." Nat had left a few minutes after me to ride his bike to school and collided with a car in an intersection a few blocks from our house, catapulting over the vehicle and breaking the driver's-side window with his elbow as he flipped. Heart in my mouth, I raced to the ER and met the incoming ambulance. Nat was there for hours of tests but released around noon with nothing but scrapes, thank God. I should have known he was a future Marine when I got home that night and he said, "Dad, let's go to the bike shop. It closes in fifteen minutes and I need a new helmet to replace the one I busted today."

Nat eventually decided I needed to upgrade my rolling stock. By now we realized that used bikes were the way to go—so many folks buy new bikes and then put them up for sale after only riding them for a few miles, losing a lot of money in the process. Nat bid online on my behalf and I ended up with a used Specialized Allez with a Columbus steel frame and Campagnolo components. It rides like a dream, with steel so comfortable on long rides even though it's a little heavier than carbon or aluminum. That bike has now lasted for about fifteen years of weekend rides, my second century ride with police officers from all over Virginia when I was governor, another Bike Virginia tour, rides on the many rails-to-trails around the state (one of which I helped add to our state park system), and also on the capital-to-capital trail connecting Richmond to Jamestown that I cut a ribbon for many years ago.

In planning for this trip, I realized that my bike had been gathering dust the last two years, so I got our local bike shop to do tune-ups both for Anne and me in February—just a month before COVID-19 pushed many people into bike shops to buy or repair their equipment as they sought to find outlets to avoid going stir-crazy indoors. (They did warn me: "You might want to get a new rear cassette, better for hill-climbing, if you are going to be riding on the parkway." I should have listened!) Anne and I had fun doing twenty- to forty-five-mile rides during our spring quarantine, when our normal scheduling would have had us going here and there all over the state.

Riding with my wife and friends reminds me of the simple beauty of bicycles. Is there any more useful and universal machine? I went everywhere by bike in Honduras and have seen them used as cargo carriers, kids' beloved toys, commuter vehicles, exercise companions, military and police cruisers, and message couriers all around the world. Since our trip this year often parallels my AT hike, I notice that I usually travel in ninety minutes on a bike what I needed a full day to walk last year. How freeing!

In fact, bicycles were viewed as "freedom machines" by American and English suffragists and helped lead to reforms in women's apparel, chasing out long dresses and corsets that interfered with biking. More than a billion bicycles on the planet and—while there are always innovations and improvements—the basic design has stayed remarkably consistent since the first chain-driven model was pioneered in the 1880s.

So many have praised bicycles in lyrical terms:

"Few articles ever used by man have created so great a revolution
in social conditions as the bicycle." US Census Bureau (1900)

"I think it has done more to emancipate women than any one thing
in the world. I rejoice every time I see a woman ride by on a
wheel. It gives her a feeling of self-reliance and independence
the moment she takes her seat; and away she goes, the picture
of untrammeled womanhood." Susan B. Anthony

"Nothing compares to the simple pleasure of a bike ride." John F.
Kennedy

"When the spirits are low, when the day appears dark, when work
becomes monotonous, when hope seems hardly worth having,
just mount a bicycle and go for a spin down the road, without thought on anything but the ride you are taking." Arthur
Conan Doyle

"The bicycle is the most civilized conveyance known to man. Other
forms of transport grow daily more nightmarish. Only the
bicycle remains pure in heart." Iris Murdoch

"It is by riding a bicycle that you learn the contours of a country
best, since you have to sweat up the hills and coast down
them." Ernest Hemingway

"Cycle tracks will abound in Utopia." H.G. Wells

The rhythm of these long rides is addictive—up and down hills,
magnificent views, stopping for food every fifteen miles or so, casual
chatter with friends. After the opening uphill slog, we do a swift
downhill to Rakes Mill Pond, a beautiful old pond along the parkway.
There, we stock up on snacks as we sit by the outflow and tumbling
creek below. (We pass through Sweet Anne Hollow along the way and I
salute my wife!) Then, an eighteen-mile stretch to Devils Backbone—a
towering overlook where we'll meet Phillip for lunch.

About three miles before our lunch stop, Scott and Charles spot a rundown train-car BBQ joint off the parkway and can't resist, even though we have lunch waiting for us at the van. Some of the rest of us power ahead while they fill up on local pork and a muffuletta—definitely not a Virginia specialty, but they swear by it when they arrive at the overlook where we've all stopped to eat.

At Devils Backbone we look down into Franklin and Bedford Counties and see pocket storms spread here and there across the landscape. We glimpse Peaks of Otter in the distance; we'll be riding through those mountains tomorrow. And we take our time as Jim fixes a flat on Dave's back tire, one of only a few technical glitches we experience all week.

The last stretch is a mostly downhill eight miles to Adney Gap. Somewhere along the way, Roger sees a black bear amble across the parkway just ahead. Glad it was him—he played football in high school and would still be the most likely among us to defeat a bear in a wrestling match. We cruise through a light rain for about thirty minutes, just enough to cool us off, before seeing the van parked by a barricade marking a recent closure of the next section of the parkway due to a rain-driven road collapse.

Tonight, we take the van into Roanoke—the Star City of the South and my wife's hometown. Jim has to leave for the airport early tomorrow to fly home to Chicago, so we celebrate with a good dinner at a restaurant in the City Market with an outdoor patio. We each bring up a favorite memory from an earlier Nightwing trip. A Christian gospel group is playing upbeat music around the corner to a sizable crowd. The music is good but their patter occasionally jars as we hear pro-Trump preaching drifting our way.

I am on the bike this week to escape politics, but that is virtually impossible in the dire straits Americans are living in. My one comfort? Virginia would have embraced Trump when I moved here in 1984. Now, though he has a loud minority of supporters, most Virginians have progressed dramatically and see the guy for the narcissistic, anti-science, bigoted bully he is.

Back at the hotel, we play a whiskey-fueled card game—Quiddler, a cross between gin rummy and Scrabble—and no one is surprised when the law professor wins. Jim was the most literate guy I knew at Mizzou and retains that distinction. The table talk during the game is deadly serious: What are the most idiotic rock and roll lyrics of all time?

Before we turn in, I do throw out a project: writing a country song. I have the perfect title—"Self-Unemployed"—and the basic storyline about a guy bragging about his life after he leaves the working world. But no lyrics or music. We retire, pondering this challenge.

3

Today was to be a forty-six-mile ride from Adney Gap to Peaks of Otter. We were looking forward to the first fifteen miles—virtually all downhill—and not looking forward to the last thirty-one miles, much of it a steep climb to a mountaintop lodge on the parkway. But we get lucky—or do we?—as rain has caused road failure, closing off the fifteen-mile downhill stretch. The shorter day enables us to sleep in and we drive back to the parkway in the late morning facing our longest climb of the trip—a twelve-mile uphill, followed by some up-and-down stretches, followed by a final six-mile climb to the lodge. My lack of good uphill gears slows me down and I soon have tiny bruises on the inside of both calves as blood vessels pop while I push the crank extra hard to climb.

The weather as you follow these mountain ridges is quirky. All during the day, we can look west into the Great Valley of Virginia or east into Bedford County and see small storms moving swiftly across the landscape. We round bends on the parkway and hit wet pavement for six hundred to eight hundred yards, evidence of recent microbursts. But we feel not a drop of rain during today's ride.

When we eventually reach Peaks of Otter, where a one-mile down-hill at the finish makes us look sporty upon arrival, we are beat from the climb but exhilarated by the beauty of the natural setting: a small valley, high in the mountains, with a lodge right on the parkway next to Abbott Lake. Sharp Top Mountain towers above the lake, visible from every room in the lodge. (Two other nearby mountains—Flat Top and Harkening Hill—form the plural peaks that give the valley its name.) This bucolic spot has attracted tourists since the 1800s and it's obvious why. We are still in August, but it is now cool at night with a feeling that fall weather, and the beautiful color change that turns these mountains into flaming red/yellow/orange, is coming soon.

After we check in, we gather to hike around the tranquil lake, now down to five without Jim. And we find that our conversation, more so than in past times together, really centers on our adult children. Perhaps it's the season of our lives that makes this so, but I also think that the tough reality of the last few months—health scares, economic uncertainty, the difficulty of finding relationships during a time of social distancing, some kids moving back home to wait out the pandemic—has made us focus even more on our children. And so, with eight days together, many questions are posed that are deeper than one might normally discuss: *What effect does success of the parents have on children? Is it a good thing to set high achievement standards and, through success, provide kids with an example and set of experiences that none of us had growing up? Does our success impose undue pressure on our kids, or cause them to worry that they will not be able to achieve similarly? Does growing up with financial success and comfort, which our kids have experienced, reduce self-sufficiency and resilience for the inevitable challenges in life? Can we help them appreciate their many privileges without sounding obnoxious?*

Perhaps the most important question we ponder is, *What is the place for marriage and long-term relationships?* We are all in decades-old marriages that have survived the same uphill struggles and downhill coasts that we experience on this trip. But of our eighteen adult children, only three are married. Some of the others are in long-term relationships, but many are not. Some of our kids are LGBTQ+, thankfully better accepted by family, friends, and society than they would have been had they grown up when we did. Some have survived tough experiences of sexual assault or harassment or mental illness. While each of the eighteen are unique and different, when looked at as a group, it seems clear that there is real difference between us and them in how they view life partnership.

How do we answer our kids when they pose the question, "Why bother to be involved in politics or civic life? It's corrupt and nothing gets done. Look at how much you adults have messed up society." There's evidence all around that this is true—climate change, racism, and the unrest over its persistent hold on large segments of American society, the pandemic, economic collapse. In general, our kids don't seem as optimistic as we were at their ages. On the other hand, they are all unusually altruistic and engaged in helping others as teachers, nurses, Marines, activists, budding public-interest lawyers, international aid workers, volunteers, health caregivers, artists, scholars of spirituality, environmental activists, policy advocates, bike mechanics, etc. Their commitment makes us proud of them.

Or a related question—posed by our children to all of us as we work to improve our communities and world in our own ways—"Why are you so moderate? Such an incrementalist? Don't we need much bolder change than what you are doing right now?" I am somewhat used to these questions from young people because I am in politics and so often speak to groups of students in my daily work. But I am a little surprised that my friends who are not in politics—and who are all generous to charitable causes and engaged with important community efforts—get the same question from their children.

We return to these topics again and again in the days to come. Today's discussion carries on as we eat fried chicken and meat loaf in the lodge's restaurant, our table distanced from others due to the pandemic. The place is only half full. As we eat, a storm comes hard with lashing raindrops against the wall of windows looking out over the lake that seemed so peaceful just an hour ago.

These are hard questions to answer. I was talking to a group of college students recently—in a Zoom session, of course—and one young lady posed the "What's the point?" question, seeking some word of motivation for civic engagement when so much is going wrong in the world. Normally, I would answer with an example of issues of importance (climate, racial equality, immigration reform, gun safety) to young people. But I now found myself giving her a very different answer:

"I was born into an America where most couldn't sit in a classroom with someone of a different race and women couldn't attend many of our universities. When I was five, I came home from kindergarten and saw my mom crying in front of the TV because our president had been assassinated. I read newspapers every day with stories about Civil Rights protests and the Vietnam War, where sixty thousand Americans and hundreds of thousands of Vietnamese were killed. When I was ten, I saw the TV news bulletin about MLK's assassination and then, two months later, the murder of Bobby Kennedy. Kids not much older than me were gunned down by the National Guard and law enforcement at Kent State and Jackson State. We accepted the possibility of nuclear war as a fact of life. When I was sixteen, a president resigned to avoid impeachment because of his corruption. I felt just like you do—that the adults had really screwed the world up. But I saw how young people marching helped bring about better civil rights laws, and how young people protesting helped end the Vietnam War. So when I turned eighteen, I registered to vote as fast as I could to make things better. And I've been in the vineyard and seen a lot of things get better, in my state and my country, especially when young people put all their passion and energy into improving lives. Now you see things that make you angry. Good! They'll get better if you throw yourself into solving them in your own way."

This message—which now becomes my go-to answer when talking to skeptical young people—connects with a broader thought I have been pondering about societies undergoing struggle. It's easy to focus on folks who are dragging us down or backward. They are obvious and loud right now. But I've reached the conclusion that bad things don't really happen—no matter how diabolical bad leaders are—without massive numbers of bystanders. When things go south, there are always huge numbers of people enabling destruction with their silence and passivity. Name one thing that gets better when people disengage.

An example of this is 2016. Sixty-six million people voted for Hillary Clinton for president and sixty-three million for Donald Trump. But well over one hundred million people who were eligible to vote chose not to vote at all. And their passivity was key in creating the chaos of this moment, chaos that often hurts most the very people who choose not to participate.

I see the same thing with some of my Senate colleagues. There are those who sincerely believe Donald Trump is a great American leader. I disagree with them, but they are candid about their views and entitled to them. But many others will share with me in private their disagreement, disappointment, and, yes, even fear about what our president is doing to our country, yet never say or do anything publicly to slow down his destructive tendencies.

Rabbi Abraham Heschel taught it so well: "Indifference to evil is worse than evil itself. In a free society, some are guilty, but all are responsible." It's the bystanders in life who drive me nuts. I see evidence of hope in peaceful protests and voting turnout in the last few years that we'll have fewer bystanders going forward. God help this country if I am wrong.

We talk into the night. When we're finally turning in, Charles offers me bike clothes he has brought that he is not going to wear. Being in the entertainment biz, he gets a lot of swag and that has included bike clothes from the Tour of California and charity bike events that he threw into the suitcase as he packed to fly east. I notice some good socks and take two pairs. Life is too long to go through it with cheap socks.

4

The weather report for today is hot and we have a few long climbs so we get started early. Peaks of Otter is high up, but we have nine more miles of climbing to Apple Orchard Mountain, the highest spot on the parkway in Virginia. I hiked over this mountain last year, and for northbound AT hikers, you don't hit a mountain this high again until you reach Vermont.

Starting a day with a long climb is daunting but much easier than finishing a day with one. When we crest Apple Orchard, we hit our longest downhill, thirteen miles to the James River. The elevation falls from four thousand feet to six hundred feet, and it is a rush. In fact, it's a little scary at times: rounding curves, accelerating quickly at times, keeping your eyes peeled to avoid rocks, branches, or small potholes in the road.

I notice my age more on the downhills than the uphills because I am not as willing as I used to be to open it up and let 'er rip on the way down. Even amateurs could easily get their speed into forty-plus miles per hour on a downhill this long, but my memories of breaking a collarbone on an inn-to-inn trip with Anne in Vermont keeps my hands on the brakes and my speed in the thirties. Occasionally, the road opens up to views north and east as the James River cuts through the Blue Ridge Mountains.

When we cross the James River, I look upstream where the AT crosses on the Foot Bridge I walked over almost exactly a year ago. And, God willing, I will canoe under this bridge in 2021 as I voyage the length of the James River. This spot is the only place that each leg of my Virginia Nature Triathlon will touch.

We climb slightly for six miles north of the river to a picnic area on Otter Creek and take our time eating salmon and salad by a tiny rushing stream. We're now four days in and we feel confident, having already done the longest climb and the longest downhill of the week. No injuries or falls so far, and Phillip's good-humored stewardship keeps us well stocked with provisions along the way.

The close of the day is a twelve-mile stretch to Humphrey Gap, where US Route 60 crosses the Parkway. It's an eleven-mile climb, with a tunnel long enough to require headlights, and a short drop down into the gap at the end. It is the hottest day of the trip and there isn't much shade to be had except in the tunnel. You start to notice how dramatically different the ride feels as you move back and forth from sun to shade. We are all glad to hit Route 60 and hop into the van to drive twelve miles into Lexington for the night.

Lexington is a college town where two schools—Washington and Lee and Virginia Military Institute—are built side by side. We stay downtown at a renovated old hotel a block from an inn where Anne and I honeymooned thirty-six years ago. The small town is historic and normally placid. But these are not placid times. The nation's painful grappling with racial injustice, sparked by the murders of George Floyd, Breonna Taylor, and Ahmaud Arbery, is causing rethinking of so much, and Lexington is in the midst of it as well.

We are overnighting at the Robert E. Lee Hotel—or rather, what was once the Robert E. Lee Hotel. Since its construction in 1926 it was known as that until the name was changed to the Gin Hotel recently. Washington and Lee is in the midst of a decision-making process over whether it should remove Lee from its name. Virginia Military Institute, a state military college that was all-male until the Supreme Court, in a 1996 opinion written by Ruth Bader Ginsburg, held that a public college could not deny equal access to women, is grappling with its own history and its continued veneration of former professor and Confederate general Stonewall Jackson.

The crew walks around town before dinner. As we eat outside

at a nearby restaurant, we talk about the importance of names and symbols. A few months ago, I supported Elizabeth Warren on the Armed Services Committee as she successfully promoted a provision to require renaming of any military bases or other defense facilities named for Confederates. During my hike last year, my neighborhood was grappling with changing the name of my street—Confederate Avenue—and those discussions recently led to a new name (Laburnum Park Boulevard) being presented to Richmond City Council. The Richmond mayor ordered the city's prominent Confederate statues be taken down following extended protests by a diverse group of mostly young activists during the spring of 2019.

Predictably, these debates raise controversial questions. Is the changing of names and statues progress or an unacceptable effort to erase history? Is it worth spending time on names when other priorities—COVID-19, economic devastation, police reform—might seem more pressing?

My own conversations with young people, especially young African American friends and staffers, have altered my perspective on these questions. When I was active in state and local politics, we generally viewed the Confederate statues as a symbol of a painful and incomplete past. Painful because of the history they represented; incomplete because there were so few statues or buildings named for the myriad of Richmond figures—black and white, men and women—whose accomplishments were not during the Civil War. Our task was to fill out this history by recognizing more people—Arthur Ashe, Maggie Walker, Abraham Lincoln, and Barbara Johns. There are now bridges named after Civil Rights heroes like Sam Tucker and Curtis Holt; a new court building named for *Brown v. Board of Education* lawyer Oliver Hill.

I've listened to people describing why this solution—filling out the historical record—is, while appreciated, still insufficient. This spring, a younger staffer said to me, "You view the Confederate statues as a symbol of a painful past. But to many of us, they are symbols of a painful present and maybe even predictors of a painful future. When the city and state take care of these monuments, tending to them and marketing them to tourists, what's the message to us? Especially now, when African Americans are disproportionately getting COVID, dying from it, losing their jobs to it—and when we're seeing Blacks killed by police on our television screens daily. Will we ever be treated equally? A society that still venerates those who enslaved us makes us doubt whether the equality promise applies to us at all."

Such a compelling argument, and it advanced my thinking. We can't change history, nor should we try to erase it. But there's a difference between telling history and honoring someone. And there is no reason, in 2020, to honor those who tried to divide our nation so that they could continue to hold fellow humans in bondage.

And to those who dismiss the focus on names, symbols, and statues as unimportant when compared to reforming our education, health care, and criminal justice systems—I have long believed that names matter a lot. One of the wise details in the Adam and Eve story—written in about 500 BC—is how God creates everything but then gives to mankind the power to name all creatures. God could have done it but instead gave mankind the naming power. The recognition that the power to name is a unique and special responsibility still carries an impact.

As we're eating dinner, the guys point out that the young waitress knows who I am and seems nervous to be serving me. Their observation proves true as she stumbles while bringing water and dumps a full glass—ice and all—in my lap. Her embarrassment magnifies as my friends and diners at other tables laugh but it's also an icebreaker. We get to know her a bit. She isn't nervous—just overexcited because she is a recent college graduate, the child of Mexican immigrants, who has her heart set on going to law school and then into public service of some kind, possibly politics. She is altruistic and optimistic in the way so many immigrant children, especially first-generation college kids, are.

We take a picture together and that starts a line of folks from other tables who want to come by and say hello or take pictures as well: a mom and dad with two young kids visiting from Virginia Beach on a short vacation; another family bringing their son to start his freshman year in college; the leader of a local community health center (who coincidentally will find out tomorrow in an announcement from my office that the center has received a sizable federal grant to help them deal with increased health needs driven by COVID-related job losses); three senior citizens at an adjacent table who want to talk politics. One of them is the world's biggest Hillary Clinton fan. When we get up to leave the outdoor patio, she has paid the tab for our whole group, so we take our dinner money and turn it into a generous tip for the budding politico who drenched me with ice water. I hope she's doing well.

5

It's our last day on the Blue Ridge Parkway, where we have forty-seven miles to go between Humphreys Gap and Rockfish Gap. From there, we will transition to Skyline Drive for the next three days. Today's ride is remarkable because it involves a lot of ridge running instead of the steady up and down of the first four days. We stay up on the ridge, affording us one beautiful view after the next—east toward the Piedmont or west to the Shenandoah Valley.

Our August ride has been dogged by worries about COVID-19. Each of my friends faced some concern from their families about whether they should even come on the trip at all. The first two nights were in a part of Virginia experiencing a dramatic rise in COVID cases. We didn't dwell on it, but everyone was checking local health websites and was aware of it. We try to do everything outdoors (except sleeping) and cross our fingers for luck in avoiding the virus.

I might be the least worried, since Anne and I have both had COVID already. But with so much still uncertain—including how much protection antibodies give you—we are trying to be very careful. Our cases, though mild, showed how tricky the virus is and ushered in an unexpected set of experiences for us during the first half of the year.

I was diagnosed with the flu in February and could never completely shake a congested cough. As COVID cases started to climb in March, I sent my Senate staff home on March 11 to telecommute. I worked with my chief of staff in the empty office until March 26 when Congress passed the CARES Act, injecting trillions of dollars into propping up our health system and helping businesses and families deal with the economic devastation caused by the pandemic.

What a horribly frustrating time. I had warned folks in 2016 that President Trump's anti-science attitudes about climate change would likely extend to other areas as well. And his refusal to take the COVID challenge seriously at a time when other nations like Germany, Canada, and South Korea were doing the right thing led to a confused federal response that magnified both the American death toll and the economic destruction that hurt so many. As someone who has managed disaster responses at the local and state levels, the catastrophic mismanagement of this serious crisis by the Trump administration has made me enormously sad for our country. It didn't have to be this way.

While we worked on the CARES Act in a near-empty Capitol in late March, community spread of the virus was in the building, like the plague in Edgar Allan Poe's "The Masque of the Red Death." A few senators and House members, together with staff, got infected then. I got hit with a bewildering variety of symptoms—allergic reactions gone wild. My nerves tingled; skin rashes would appear and then disappear twenty minutes later only to show up on another part of my body later in the day; I experienced conjunctivitis and abdominal pain. But I had none of the COVID symptoms thought most common then—shortness of breath, dry cough, fatigue, loss of taste or smell, sore throat. I assumed I was dealing with seasonal allergies in an unusually high spring pollen wave in DC.

When we passed the CARES Act, the Senate went into a public health recess until May 8. Anne and I spent nearly forty days together in Richmond, just the two of us—the longest period of one-on-one time in our thirty-six years of marriage. Of course, within a few days of quarantining together, Anne got hit with the virus too. We went for a walk one morning but by 2:00 p.m. she felt sickness coming on like a freight train. She got in bed with fever and body aches, but no cough—at the time the best-known symptom. By the next day, she felt a dramatic improvement except for lingering cold symptoms. Five days later, we did a forty-five-mile bike ride together. Shortly thereafter, she developed a cough and we began to suspect we had encountered the virus ourselves.

We talked to both our doctors who said we likely had COVID. But we weren't tested—partly because tests were still in short supply, and partly because our doctors told us that we would almost certainly be positive. If we were, their advice would be to do exactly what we were doing now: staying at home and seeing whether we would recover on our own. By mid-April, we both recovered. By May, antibody tests confirmed that we had each contracted the virus.

Just as it was for all Americans—let alone the entire world—the spring of 2020 was surreal for us. We were both sick. Two of our three children were laid off from work for months. We knew multiple people who died of COVID.

We worked remotely: Anne leading her university in switching thousands of classes from in-person to online from our dining room, and me doing Zoom calls with staff, constituents, and senators from my small home office. We could see the dogwoods and redbuds in bloom. We went for a walk or bike ride every day. We made dinner every night (or did our patriotic duty by supporting local restaurants with take-out orders) and then watched movies, listened to music, or played cards. In the midst of so much suffering, our time of intense togetherness was magical.

During this time, I was often reminded of The Who's song "Amazing Journey," but unlike the song, it wasn't as if this sickness took our minds to dramatically new places. Instead, the time of enforced togetherness was the amazing journey. Anne and I slowed down, rediscovered that we still love spending time together just as we did when we started dating, and got more intentional about counting our blessings—even ones caused by a pandemic. We also pondered anew the injustices we have each battled during our public-interest careers, now made even more obvious by the disparities in who is afflicted by the virus and its economic consequences.

Mark Warner often chides me for being overly optimistic, and the events of the last few years—especially during this pandemic—have convinced me that he's right. (I hate to publicly admit that!) But since I find optimism often leads to the will necessary to achieve things, I will myself to always look on the bright side. This attitude has helped me achieve, but it often makes me insufficiently objective about the scope of challenges or the negative influences that must be reduced to make progress. COVID has been a time of recalibration for my worldview, even at age sixty-two. I now find myself a little less optimistic—but because of that reduced optimism, I am now a little more resolved to battle for what's right and protect those who are under such stress in American society today. I can't simply assume things will work out; I have to lean in more to do my part. I probably needed that rebalancing.

The other recalibration during the first months of the pandemic is my physical health. Anne recovers from COVID with no after-effects, but I end up with two enduring symptoms that won't go away. From the onset in March, I felt as if every nerve ending in my body was tingling 24/7, like my skin was dipped in a fizzing Alka-Seltzer. Not painful or debilitating, but just an ever-present nerve sensitivity that I had never felt before. And while my randomly appearing rashes went away quickly, they were replaced by something similar—a frequently occurring sensation that portions of my skin are heating up, as if someone has applied a heating pad to my arm or leg or back or stomach for ten to fifteen minutes at a time.

Of course, many COVID patients are now suffering serious "long-haul" symptoms—horrible fatigue or muscle weakness, respiratory issues, heart problems, mental confusion, balance problems. My weird nerve sensations don't get in the way of daily functioning, but they are odd nonetheless. As I write these words, they seem like a physical equivalent to my attitudinal shift from over-positivity—possibly approaching complacency—to heightened awareness and, hopefully, a more vigilant attitude about the world and how others are treated by it. Had I become comfortably numb? My post-COVID neurological activity is the opposite of numbness. The good news is that my nerve symptoms don't affect my energy or physical strength. They make sleep a little harder to come by, but this is such a minor inconvenience, compared to what other long COVID patients suffer.

But I digress. Today's ride might be the best one of the week, with remarkable views of Yankee Horse Ridge, Three Ridges, The Priest, and Humpback Rocks—places I struggled to climb with a full pack last summer on the AT.

At one point, we see a climb ahead and notice the beautiful stone-work laid by the Civilian Conservation Corps workers who built this road. Roger's grandfather worked for the CCC during the Depression on the parkway in North Carolina and his dad was a highway engineer. He draws our attention to the craftsmanship on this stretch, so often invisible as we zip along. And as we complete the climb and round this bend, we start a gently curving seven-mile downhill stretch that ranks as the most enjoyable of the trip.

We finish later with another long downhill stretch at Rockfish Gap, milepost zero on the parkway with the southern terminus of Skyline Drive just across the bridge. We hop into the van and drive through beautiful Nelson County for about forty-five minutes until we reach Scott's family farm, right on the James River south of Scottsville. Scott's mom, Judy, and one of his children, Krista (an economics policy analyst in DC), are there to meet us—with cold beer, a washer and dryer for our laundry, and a salad and lasagna dinner on the porch where we share with them the details of the trip thus far. We have all been on this porch many times during our forty-year friendship with each other. And we retell stories from our earlier visits as the sun sets and brilliant stars fill the sky.

6

We are treated to homemade cinnamon rolls, fresh fruit, and black coffee before we load into the van to head back to our ride. Having counted down 217 miles of the parkway from the North Carolina border, we now will take three days to ride the entire 105-mile Skyline Drive—Rockfish Gap to Thornton Gap, Thornton Gap to Swift Run Gap, Swift Run Gap to Front Royal.

Unlike the Blue Ridge Parkway, which for much of its length is a long, linear park—barely wider than the right-of-way itself—Skyline Drive sits in the midst of the vast Shenandoah National Park. The park is more than two hundred thousand acres and its creation was initiated by an act of Congress passed in 1925. Yellowstone was the first national park, created in 1872; other parks were added over time, all in the West. Shortly after the National Park Service was created in 1916, Acadia National Park in Maine became the first national park in the East, and Shenandoah and Great Smoky Mountains National Park followed a few years later.

The process of creating the park took ten years, with the long-awaited opening at the end of 1935. The authorizing act stipulated that the land would need to be provided by the Commonwealth of Virginia, and determining who owned the more than five thousand parcels in these hills and hollows was difficult. Even more difficult was the process of purchasing the land and displacing the families who lived there. Estimates of the total number of people displaced vary between a few thousand to as many as fifteen thousand. A handful of residents were allowed to remain in the park until their deaths—the last resident, Annie Shenk, died at age ninety-two in 1979. Many moved into nearby valley communities, and the pain of their forced removals is documented in letters and newspaper articles of the day. In recent years, the Park Service has begun to tell their stories and offer visitors opportunities to learn about life before the park was cleared for tourists and visitors.

The history of Skyline Drive is connected to Shenandoah National Park history. Herbert Hoover, who established a presidential retreat near here at Rapidan Camp where he could escape Washington to fly-fish in cooler weather, called for construction of the ridgetop road in 1929 as the land assembly for the park was underway. A groundbreaking took place in 1931, and the 105-mile road was complete by 1939.

The drive is an engineering marvel with stone fences and culverts, one significant tunnel at Mary's Rock, seventy-five scenic overlooks, picnic grounds, and numerous parking areas allowing access to a five-hundred-plus-mile trail network. Two historic lodges—Big Meadows and Skyland—sit along the drive together with other campgrounds such as Loft Mountain and Lewis Mountain. The speed limit is a comfortable thirty-five miles per hour, and vehicles are accustomed to bicycles and thus more accommodating than just about anywhere. Since hunting is not allowed in the park, wildlife sightings—bear, deer, wild turkey, raccoons, coyotes—are common.

The construction of Skyline Drive drove two great outdoorsmen apart. Benton MacKaye and Myron Avery were the driving forces behind the AT—MacKaye the visionary dreamer and Avery the key supervisor of the trail's construction. MacKaye hated the idea of the Skyline Drive as a profit-driven intrusion into his wilderness. But Avery believed that the establishment of the drive and park would make it easier to complete the AT, bringing federal resources to it and allowing more volunteers and hikers to access it. The interchange of increasingly frosty correspondence between MacKaye and Avery over the Skyline Drive mirrors dilemmas of today.

MacKaye attempted to convince Avery and others in the AT community that the drive and parkway were incompatible with the wilderness purpose of the trail. Recognizing the unstoppable appeal of motor vehicles, he suggested an alternative that would construct a scenic Appalachian road routed off the ridge so that the AT could continue to have a pristine wilderness presence. He summarized the different approaches in a letter to Avery:

> Here then is the first issue between us. You are for a connected trail, whether or not wilderness. I am for a wilderness trail—whether or not connected.

Avery replied with a classic doer-versus-dreamer letter:

> It is very pleasant to sit quietly at home and talk of primeval wilderness, and to think of a Trail that will make and maintain itself. But to bring such a Trail into being requires hard work, hours of labor under broiling suns and pouring rains, camping out in all kinds of weather, as well as incessant "office work" in connection with guidebooks, maps, markers, publicity, and a thousand and one other details. It is, don't you think, significant that the majority of those who are loudest in their demands and in their abuse of workers, have covered little of the Trail and have done little physical labor on it.

MacKaye waited a few weeks before sending a response back, ending their partnership. They never spoke again. MacKaye stopped any connection with the AT and helped found The Wilderness Society, designed to protect natural areas and federal public lands. Avery continued his work on AT construction and maintenance until it was completed. He became the first person to walk every mile of the trail and led the Appalachian Trail Conference until his death in 1952. Both were inducted as charter members of the Appalachian Trail Hall of Fame in 2011.

Today, we start with a six-mile climb from Rockfish Gap and get back up on ridges with beautiful views. My chain snapped at the end of our ride yesterday because I was having to torque the pedals so hard uphill due to lack of good climbing gears. I now ride an extra road bike that Phillip brought just in case and it's a revelation. The carbon-frame bike is much lighter and the rear cassette is built for mountains. No more straining up hills and no more burst blood vessels in my calves.

Our first stop is at Moormans River Overlook, a sunny spot looking eastward to Sugar Hollow, a valley with a lake formed by a dam on the headwaters of the Moorman River. We have lucked out on weather all week—a little hot, and thirty minutes of rain on each of our first two days, but mostly clear enough so that the natural splendor of the views is overwhelming mile after mile. It is late August now, too early for the advance in fall color that will peak in six weeks, but we occasionally see flashes of red or yellow from peculiar trees making their autumn fashion statement early.

We stop for lunch along the drive at the Loft Mountain Wayside. This is the spot where I bushwhacked off the AT a year ago to get a milkshake only to find the milkshake machine broken. Would my luck change on this trip? No. We arrive and find that the camp store is open but the dining room is shut down due to the pandemic. Of course I have made things worse by promising my crew all day that we could get a milkshake at lunch. At least they are a forgiving bunch—or maybe they naturally discount a politician's promises?

As we ride along, we are all struck by the incomparable gift of the two great national parks we experience on this trip. Our national parks, together with national forests, state and local parks, wildlife preserves, and the myriad of other protected open spaces, are a soul restorative in exactly the way Benton MacKaye intended. We've all been stir-crazy during the pandemic, and this outdoor time—exercising and observing nature's bounty day after day—is an antidote to the challenges of the last months.

I'm proud that, earlier this summer, we passed the Great American Outdoors Act to address the huge maintenance backlog in our national parks and expand land and water conservation efforts. And, as governor, one of my signature accomplishments was land preservation. Working together with my team, we created new state parks, state forests, wilderness management areas, and natural area preserves. We used federal, state, and private funds to save all or parts of nearly twenty Civil War battlefields. And we used a robust transferable tax credit to encourage private landowners to place more than four hundred thousand acres of private land under permanent conservation easements, promising never to develop those acres.

We chose land preservation as our chief environmental goal because of the multiple benefits to be gained. Preserving open space preserves the endless beauty we enjoy but also helps improve air and water quality and, through forest maintenance, serves as a brake on climate change. It was a bipartisan priority—though my Republican Speaker of the House and I disagreed on most things, we found common cause on preserving our natural beauty, including Chesapeake Bay restoration. And, unlike most things in public policy that can be undone by a future law or court case, tools such as conservation easements can last forever, at least so long as America still has a legal system that will honor deeds permanently recorded in local courthouses.

The last stretch of the day is a long downhill to Swift Run Gap. We then load up with Phillip and drive fifteen miles north to spend the night at Big Meadows, a prominent and popular spot on the drive that includes a lodge and cabins, camping sites, and a massive open meadow filled with wildlife and one of the best places to stargaze that I know.

We stay in a 1930s-era cottage with adjoining rooms and sit outside on the lodge's porch for dinner, gazing down into the Shenandoah Valley below. Charles gives no love to the dinner special, turkey and stuffing, but all agree that the blackberry pie à la mode more than makes up for it. It is the first night this summer where I've needed a long-sleeve shirt to be outside, a signal that the heat is breaking and cooler weather is on the way.

7

The lodge where we've spent the night is actually the halfway point of today's ride. The plan is to drive the van back to Swift Run Gap fifteen miles south and then do a mostly climbing stretch up to Big Meadows, before twenty miles more of up and down to Thornton Gap. As you might imagine, the temptation to sleep late and skip the first fifteen miles of climbing is very real. I am determined to do every mile, however slowly, as part of my quest. (When I'm forced to skip fifteen downhill miles near Roanoke due to a closed road, I wait for months until repairs are done so I can return and complete the stretch.) Though none of my companions are under any such compulsion, I am proud of them—none flake out to sleep in.

Today is the busiest stretch of the trip. The drive is little more than an hour west of DC. It is late summer 2020, and people are stir-crazy to get outside. When the fiscal year ends on September 30, park visitation is up 14 percent over the previous year even though COVID completely closed the park for six weeks in the spring. And in October 2020, park visitation spikes more than 50 percent from 2019. Being cooped up inside by the virus has created a huge demand for outdoor time.

It is a Friday, one week before Labor Day weekend brings the unofficial end of a summer that never was for many people, as folks still aren't traveling much. This stretch of the drive has the two popular places—Big Meadows and Skyland—each with lodges, dining rooms, and parking areas with access to hiking trails. We have to battle more vehicles than normal today and even a one-mile road construction project that slows traffic to a standstill for five minutes at a time as groups of cars (and our bikes) slowly follow a flagged pickup over fresh-laid asphalt.

We pass Dean Cemetery just off the drive on the climb to Big Meadows. There are many tiny family cemeteries scattered throughout the park, some on fire roads and some deep in the woods. This one is larger than most, with a parking area and clearly organized mainte-nance, likely by a combination of Park Service personnel and family members of those buried here. I pull my bike over to pay respects and fall behind the others.

By Lewis Mountain Campground, a few miles farther up the road, I have now caught up. I camped here with my boys once many years ago in the early spring and worried all night long about dead branches falling as the wind roared through the trees. And last year, while hiking the AT, I spent the night in a nice cabin here with my friend Ned. It took until 1957 for the National Park Service to fully integrate the park, reasoning correctly that Virginia would not ask for the land back. (Virginia did keep its state park system segregated until 1965, even closing Seashore State Park for many years beginning in the late 1950s to avoid having to integrate the Virginia Beach facility.)

We stop for snacks at Big Meadows and then for lunch ten miles later at Skyland. Construction of the Drive began at Skyland—a preex-isting mountaintop resort—in 1931. And FDR came to Big Meadows on July 3, 1936, to dedicate the park, declaring that it was "for this and succeeding generations of Americans for the recreation and re-creation we find here." A photo of the event shows an apparently all-white crowd with only men on the stage, dressed in coats, ties, and hats even in midsummer.

The gently curving roads and comfortably rustic amenities of the drive belie the tough years of work that went into building the drives we have been traveling on this week. While the idea for the road-ways was hatched in the 1920s, it was arguably the Depression, oddly enough, that brought these scenic routes to life. The AT and other hiking trails were already being built by groups of volunteers like the

Potomac Appalachian Trail Club, Roanoke Appalachian Trail Club, Natural Bridge Appalachian Trail Club, and numerous others from Georgia to Maine. But the Blue Ridge Parkway and Skyline Drive really came to life because of the Civilian Conservation Corps.

Not all of FDR's New Deal projects were popular or successful. But the CCC, which put three million young men to work from 1933 until 1942, was a home run and remains a beloved part of our history. Building on a similar program that he initiated as governor of New York, FDR started a program that would recruit out-of-work men to do reforestation, park construction, and other outdoor projects. Recruits would sign up for six-month stints and could re-up to work for a maximum of two years. The program was limited to three hundred thousand men at a time. Pay was thirty dollars a month, with five dollars staying in the workers' pockets for spending money and twenty-five dollars sent home to help their families get through the Depression. The workers lived in camps near their projects, supervised by Army officers, and built a robust life of work and recreation.

CCC camps existed all over America. FDR proposed the idea immediately after his inauguration in March 1933, and the plan passed Congress on a voice vote that month. The first enrollee was selected on April 8 and the first camp—Camp Roosevelt, of course—opened near Luray, Virginia, on April 17. By June, there were more than 1,400 working camps and more than three hundred thousand enrollees. The speed of starting the program puts our current Congress to shame but also shows just how desperate people were for a solution to the achingly stretched out joblessness of the Depression.

Memorials and museums to the CCC abound. One at Pocahontas State Park near where we live in Richmond features original wooden buildings and a museum with memorabilia from the time—uniforms, photos, camp newspapers, cooking gear, tools, construction blueprints. There is also an iconic CCC statue—a life-size bronze figure—shirtless, fit, wielding a pickax and wearing a beat-up fedora. One stands outside the visitors center at Big Meadows, and there are numerous others all across America.

The CCC was constrained by the prejudices of the day. No more than 10 percent of the enrollees could be African American and they mostly worked in completely segregated units. Some Southern states excluded Black men entirely, only willing to accept a government safety net program if it was for whites. This trend continues today as the reality of racial discrimination leads the US to have a less robust set of social insurance programs than other similar nations who have not grappled with our legacy of slavery.

Eleanor Roosevelt was struck by the need to offer young women a similar opportunity and worked with Labor Secretary Frances Perkins to found She-She-She Camps. But there was little public support for the idea. Red tape, ridicule, criticism of using public funds for women, and suggestions that the program was too left-wing all conspired to cripple an initiative that only enrolled 8,500 women before it was closed down in 1936.

Still, the enduring memorial to the CCC is the sheer number of projects the "CCC boys" worked on that still exist today: scenic roads, local/state/national parks, forests, irrigation projects, dams, tree planting, battlefield restoration. Virginia's first state parks, opened in 1936, were built by CCC volunteers. In addition to employing people at a tough time and giving them employable skills, the project also helped create new appreciation for America's outdoor spaces. And when the war came, the CCC veterans were prized recruits, already used to military discipline and hard physical work and able to join up at an advanced rank due to their previous service.

With the war, a draft was needed, so Congress stopped funding the CCC. But many states, local governments, and nonprofits have continued the tradition, together with student internship programs run by the National Park Service. I honored Virginia's Youth Conservation Corps as our best volunteer program when I was governor. These programs, and others, raise the question of whether a new national public service program—no longer primarily for white males—could work again to perform worthy projects and introduce America's young people to each other as a way to break down our growing tribalism and political polarization.

As we lounge around eating lunch-meat and peanut-butter sandwiches at Skyland, we talk about the meals of our youth—culinary trends like casseroles with ubiquitous cream of mushroom soup that were popular in Midwestern middle-class homes in the 1960s. Our entire crew were kids from the Midwest when we first connected back in Cambridge—with the exception of Roger, who grew up in Gainesville, Georgia. Maybe it was the Midwestern connection that drew us together. Dave still lives in Des Moines and Jim in Chicago, but the rest of us have decamped to live near the coasts.

From Skyland north we have managed to escape traffic and have a thrilling downhill to Thornton Gap, zipping through our second tunnel of the week beneath Mary's Rock. When we finish, we have a treat in store for our last night together. Dave's son Mike and daughter-in-law Jen have a farm a few miles away near the town of Sperryville. We hop in the van to their farm and sit on the porch outside enjoying cold beer, crab cakes, and homemade pizza from their wood-fired pizza oven. Anne drives up from Richmond to join us for our meal and gets caught up on the adventures of the week.

Dave and his family are unfailingly generous—just as he was when I first met him forty years ago. As we talk late into the night, we get hit with a massive storm, the remnants of a hurricane that landed on the Gulf Coast a few days ago. And we realize that, for our last day tomorrow, our good luck with weather this week has officially run out. Take that, Mr. Blue Sky!

8

It storms all night long and the rain is falling steadily through fog when we start on Saturday morning. We have a relatively simple thirty-two-mile ride to Front Royal to finish our journey—climbing for the first half to Hogback Mountain and then a long downhill to the Park Service entry station at mile zero on Skyline Drive.

There is much back-and-forth about whether we should even do the ride in the rain. The fog makes visibility poor and the road is very slick, especially challenging on the downhill stretches. But we've come all this way. So after getting fortified by ham biscuits, we hatch a plan with Phillip. Instead of setting up at a midpoint for a snack break, he will simply ride ahead of us to each overlook, stopping every few miles in case conditions get too bad or our wills fade. We can pull over to climb in the van if we want or give him a thumbs-up as we cycle past. And so we start.

For some stupid reason, I am wearing black shorts and a black shirt and riding the all-black extra bike that Phillip brought along. No light on my bike. In the fog, I can barely be seen. Dave notices this and encourages me to stop at the van at the first opportunity to pull out a bright blue rain jacket just so I can be seen by traffic. We slog on.

Hurricane Laura dumped massive rain on the Gulf Coast a few days back and then swept quickly on a northeastern arc. We are hitting the tail end of the weather system today and it is oddly beautiful, certainly different than what we've experienced during the first seven days. The rain is steady and the fog is swirling, giving every overlook and blind curve a ghostly appearance. The weather has kept normal Saturday crowds home—no backed-up traffic like yesterday. But the wind is not too intense and the temperature is warm. No danger of hypothermia. Just stay on the bike and no falls!

Today's ride is the shortest and the easiest, but I find myself riding pretty slowly. I watch the mileposts count down from thirty-two and realize I'm dawdling because I don't want the trip to end. These friends have meant so much to me for forty years, and this has been one of my favorite times with them. We've been through it all together. They committed to join me on the trip nearly a year ago and never wavered even as COVID made traveling seem unwise to many. And the ability to spend eight days together made for conversation that was both leisurely and deeply introspective. Exercising together to the point of physical fatigue is an inducement to good discussion.

Cycling this great Virginia route has also given me additional personal perspective, the kind of thing that can happen when you step away from the busyness of your routine. Last year, and again this year, the rhythm of straining up hills and then easing down was a reminder about the ups and downs that go along with any fully lived life. But looking down at my handlebars and shifting gears all week has given me another metaphor that seems to describe how I am feeling about my own stage of life.

The two bikes I've ridden this week are equipped with a two-ring front derailleur and a ten-ring back cassette. Some of the other guys have bikes with three front rings, the tiniest known as a "granny gear" designed specifically to climb steep hills. And if you've ridden bikes a lot, you know that you usually set the front ring and then adjust the back gears frequently depending upon gentle rises and falls on the road. You change the front ring much less often, normally when there is a big change in terrain.

Most of life is making small shifts on the back ring. For big life transitions, you shift the front ring. At sixty-two, I feel like I am making a big front ring shift, the third in my adult life. My first phase—from law school at twenty-one through my election to Richmond City Council at thirty-six—was a civil rights phase. I trained for it, was inspired to pursue civil rights advocacy by my time in Honduras and early mentors, and then built a satisfying career fighting racial discrimination, the death penalty, and other injustices in the court system.

When I was elected to my first office, I shifted into a public service phase. Just as there are overlapping gear strengths in derailleur-equipped bikes, the shift from civil rights to public service was not a clean break. I carried the civil rights passion with me and found new venues (city hall, the governor's office, the US Capitol) other than a courtroom to express that.

Now—perhaps as a part of aging and with months of COVID altering life around me—I feel myself shifting again, this time to a phase more focused on spiritual and creative endeavors. Again, I carry the civil rights and public service passions with me into this new chapter, but I find myself eager to embrace the contemplative ring alongside the task-focused ring as I grapple with the challenges of my life and the life of the community I serve.

Anne and my children, my parents and brothers, and Anne's extended family have been supportive at all phases of the journey. And I have been enormously blessed with friends—friends from my Kansas City childhood, Richmond neighborhood and church friends, some deep friendships I have made through my political travels across Virginia and across America. But these Nightwingnuts, who have stuck together to offer a support network to each other for forty years now, are unique and special. I know how lucky I am to know them. And I think they each feel the same about the group. It's central to our lives in ways both easy and hard to articulate.

As I meander along and the mileposts count down, I see the guys stopped ahead at the Signal Knob Overlook, about seven miles from the end of the trip. I pull over and ask what's up. They tell me that they have determined that I should finish first with them tailing as my wingmen for the last few miles. By now the rain has stopped and there is even sun peeking through from the west as the storm is moving quickly out toward the sea. We speed down the last curves under a deep tree cover, hardly needing to pedal at all. The Dickey Ridge Visitor Center passes by and then, a few minutes later, the ranger station comes into view with Phillip's van parked just beyond it. And just like that, the trip is over.

As we load the van, Phillip indulges his tradition as a guide by bestowing a cowbell on one of the riders. If you watch the Tour de France, you often see spectators lining the route ringing cowbells as the peloton speeds by. He chooses Roger for the honor out of respect for how heavy a bike he rides while still making the hills look easy.

We reclaim our cars at Mountain Home and, deprived of milk-shakes all week, stop in Front Royal for cheeseburgers and frozen custard before heading home. A quick survey: no falls, no injuries, no major mechanical malfunctions, no one showing symptoms of COVID. Sore muscles and a few minor bike issues that were easily remedied. All of us proved that our trip across Iowa twenty-four years ago was no fluke—we handled this more challenging terrain like champs. Middle-aged champs, but champs nevertheless.

Dave drives west for Des Moines, Scott and Roger load up to head north to Boston, and I take Charles on a leisurely backroads route to Dulles so he can hop his flight back to LA. And within hours, the group email exchange of pictures, memories from the week, and discussions about our next adventure together begin anew.

AFTERMATH

I get back to the Senate after Labor Day with the 2020 presidential election rushing toward us like a freight train. It dominates everything. We need to pass another bill to help people and businesses hurt by COVID. The Republican Senate wastes all summer, not even voting until mid-September on a woefully inadequate proposal. No rent assistance, no mortgage assistance, no SNAP benefits or food aid, no aid to state and local governments. The Democratic House passes such a bill in May but Senate Republicans show little interest.

What Senate Republicans are motivated by is the chance to rush filling the Supreme Court vacancy left by the death of Ruth Bader Ginsburg. Despite their loud claims in 2016 that a vacancy occurring in an election year should only be filled after "letting the people decide" who will be the next president, the Republicans break all speed records (and their own promises) by filling the vacancy before the election. Why? Because they can.

Also, the Supreme Court is scheduled to hear a case one week after the election that could finally achieve the GOP dream of killing Obamacare. Filling this seat as soon as possible increases the odds that they will finally succeed in taking health care away from millions or succeed in their biggest goal: the recriminalization of abortion.

Because of laudable changes to Virginia election laws, we start early voting on September 18, and Anne and I go to our local registrar that day to lead what we hope will be a surge of 2020 participation. I campaign with a local congresswoman later in the day in a rural county and witness two maskless MAGA provocateurs shouting at senior citizens who have come to vote early. I have to escort some folks away from the shouters to calm them down—not only were these MAGA folks harassing people, they were frightening them with the threat of super-spreading the virus.

As we enter the month of October, the president contracts COVID, battles with his own science advisors, backs out of a debate, and continues to conduct his campaign at packed rallies, endangering the health of his followers. Smart law enforcement disrupts a plot by white supremacist militias to kidnap the governor of Michigan. Coronavirus cases start a massive surge in many states as dropping temperatures drive folks back indoors. Joe Biden and Kamala Harris conduct a COVID-appropriate campaign to help keep everyone safe.

I get drafted a few times a week to do press for the campaign in Virginia or Spanish-language media around the country. I was at the center of things in the 2016 campaign but am a peripheral player now. This feels both wistful ("what might have been") and liberating ("I'm free for a bike trip with friends"). The polls look good, but the possibility for electoral interference is high, and many worry that the president will not accept a result he dislikes.

I tell people that their 2020 vote will be the most important of their life. 2016 was important to me, obviously, and I plan to live long and vote many more times in the decades to come. Still, 2020 will remain the most important vote of my life. It's about many issues, of course—climate change, racial justice, economic fairness, an impartial court system. But it's also about whether we still uphold the values that have made our nation great. It's about whether we retain a wonderful American trait: the capacity to recognize a mistake and improve upon it.

We are not a perfect nation, just as none of us are perfect individuals. America has made many mistakes, and we always will. But we chose wisely in setting the equality of all as our moral North Star. And when we get it wrong, as we often have and will again, we have a way of realizing it and then readjusting back to our professed values.

We got it wrong in 2016, but that's not unusual. The question on the 2020 ballot is whether Americans can admit that and, as we have in the past, resolve to make things better. And when we do make such a resolution, we normally achieve great things.

Having shifted my "front ring" to a more contemplative gear puts me in a weird place where I am both at the center of the action but also removed from it. A common phrase with biblical origin is to be "in but not of the world." And my trips in nature—whether this Virginia Nature Triathlon or my weekend hikes and bike trips with Anne and my neighbors or even my daily walk to work on Capitol Hill—help me find a spiritual equilibrium even as the consequences of COVID, economic distress, racial injustice, and chaotic leadership pile up all around us.

One night, seeing a beautiful full moon rise above my backyard in Richmond, my subconscious surfaces a stray line I read decades ago: "The moon lifts, radiant with terror." I search for it and find the Robert Lowell poem "Fall 1961" about political anxiety, parenthood, and nature. It is nearly sixty years old. I get a shock of significance when I see it was published in the *Blue Ridge Review*.

I finish these notes from our bike trip on October 24—ten days before the election. It is an absolutely beautiful fall Saturday in Virginia. I step outside at sunrise to get the paper and revel in the cool air, multihued trees, and pumpkin-adorned porches in my neighborhood. Then I read today's front-page headline: "US Sets One-Day Record for Infections."

PADDLE
2021

Where to begin?

From the October morning when I finished writing about the bike trip, COVID deaths in the US rocket upward. Joe Biden and Kamala Harris are elected to be our next president and vice president, earning seven million more votes than the Trump-Pence ticket and handily winning the once reliably red Virginia by ten points. But the normal response of a losing candidate—a concession—is not possible for the insecure forty-fifth president of the United States.

Instead, we see a carnival of lies, stunts, and dangerous provocations during the months of November, December, and January. Donald Trump preaches his biggest lie: that the election was stolen from him and that he would prevail in overturning it. State election officials review and then rereview the results and confirm the Biden win. Dozens of state and federal courts confirm the Biden win. But still Trump persists in his dangerous folly, ultimately urging his followers to come to Washington on January 6 for a "wild" gathering to upend the result.

Trump's disgraceful effort occurs at the same time as two runoff Senate elections in Georgia stand poised to determine who will have the majority in my chamber. For Democrats to go two for two in Georgia to take the majority seems improbable. In talks with my supporters during those months I often say, "We need three things to win. First, we need great candidates. In Raphael Warnock and Jon Ossoff, we have them. Second, we need energized Democratic turnout. With all eyes on Georgia and with the recent Biden win, we'll have it. But that's not enough. We need an internal dispute within the Georgia Republican Party that will depress Republican turnout."

Donald Trump ignites that dispute in exemplary fashion, lashing out at the Republican Georgia governor and other Republican officials for their sin of allowing Joe Biden to win Georgia's electoral votes. His actions force the two Republican senators from Georgia into an awkward dilemma—should they trash the legitimacy of their own state's election and the Republicans who managed it, or break with Trump and acknowledge the obvious truth of the election results? Their inability to wholeheartedly do either is apparent and suggests weakness.

The morning of January 6 dawns clear and cold on Capitol Hill. The Georgia elections the previous day delivered a win for Raphael Warnock. The Jon Ossoff race is too close to call. I walk the mile to the office early, hoping to avoid any protestors arriving for the Trump rally that day. I am inside the Russell Building by 7:15 a.m. and work there in my silent office—accompanied only by my chief of staff—until senators are called to the Senate floor to consider Ted Cruz's objection to accepting the Arizona certification of its electoral votes.

Senators can travel from their offices across the street to the Capitol by underground tunnel, and that's what I do. Having successfully weaned myself from permanent attachment to my cell phone while on the AT, I leave it in my office because I don't want it to distract me during the possibly significant debate. The fact that I came in early, walked to the Capitol through the tunnel, and left my phone behind means that I am somewhat oblivious to the crowd gathering outside the Capitol.

As we begin the debate in the Senate Chamber, I am struck by how different this day is than four years earlier. It took all of about twenty minutes to open the letters from each state and certify the 2016 results. My name was on all those letters, but it was nonetheless an inconsequential formality. Of course, Hillary and I had conceded the election in public speeches delivered about twelve hours after the last US polls closed that November. But today is different because Trump and his enablers determine to try something wild.

I know Ted Cruz well. We came into the Senate together in 2013. He has an IQ second to none and academic credentials—double Ivy League education, Supreme Court law clerk—that put him in the very top ranks of the legal profession. I have no doubt that he objects to the Arizona result despite knowing full well that Biden won the election and Trump lost.

As the debate goes on over the Arizona result, James Lankford of Oklahoma takes the floor. While he is speaking, security officers usher Vice President Pence from his spot on the dais where he is presiding over the debate. I still don't have my phone, so it is unclear what's occurring because Iowa Senator Chuck Grassley takes Pence's place and debate continues. Perhaps Pence is ushered out to take one last pleading phone call from Trump—we had all seen that occur during the Republican effort to kill the Affordable Care Act in August 2017 as John McCain was summoned from the chamber to talk to the president before his pivotal vote that saved the ACA.

That moment was one of the most exciting in my public life. As chair of the Democratic Party, I stumped for ACA passage all over the country and was determined to block any effort to repeal it. But we were in the minority; Democrats needed three Republican votes to save the ACA. Susan Collins and Lisa Murkowski were rock solid. But McCain, just released from the hospital after being diagnosed with brain cancer, was casting preliminary procedural votes as if he were onboard with ACA repeal. On the day of the final vote, I'd never seen Democratic leader Chuck Schumer so depressed. I told some colleagues: "I know the signs are that McCain is against us, but I cannot believe he will come out of a hospital, where he's been surrounded by people who are fighting for their lives, and cast a vote to take their health care away." Hours later on the floor—about fifteen minutes before the final vote on ACA repeal—McCain sidled up to Amy Klobuchar and me and said, "I'm with you guys." And that began the slowest fifteen minutes of my life, as the clock ticked down and his GOP colleagues, Mike Pence, and the president waged an increasingly frantic effort to get him on board. John's dramatic no vote—thumbs-down as though he were in *Gladiator*—was political courage with the dash of drama for which he was justly famous.

Today, I see Mitt Romney stand and bolt out one of the Senate doors into the hall that goes down to the House Chamber. (I learn later that he has been notified by his staff that the Capitol is under attack.) When he quickly comes back into the Senate Chamber with a worried look, I know something is wrong.

At this point, Senate security takes the dais and Senator Grassley recesses the proceeding. We are told that the Capitol has been breached and we will be barricaded into the Senate Chamber. The slamming of doors—first the ornamental glass doors and then the set of heavy wooden security doors—is eerie. We begin to hear noises from the insurrectionists. At one point, Amy Klobuchar, sitting next to the door leading the House Chamber, says, "There's been gunshots." A sense of dread, confusion, and anger is thick in the air.

We are in the chamber for about forty-five minutes before Capitol Police secure a path down a flight of stairs, through a hall, down another flight of stairs, and into the underground tunnel that will take us back across the street where we can assemble in a committee room. At two points along the route, we can see the attackers just yards away.

When we finally gather in the committee room, Senate security informs us that we can complete the work there. I am proud of all my colleagues because, without any discussion, we speak in a single voice: "We won't do the work here. Clear the chamber and we'll go back and finish there in full view of the American public."

We stay in the committee room for five hours—one hundred senators and nearly fifty staff, packed together at the peak of the COVID epidemic. (All but one wear a mask.) Television monitors are rolled in and, for the first time, I can see what is happening outside. Suddenly, I miss my phone and want to let my family and friends know that I am safe. I borrow a phone from Martin Heinrich of New Mexico and call Anne and my chief of staff.

Two notable things happen in that room before we go back to the chamber to defeat the Arizona objection and the even more ridiculous objection lodged by Missouri Senator Josh Hawley against the Pennsylvania result. First, the coverage of the Capitol attack is interrupted by the breaking news that Jon Ossoff is declared the winner of the second Georgia Senate seat, giving Democrats the majority. The timing seems providential. The Trump era ends in an orgy of unnecessary death and chaos due to his mishandling of the pandemic and a soul-sickening domestic insurrection. The decisive Georgia race being called during the attack seems like the American public repudiating the destruction and declaring that new management is needed.

I go up to my friend Lindsey Graham and tell him that Democrats never could have taken the majority except for the Trump antics challenging the election. He doesn't disagree. I say the same thing to Mitch McConnell, and though he does not respond, I can see a level of anger in his eyes that I have never seen in my life. He is clearly thinking what I am—that Donald Trump is behind both the disgraceful attack on the Capitol and the loss of his Senate Republican majority.

The second event—very personally meaningful—comes when the television monitors show a line of Virginia State Police cruisers arriving to assist the Capitol Police. Our colleagues start to applaud and tell me and Mark Warner to pass their thanks on to our governor. These state police would be promptly joined by thousands of Virginia

Guard members, who had repeatedly been pressed into service during the pandemic for COVID testing, food distribution, and vaccination assistance.

At that moment, I recall that our nation's largest domestic insurrection had been supported by Virginia in the 1860s. Now here we are, with an attempted insurrection against the Constitution led by the president, and Virginia is coming to the rescue of the union! A flood of emotions washes over me in that instant. I try to communicate this to Mark Warner but choke up. He understands what I am trying to say and feels the impact of it too.

We finish the electoral count in the wee hours of January 7. New York Senator Kirsten Gillibrand and I gather in my office with our chiefs of staff to share a drink and toast the Constitution. My chief gives me a lift home and I fall asleep pondering what is happening to our country. I recall telling folks after the 2016 election that "we're about to go through a stress test of our democracy." It's clear that we've not yet passed the test.

A few hours later, after a fitful night of tossing and turning, I walk back to the Capitol to get my first vaccination shot. (The prompt development of effective vaccines was a real bright spot in the Trump administration's generally shoddy COVID response—how odd that Trump later encouraged vaccine denial rather than leaning into his own success.) The day is clear and calm, but the ravaged Capitol is near empty. A Capitol Police officer pulls me aside as I enter the building and says, "You need to do everything you can to get to the bottom of what happened, even if it makes people in my department or in Congress very uncomfortable."

The officer's comments and the events of January 6—indeed, of the last four years—start a slow-growing awareness of a reality I have not previously contemplated. I came to the Senate in 2013 to do good things for my country and Commonwealth and fight for people I care about. I would not have described my job as "preserving democracy" because I took that for granted and assumed that all members of

Congress did as well. But I now see that it cannot be taken for granted and that much of the labor of the past four years has been about more than the daily issues that we were voting on. It has been about the basic work of preserving democracy.

Inauguration Day is bizarre—there's no crowd, and the Capitol is surrounded by barbed wire and troops. The outgoing president is unusually but thankfully absent after slinking out of town. I am relieved to see my friends Joe Biden and Kamala Harris take their oaths of office. I have no doubt that they will support and defend our Constitution. The day *should* feel like the start of a new chapter, but the lingering shock of January 6 greatly dampens the mood.

That "new chapter" feeling kicks in about six weeks later when I stand on the steps of the Capitol at sunrise after an all-night floor session passing the American Rescue Plan, the Biden administration's first big bill, providing relief to American families, small businesses, health care providers, schools and universities, state and local governments. Because no Republicans would vote yes, the Rescue Plan passes by one vote. My mind flashes back to my ambivalence in 2011 about whether I should run for the Senate. I have now been part of two near-existential issues—saving the ACA and passing this Rescue Plan—that were decided by a single vote. Perhaps these moments are the reasons I am here.

Together with a rapidly escalating vaccination campaign, the passage of the Rescue Plan creates a palpable hope as we see a way out of the unmitigated disaster of the past year. With a Democratic majority, I am now chairman of two Senate subcommittees dealing with foreign policy in the Western Hemisphere and US military installations and acquisition. It feels as though things may finally turn a corner. With this fresh start in mind, I start planning the final leg of my outdoor journey. It will be 348 miles on the James River from Iron Gate in the Allegheny Mountains to the Chesapeake Bay.

I learned last year that planning a mostly solo hike is different than a group bike trip. And equally so for a canoe trip with someone in the front of the boat with me most days. Each day's route—who will join me, where to stay, how to get cars shuttled up and down river, how much food and gear to carry in the canoe, interesting stops along the way—has to be carefully planned out.

But the planning isn't a burden. It builds a sense of anticipation. And thinking about the journey—with each leg planned, undertaken and later written up as a journal entry—makes me understand life's moments in a new way. Each moment is thrice-lived: first, anticipation; next, experience; finally, recollection. (Actually, each moment is lived four times—with the sharing of the memories a separate reality from any of the listed three. This is also probably the most meaningful.)

I learned on the AT that dividing the walk into spring, summer, and fall segments worked well because I experienced the natural beauty of the trail in distinctively different seasons. I plan the James River trip during Senate recess weeks in a similar way—a week around Memorial Day from Iron Gate to Lynchburg, an August stretch of nearly two weeks from Lynchburg to Richmond, and an October finish from Richmond to Fort Monroe. I am expecting the trip to take about twenty-five days, but I have no need to rush it.

Before I begin, I have to fix my canoe: an Old Town Camper that Anne and I were given as a Christmas gift by her folks when we were newlyweds. It has seen so much action—and its rubber/plastic composite shell has the dents to prove it! But it's been sitting behind my garage for about ten years with little use—wrapped in vines—and I wonder whether I can rescue it.

Thank God for American craftsmanship. The cane seats, repaired by my friend Fay more than fifteen years ago, are still fine. Just the wooden yoke and thwart—necessary for stabilizing and carrying a canoe—are rotted through. Old Town lets me order the parts online, and with a drill and my neighbor John, the canoe is brought back to shipshape one Saturday morning in winter.

Anne and I take it for a trial run the following April—canoeing into the Great Dismal Swamp National Wildlife Refuge, an amazing natural marvel in southeastern Virginia. Its history is as a home for the Nansemond Indian Tribe and haven for thousands of African Americans who came here to escape slavery and form their own communities in the middle of what was once a million-acre wilderness. I am working with other members of the Virginia congressional delegation to have this human history recognized with a National Heritage Area designation. We have a beautiful trip, testing the canoe and indulging Anne in her pandemic hobby of bird-watching. The swamp is a treasure trove of birds, and we are there at the perfect time to see the migration of warblers that arrive in April and May every year.

So—knowing the canoe doesn't leak—I tinker with the gear and plans until the start of this final leg. Annella and her writing partner, Fern, will come down from New York to join Anne and me for a few days over Memorial Day weekend as we start the James River adventure in the town of Iron Gate—a small village, really—where the Jackson River and Cowpasture River cut through mountain passes and join together to form the James.

After a grueling week in the Senate, passing a bipartisan bill to meet the China challenge and failing on an effort to create a bipartisan commission to investigate the roots of the January 6 attack, I beat a quick path to Richmond, put the canoe on top of my Ford Escape, and caravan to the town of Buchanan by the James River in Botetourt County. We call the Anchorage House—a renovated historic home now run as an inn—and ask if they allow camping on their grounds. Of course! So we arrive near sunset and Annella and I set up tents in the backyard while Fern and Anne scour the town for takeout. We end up with hamburgers on the front porch, visiting with the other guests—weekend visitors who are here for the river and bicycle trails nearby and Appalachian Trail thru-hikers. We are about ten miles from the trail. Chris—a Marine veteran and one of the owners of this inn—will shuttle hikers to his place. We soon retire to our tents and the skies open up with a thunderstorm. But we are dry, the sound is heavenly, and sleep comes in an instant.

1

We awake to rain. Each of my three trips starts this way! The tents are wet and the forecast calls for cold and more rain today when we are on the water. But we pack up, and Spring—one of the inn's owners—has hot coffee and breakfast sandwiches to fuel us along the way.

The town of Buchanan is like many in this part of the country. Founded in 1832, it thrived because it was on the river. And as the western terminus of the James River and Kanawha Canal Company—begun in 1785 with the intent of linking the Atlantic, James River, Kanawha River, Ohio River, Mississippi River, and Gulf of Mexico—its prospects must have seemed bright. But railroads and highways overtook water as the transportation of choice, and river towns declined for a long time. The canal right-of-way was eventually converted into a railroad line in the late 1800s. Buchanan now has about 1,200 residents.

People coming back to nature are breathing new life into Buchanan (an easy commute to Roanoke) and other small towns in Virginia—Scottsville, Marion, Waynesboro, Front Royal, Sperryville, Abingdon, St. Paul, Floyd, Chincoteague, Damascus. I think the pandemic may accelerate this trend—why not work virtually, live in smaller communities, and spend more time outdoors?

We drive five minutes to Twin Rivers Outfitters, a local outfitter started by twin brothers who love the Allegheny Mountains and the rivers in this region. They rent canoes, kayaks, and inner tubes; shuttle visitors hither and yon; and own three campsites along the Upper James, which local tourism pros have dubbed the Upper James River Water Trail: sixty-four miles of the most pristine and free-flowing water from the confluence until a stretch of seven dams starts to back up the river above Lynchburg. My goal this week is to do the nearly ninety miles to Lynchburg—accompanied by family the first three days, environmental advocates from the James River Association for two days, and my reliable friend Ned through the gnarly dam section above Lynchburg for the last two days.

The Twin River folks take us up to Iron Gate and we put into the clear, swift-flowing, narrow water. The river here is pools and drops with class-one to class-two rapids just frequent enough to keep your adrenaline up. (Boaters usually class rapids from class one to class six, with class-one rapids easy and class-six rapids life-risking.) We see black minks swimming in the water soon after we put in—beautiful and agile.

Anne and I fall into an easy rhythm in the canoe after so many trips together. She sits in front and uses her binoculars to scout birds while paddling occasionally until we get to rapids, when she helps power us through. The best bird today is a common merganser—a beautiful duck with a rust orange head that is actually not so common in Western Virginia in late May. In fact, we've never seen one before, but they are ubiquitous for the next few days.

Annella and Fern do fine on the water. Growing up in Richmond, Annella and her brothers grew up with the James River as their playground. Canoeing with Mom and Dad, kayaking in a great summer camp located on an island right in the middle of downtown—she knows how to handle a boat and chart a line through rapids. Fern is from Northern California and is comfortable on the water. Because she's spent so little time in the South, she does unintentionally surprise us at times: "Why are there so many Trump signs still up? What's up with the Confederate flags? Why don't any of the markets have fresh fruit and vegetables? People are so friendly here!"

The shuttling upstream means a later start and a light day—just eleven miles to a Twin Rivers campground in Gala. We have tents and gear, but this campground has preset canvas tents on wooden platforms. Thank goodness! It rains most of the day on the river and into the evening. We haven't brought warm enough clothes or sleeping bags for this first night. But we play cards and sing in the tent and get lucky with a two-hour break from rain when we fire up a freeze-dried dinner with my trusty Jetboil stove and start a roaring campfire. Even though the conditions aren't ideal, I am so happy that Annella made time to come down from New York to do this trip, just as she made time to hike with me two years ago.

We turn in and try to stay warm. Only Fern has a real sleeping bag. The rest of us—at my suggestion—are relying on thin sleeping bag liners that I was sure would be sufficient for nighttime temperatures in late May. Oops! So we wrap clothes and tarps around ourselves and pass a restless night.

2

Today we will be on the water for seventeen miles from Gala to another riverside campground at Horseshoe Bend. The weather is markedly improving—temperatures will be in the sixties with no more rain expected for the next few days.

This stretch of the river brings back strong memories. I have done it twice before. It is one of the premier fishing stretches of the Upper James—smallmouth bass and now muskie are prized here. On one of my trips, I canoed with an eleven-year-old Annella in the front of the boat. A friend in a nearby boat launched an errant cast and put a fishhook on a lure right through Annella's scalp. We pulled to shore, clipped the barb off the hook, and backed it out with some drama and tears that we laugh about now. The bad parts of trips—a fishhook through the scalp, the cold, rainy weather yesterday—become the most fun stories later.

We canoe all day—pools and short rapids to keep you on your toes. The most notable rapid is Gwynn Lock, a rapid below Eagle Rock where the ruins of an old dam and mill operation stretching from river right across the channel combine with the ruins of the old canal lock on river left to funnel the river into standing waves over the derelict man-made structures that have collapsed over centuries into the river. I remember this spot from earlier trips—we all go through happy and bouncing up and down over the waves without incident, and we stop to snack on a beautiful gravel bar just below the rapid.

Just as hiking the same trail in different seasons and weather means that the trip is always different, a river trip is always new, even when you are on a stretch you've done before. It's not just differences in seasons and weather. The rising and falling river levels create different challenges in the water. Some stretches get harder as the water level rises and the volume amps up the current and waves, pushing you harder toward obstacles. But some stretches get harder as the water level drops and more rocks are exposed.

The Greek philosopher Heraclitus captured the variability of a river thousands of years ago: "No man ever steps in the same river twice, for it's not the same river and he's not the same man." While a river trip is infinitely variable, every river trip is also the same in one important way: each river leads to the same place. A trip down a river—like the one I am undertaking on the James—normally finds the ocean, and its waters merge with those of all other rivers and streams. Hiking and biking trails don't all end in the same place.

The Book of Ecclesiastes says, "All the rivers run into the sea, yet the sea is not full. To the place from which the rivers come, to there and from there they return again." The words were written between 450 and 200 BC. Already the writers understood that one sea covered much of the earth, that all rivers eventually became part of it, and that the sea never overflows because the waters there are recycled back to their multitude of sources. The same writers posed the existential question that preoccupies the book: "What profit hath a man of all his labour which he taketh under the sun? One generation passeth away, and another generation cometh: but the earth abideth forever."

Rivers (and river trips) are about cycles and returns. They are about transition from individual to collective—the growth of a tiny stream into a larger stream before ultimately merging with all other streams in the ocean. They are about birth and death: there is a starting point—a confluence or lake outlet or spring—and then eventually a final destination where the river's identity ceases. They are about the mortality of man against the persistence of nature: "The earth abideth forever." And they are about rebirth: miraculously, the small springs and headwaters keep producing the trickles of water that not only feed the ocean covering 71 percent of the Earth's surface but also become the very source of life for mankind and all species of flora and fauna.

The eternal cycle of a river's life was captured by a book released on this day in May of 1849, Henry David Thoreau's *A Week on the Concord and Merrimack Rivers*. A journal of a journey with his brother, John, written years after the trip by Thoreau as he sojourned at Walden Pond, this book—combining memories of the river trip with reflections on nature, society, and friendship—has been a touchstone throughout my life. I am sure that part of the reason I embraced this Virginia Nature Triathlon, finishing on the James River, was my deep love for Thoreau and his mystical reflection about rivers.

My own river journey will trace the abiding cycle from start to finish along the river that really defines much of Virginia, with a watershed of more than ten thousand square miles that is home to a population of nearly three million people. The grand scale of this seems out of whack with the still-small stream we are negotiating today.

In the early days of the pandemic, Anne and I hit upon a project—every day we spent together, we would find a walk or bike ride or canoe segment to do together. And the most important rule was "No repeats." We could do a hike that we had done pre-pandemic, but the idea was to get outside together every day we could and find something new to do.

Beginning in late March 2020, it's been parks, forests, cemeteries, refuges, battlefields, wildlife management areas, natural area preserves, trails, rails-to-trails, rivers, creeks, lakes, swamps, undeveloped drainage areas, single-tracks, neighborhoods, beautiful hidden alleys, college campuses, high school tracks. Truly a physical and spiritual haven during a tough time. And along the way we fell into a good pattern. I have freakishly good faraway vision. So I'd see motion in a tree and a flash of yellow and then direct Anne's eyesight toward it. She'd find it and then want to know what kind of bird it was.

Soon she started bringing binoculars on all our excursions. In October 2020, she began a bird list and has well over one hundred birds on it by the start of our trip in May. She gets CDs and an app to help her identify them by song as well as sight.

The Upper James is filled with great birds—ducks and geese, eagles and hawks, cardinals and orioles, swifts and bluebirds, finches and swallows, tanagers and meadowlarks—and Anne is fixed to her binoculars during much of the day. As we get ready to land for the night at our campsite, her eyes glued to the binoculars cause us to run up on a barely submerged rock and the boat starts to spin around and lean dangerously. I jump out of the boat—knowing that the move will cause the canoe to immediately right itself—pull it off the rock, and then hop back in to paddle us to the bank. No capsizing or submarining, but I am soaked. And I then have to swim after a spare paddle that fell out of the boat as it was near tipping. Annella and Fern are highly amused.

We set up camp—again using the campsite's preset tents rather than those we've carried—and the night couldn't be more different than last night. Still cool, but clear now with a beautiful sunset and plenty of dry firewood to warm us up. After dinner, we play music around the fire, taking advantage of the beautiful voices of our two New York theater companions. Annella plays the mandolin, and one of my greatest parental joys is playing with her and seeing the progress she's made on the instrument since the last time we were together.

A half dozen young public servants from Washington, all connected through a public policy fellowship for scientists, are also at our campground. They recognize us and come over bearing beer to join us by the fire. They each describe the work they do—fighting COVID and human trafficking, wildlife biology research, protecting endangered species—as we work our way through songs whose words and music we've memorized enough to play in the dark. I gain so much optimism when I encounter young public servants like these folks. Their enthusiasm for their work and love of the outdoors combine with their beer, my bourbon, and our campfire to create a glow of good feeling that lasts long after they depart.

3

Today is a fifteen-mile day divided into two sections. The four of us will float eight miles to Buchanan where Anne, Annella, and Fern will grab their car and head home. And I will then canoe solo seven miles to Arcadia to camp for the night. Bill Street of the James River Association will meet me there and then canoe with me for the next two days, educating me about the river and leading me through the tough Balcony Falls stretch of the James.

It is Memorial Day, and after two cool days the weather finally feels like summer: sunny, humid, and likely to be hot as the day wears on. We slather on the sunscreen and set out on the water by 8:45 a.m.

The James begins in the Allegheny Mountains, and then enters the Shenandoah Valley between the Alleghenies and the Blue Ridge. The magnificent Shenandoah Valley stretches 180 miles from Roanoke northeast to Winchester between these two mountain ranges. It is anywhere from ten to thirty miles wide and bisected in the northern portion by the fifty-mile-long Massanutten Mountain. It's named for two forks of the Shenandoah River that run north before joining in Front Royal near the northern tip of the valley. Then the Shenandoah proceeds farther north to Harpers Ferry, where it joins the Potomac River, right at the spot where I took my first step on this long journey in May 2019.

The James is somewhat unique in that it comes out of the Allegheny Mountains, crosses the valley, and then slashes through the Blue Ridge on its way to Richmond and the sea. Other rivers and streams drain into the valley, but only one cuts across it and powers through the Blue Ridge. We start our day in the mountains, negotiating ledges and

234

small rapids beneath towering cliffs, but then enter the valley, traveling under Interstate 81 with the first loud traffic we've heard in days. And soon the town of Buchanan emerges on river right.

I help Anne and the girls unload their canoe and pack their gear into Anne's car. I have four and a half days of fun ahead but still feel down as they depart. I leave my canoe and gear on the bank and drive back up to Anchorage House to get lunch before finishing the trip to Arcadia.

As I drive my car to the inn, I spot a backpacker trudging down Main Street out of the corner of my eye. When I get to the inn and find Spring at her café across the street, I casually ask about Chris. She tells me he is out "doing about twenty miles today." I assume he's doing a stretch of river on this beautiful day.

A few minutes later, Chris appears, trudging with the backpack. He briefly waves and keeps walking, not saying a word. When Spring brings my food out to the patio, I ask for specifics about what Chris is up to. She tells me that Chris is walking twenty miles in long laps around town on Memorial Day with his military backpack on to honor a friend he lost in Afghanistan. He did three Middle East deployments as a Marine and was himself wounded in an IED explosion.

I am an Armed Services Committee member with a son in the Marines and make decisions every day that affect our troops and their families. But I never served in the military. I am sitting in the sun in shorts and a T-shirt, enjoying my river trip on this national holiday. The day means something very different to Chris. I am humbled by this.

When I get back to my boat, a group of families are going out on inner tubes to do a few miles on this sunny afternoon. One of the families is Indian American and it strikes me—just as it has on both my hike and bike trips—that I don't see many people of color on my nature journey through Virginia. In our first three days on the river, we've seen campers, Boy Scouts, day-trippers, plenty of people fishing. The cool weather kept some of the normal Memorial Day crowds down, I imagine, but we've seen many people. But no racial diversity except this Indian American family. Since Virginia's minority population is about 30 percent, it seems odd.

I took a picture yesterday and posted it on social media with this caption:

> Iron Gate to Lynchburg on the James River this week. Otter, mink, bald eagles, common mergansers, Baltimore orioles, scarlet tanagers. Virginia is for nature lovers!

I almost never read comments on my social media postings. But I did read comments this time. One stood out:

> Virginia is for WHITE nature lovers. Not too safe for non-whites.

The comment was from someone out of state and contained nothing else to explain its meaning.

But it made me think.

In many ways, nothing is more accessible than public lands and waterways. Most parks are free, and the waters and forests of Virginia are open to all. I have puzzled over the lack of diversity and assumed that it must be that many people of color just don't get the same exposure to outdoor opportunities that I received growing up in Kansas, actively participating in my church Boy Scout troop. And, without that exposure, they don't pursue outdoor opportunities.

But the comment was about *fear*—and not fear of nature. Things feel okay for *white* nature lovers. But "not too safe for non-whites." The comment gave me a new insight on the lack of diversity. It's not necessarily lack of exposure or fear of nature—it could be the fear of how others will treat you when you're out in nature.

I think back to Fern's comments from two days ago: "What's up with the Confederate flags? Why are there so many Trump signs still up?" For Fern, a white woman from Northern California, those cultural markers are puzzling. For a person of color, they may seem threatening.

And they might call up a serious doubt: "How will people treat me out here?"

The fear is connected to the history of exclusion in many of our parks—the stories I've already shared of Lewis Mountain Campground in Shenandoah National Park, or the segregation that blocked African Americans from full participation in the Civilian Conservation Corps, or the closure of municipal swimming pools to block Black families from basic outdoor amenities that whites enjoyed are still well known.

More and more is being written about the lack of outdoor diversity and the fact that it will not be remedied without intentional effort. Many groups gathering diverse people together for outdoor experiences— climbing, hiking, cycling—are forming to give people of color supportive groups of friends to join with in tackling wilderness adventures.

I canoe solo for seven miles to Arcadia, realizing that I have not done solo canoeing in moving water except once or twice in my life. The lack of weight up front makes the boat ride a little higher and it becomes easier to turn, but also more susceptible to wind pushing it one way or the other. But I make good time in the lighter boat and find my campsite by midafternoon. No glamping tonight—I set up my tent and relax for a few hours, hearing birds singing, trains rolling by periodically, and goats bleating somewhere near in voices that sound eerily like babies crying.

A little before dinner, Bill pulls his truck into the campground to set up his tent. He will join me for a few days on the river. I have asked him to come talk to me about the health of this waterway. The JRA is the key environmental river keeper for the James, and Bill has been at the lead of the nonprofit for nearly twenty years. They advocate for the James, research many aspects of river health, run an amazing variety of programs for students, and publish a biennial *State of the James* report. As I make a campfire, he pulls out a propane stove and heats up a Brazilian fish stew he has brought from home in a cooler. We sit up late enjoying a real meal—not freeze-dried (!)—and red wine he has brought.

We talk about the diversity issue in Virginia and I hear about the JRA's efforts to make their staff, board, and programs more inclusive. This is an ongoing priority and struggle. We agree that one activity on the James River *is* fully diverse: fishing. Especially in cities like Lynchburg and Richmond, the crowd of folks gathered on the banks at popular fishing spots looks like the United Nations. White and Black families. Immigrant families from Mexico and Central America, Vietnam, Africa. Fishing might be the key to diversifying the river experience, both here in Virginia and elsewhere.

4

Today Bill and I will canoe fifteen miles from Arcadia to Glasgow, stopping at a campsite on river right before tackling Balcony Falls tomorrow. It's a chance to get some paddling advice from a river regular before the water gets challenging and—more important—learn a bit about the health of the James River.

I thought Bill might get in the canoe with me but he's brought his own boat—a sit-on-top kayak—and so I do what I did yesterday and paddle solo, with the canoe turned around to better balance the weight. It's helpful to learn to do all the river reading and rock avoidance on my own, and we make good time between towering bluffs, stopping for lunch on a gravel bar at about the ten-mile mark.

Bill and I talk about how Virginia's defining river is faring. JRA's 2021 *State of the James* report gives the river the same B- grade that it received two years ago. Given that the river was in a failing status in the 1970s, the progress has been notable. The James is often listed as the most improved of the major Chesapeake Bay rivers. In 2019, the International RiverFoundation awarded the James the Thiess International River*prize* award, recognizing both its remarkable history and ongoing environmental comeback.

But incremental improvement masks a sometimes-bewildering mixture of advances and retrogressions. Improvements in land protection and agricultural pollution controls are offset by worsening sediment, nitrogen, and phosphorous loads. Better conditions for bald eagles, oysters, and sturgeon are offset by significant reduction of smallmouth bass and the near-complete collapse of American shad.

All of these measures of river health are complex. The shad collapse, occurring while other species are thriving, is particularly confusing, and the JRA is digging into the reasons with the help of researchers at many Virginia universities. The American shad has been called "America's founding fish" due to its historical and cultural importance to American indigenous communities and the earliest English settlers. But the trips these fish take from the ocean to their spawning grounds on the James and other rivers expose them to a variety of obstacles—dams, water intake valves, commercial net fishing. In particular, the introduction of the non-native blue catfish in the James fifty years ago has created a voracious predator in the lower third of the river that wipes out huge portions of the migrating shad population as well as other marine species.

The effects of climate change are notable. Heavier than normal rains many years in a row bring increased runoff into the bay from farms, roads, and parking lots. This runoff carries sediment and pollutants. Two cities along the river—Lynchburg and Richmond—have old combined sewer overflow systems that link stormwater and wastewater systems. These systems push untreated sewage into the James at times of peak rainfall. As climate change amplifies extreme weather events, overflows become more common. Local, state, and federal funds are combined to fix this problem, but the comprehensive upgrade is expensive and still has a long way to go before completion.

This trip exposes me to the river as a system, rather than just a water corridor. The James is the river itself but also its scores of tributaries. About 2.7 million people get their drinking water from the James. More than six million people visit its riverside parks every year. Nearly six hundred thousand people who live in the watershed have hunting or fishing licenses. And public access is expanding as the population of the watershed expands—nearly fifty public access points have been added to the river just since 2013. Groups like the JRA focus our attention on the overall health of the James system and remind us that every person has a stewardship responsibility.

And the James is just one part of a larger system—the Chesapeake Bay watershed. The bay watershed is massive in size (sixty-four thousand square miles) and population (more than eighteen million people). We are still paddling a small stream, fifty to one hundred yards wide at most spots. But it is a key part of something truly monumental—a grand-scale, living, and ever-evolving web of connections between nature and mankind.

Today, as most days, I find myself singing tunes to keep myself company as I paddle. And the song today is a special one, right for the moment. Last year on the bike trip, I challenged my friends with a song title and basic story arc of "Self-Unemployed." About six months after that trip, I got an email from my friend Roger, the president of Berklee College of Music, with a witty lyric for the tune. A week or two later, he sent me a demo version with some Berklee students playing the song. And just before I got on the river, he sent me a version recorded by some ace musicians in Nashville.

I love music but my only "expertise" is showing up and playing live music with bands. I can't read music but just play by ear once they tell me what key the song is in, so this little project of watching a song develop from idea to lyric to demo tape to professional recording has been completely novel and fascinating. (I even have to register as a songwriter to get the song copyrighted!) And the song isn't finished, either, since Roger wants me to record a harmonica piece to add to the Nashville session. I am singing the song to myself, knowing that I will be in a studio with a producer and sound engineer a few days after I get off the river.

Bill and I repeat our campfire from last night and share food, beer, and bourbon. I break out the harmonica and we sing some songs together—old camp songs and classic rock, folk rock, or bluegrass tunes whose lyrics we can recall. I even play and sing "Self-Unemployed"—a song about a guy who hasn't quit, been fired, or retired but just decided to walk away from the rat race to fish, hunt, watch sunsets, and smell the roses. It seems to capture the zeitgeist of this river trip and, to some degree, the feelings of many during the pandemic. And as the day ends around a dwindling campfire, with fireflies sparking in the sky to background noise from crickets and frogs, I think of a title for my next song: "Bullfrogs and Lightning Bugs."

5

I am nervous about the next three days—a thirty-plus-mile stretch of the river that will take me into downtown Lynchburg, where I will finish the first week of my trip and then take off until August.

Why the nerves? Two reasons. First, there is a seven-mile stretch known as Balcony Falls, where the James River blasts through the Blue Ridge Mountains in a long and—for me—challenging run of whitewater with many ledges and falls. I tried it once about fifteen years ago with my son Woody in the front of the boat. We made it through half of the run but took on so much water that the boat sank beneath us—or "submarined"—at the base of Big Balcony, the biggest drop in the stretch. It took a long time, with the help of neighbors on the trip with us, to swim to safety, gather our gear out of the water, and pry our canoe off a rock where it was pinned. And I was in better canoe (and physical) shape on that trip than I am now. At least I'll get great scenery in the Balcony Falls section with the George Washington and Jefferson National Forests on both sides of the river, including the delightful James River Face Wilderness.

The second reason for nerves is completely different. Below the falls, there are seven dams blocking twenty-three miles of the river to Lynchburg with no easy portages. I have pledged to do the entire river but don't know exactly how to get by the dams because virtually no one does it. Even the talented river rats at the James River Association call it the "no-paddle section." They award a certificate to anyone who boats the whole James but exempt all from this twenty-three-mile stretch.

Bill has recruited his ace guide Rob, who works for the JRA in Lynchburg and has done the Balcony Falls stretch of the river many times. We meet him a mile or so downstream from our campground. He paddles his canoe out to meet us from the confluence with the Maury River, a sizable stream that adds major volume to the James.

I expect Rob will hop in my canoe, sit in the stern, and guide me through the falls. Nope. Bill, having scouted my canoe skills out yesterday, says, "Tim can do it solo if you show the way." I notice that Rob has air-filled flotation bags in his canoe to help keep it from filling with water in heavy waves and keep it floating easily if it flips. I have flotation bags too—but like an idiot I left them in the car this morning! I am very unsure if I can really do this, but now that Bill expresses confidence, I put on a game face and fall in behind Rob with Bill trailing behind me.

The Balcony Falls stretch is famous for a tragic accident in January 1854, and any seasoned guide like Rob will tell the story just to make sure you are as nervous as can be before you hit the big water. A canal boat—*The Clinton*—was maneuvering upstream in the canal on river left with forty-five railroad workers and much cargo on board. As the boat tried to cross the confluence with the Maury, then called the North River, its towline snapped and the boat spun out into the flood-swollen James just at the start of the whitewater section.

As the boat rocketed downstream, seven folks jumped overboard to swim for shore, and three drowned immediately. Five more—including the skipper—leaped from the boat onto White Rock, a massive rock jutting up in the center of the James. The Clinton kept on downstream powering over Little Balcony and Big Balcony until it got held up at a rapid called Tobacco Hill Falls with thirty-plus people still aboard.

Frank Padget, a local enslaved boatman with years of expertise on the water, recruited four others (two of them also enslaved) and boarded a smaller boat—a batteau—to attempt a rescue. He saved the passengers off White Rock and was nearing *The Clinton* when it broke free again and rushed farther downstream. Padget caught up to it and saved those passengers, too, except one who had leapt onto a rock in midriver. When Padget maneuvered his batteau to the base of the rapids, he dropped off those he had rescued, got his boat back up into the canal, took it upstream, and came down the raging stretch a second time with eight aboard to rescue the last stranded passenger. Just as they got the man aboard, the current swung the batteau broadside against a rock and crushed it. All eventually made it to shore except Padget and the stranded passenger, who were swept away in the frigid floodwaters and drowned. Five lost their lives, but it would have been dozens without Padget's bravery. A small historical marker to this intrepid hero stands nearby.

With that cheery story fresh in mind, we work our way through Flat Rock Falls, White Rock, and Little Balcony Falls. The river isn't in flood stage but it has a full springtime flow, and the sound of water drowns out everything. I stay about fifteen yards behind Rob until he motions us to pull over right above Big Balcony, a strong class-three ledge that drops into rocks and big standing waves. We exit our boats onto a gravel beach.

I assume we are here to scout the drop and am partially right. But first, Rob leads us up a 250-yard creekside path to a peaceful thirty-foot waterfall falling from a flat ledge into a pool ten yards in diameter. This is actually the Balcony Falls that gives the whole section its name. It is tranquil, filled with tiny minnows and delicate plants. I didn't know this was here. The moment of zen helps prep for what's to come.

Back to our boats, we survey the falls and Rob says, "Do what I do." I kneel in the boat to lower my center of gravity, get to river center, turn downstream, shoot the ledge down into big waves, and maneuver left immediately to avoid rocks, paddling like hell all the way. A few wobbles, but I stay dry. And then we twist and turn through more rock gardens and rapids—Willow Hutch Rapid, Tobacco Hills Falls, Velvet Rock Falls—in quick succession. At one point I don't turn quick enough and the light bow of my canoe slides onto a slanted rock and I start to tip. I remember the move I made with Anne a few days earlier and jump out of the boat into the water so that my body weight doesn't cause me to flip. I pull the canoe backwards, the boat stabilizes, and I hop back in—wet but not submarined or capsized! And then—just like that—we enter a flatwater stretch and know that Balcony Falls is done and we are in the backwater created by the first dam a mile or so downstream.

As we maneuver this mile to a take-out on river left, we pass under the Foot Bridge carrying the AT over the river. I hiked over it two years ago. Later today we pass under the Blue Ridge Parkway, where I was flying down a thirteen-mile descent on my bike last year. So much has happened in between these trips. But the river flows on, seemingly unchanged.

We pull out at a take-out just above Cushaw Dam where a tiny creek enters the river. The twenty-foot hydro dam slants diagonally across the river. And now, as we eat lunch, we have to use street smarts to figure out how to maneuver this section.

The best guide to Virginia rivers, H. Roger Corbett, has this to say about the dam section in his book *Virginia Whitewater*: "These are not easy dams to portage around . . . . The area is not recommended for paddling, but if one loves pain, it is a candidate." Virginia writer Earl Swift wrote a wonderful book, *Journey on the James*, describing his descent of the river in the late 1990s and reached a similar conclusion, shuttling his boat downstream to Lynchburg instead of hassling with the dams and slack water.

It's tempting to think about what might have been. Some say that the Balcony Falls section of the James would have been a thirty-mile-long whitewater delight without these seven dams, likely attracting boaters from all over the East Coast. But instead we have old hydro dams, some no longer operational, caging the river.

After lunch, we drive the boats about six hundred yards down an adjoining road below the dam and then carry them down a long, unofficial path that drops sharply to the river. Bill joins me in the front of the canoe and Rob drives downriver to help us figure out a later portage. On this stretch of water, some light rapids and then slack water before the next dam give Bill and me the chance to talk about the future of these dams. In Virginia, and elsewhere, getting rid of old dams—or at least creating fish ladders and boating channels around them—is now deemed progress, just like putting them up was viewed as progress a century ago.

After a mile or so, we reach the second dam, the Bedford Power Dam. It is only eight feet tall. We decide to portage this one and lug our boat up on the right bank, carrying it through a scrubby section of brush, weeds, and chain-link fence set up to block access to the rail line on that bank. Glad to do it but can't recommend it.

We put in below the Bedford Dam and experience eight hundred yards of a fun rock garden rapid that is rarely accessed. Swift water in tiny channels, tight turns around sizable rocks—Bill and I enjoy this section and take extra pleasure out of knowing how few do it. We then have two miles of slack water with some beautiful islands giving us multiple options to reach the third dam, the Big Island Dam that feeds water to a nearby Georgia-Pacific paper plant.

Here comedy ensues. As Bill and I paddle down the stream, we mistakenly believe the take-out is river left and take a left channel around Big Island. But the take-out is really on river right. Rob arrives at the take-out in his car, and rather than just sit around waiting for us, he puts his boat in and starts paddling up the slack water section on his side of the island. When we get to the end of the island and realize that we have to cross the river to the take-out, we arrive to find that Rob's car is there, but not Rob. We go back on the river—still no Rob. We start to paddle upstream to find him but quickly figure that we should sit tight at the base of the island where we can see up both channels. While we wait, gently rocking in the middle of the river, we see an otter putting on a show down near the dam.

Eventually Rob appears, having circumnavigated Big Island to find us. We pack up and drive downstream to Lynchburg, determined to get all the way to the last dam, right in downtown, tomorrow. My friend Ned—the ace hiker who doesn't like sleeping on the ground—has agreed to canoe this pitiless stretch with me if I get a hotel room. We meet up and take Bill out to dinner at an outdoor café right on the river. The initial portage efforts suggest that tomorrow—forecast to be hot in the morning and rainy in the afternoon—will be instructive but not much fun.

6

Ned and I meet Rob at a put-in just below the Georgia-Pacific paper plant at Big Island. We saw no one else out on the river yesterday, and the parking lot at the put-in is empty. The challenge today is that there are no official access points above and below the dams. Our starting place is one of only two public launch points all day. So to put in and take out of four different dammed-up segments, we'll have to be creative.

The first stretch is a four-mile flatwater float between Big Island Dam and Coleman Falls Dam. The scenery is somewhat industrial on river right but pristine wooded bluffs on river left. We decide that we needn't do an eight-mile circuit of what is essentially a lake between the two dams. Instead, we paddle upstream to get as close to the dam and paper plant apparatus as we can, then float downstream a few miles, witnessing the effect of the paper operation on the river before paddling back upstream to our car. I can't swear that our slack water lap was four miles long, but that was the goal.

At one point, half a mile below the plant, we witness multiple bubbling liquid releases in midriver. Georgia-Pacific routes pollutants into treatment ponds right next to our parked cars and then into pipes on the river bottom that release the effluent in dispersed sudsy patterns that drift lazily along for a good while before mixing into the current. We decide that swimming is not an option.

Next up is a two-mile stretch between Coleman Falls Dam and Holcomb Rock Dam, also called Perch Dam. These are high dams with no easy portage and no public access points. But we notice that a tributary of the James, the Pedlar River, enters on river left not far above Holcomb Rock Dam, so we find a bridge over the Pedlar not far from the confluence, drag our boats over a once-electrified fence and some private land (there weren't any "No Trespassing" signs!), plonk them into the Pedlar, and—after exploring that tributary as far upstream as we can—paddle down into the James for another big lap. In the whole dam section (or "whole damn section"), this undeveloped stretch is the most pristine.

Afterward is the eight-mile stretch between Holcomb Rock Dam and Reusens Dam. River right is inaccessible railroad property, but river left is a local spot for small vacation homes, one after the next built very close to shore. We find Monacan Park, an Amherst County park on river left about midway between the dams, and work on our picnic lunches while we plan our next move. As we eat, we see a brilliant Baltimore oriole repeatedly dive-bombing a crow that has perched on a tree too close to the oriole's nest. (If only its American League East namesakes, Ned's favorite team, were exhibiting such scrap.)

After lunch, we put in and paddle upriver, looking at the vacation homes and houseboats, some showing signs of life on a Thursday afternoon. Rob tells us that near here is the spot where the Bethel trading post was established in colonial times. The Monacan Nation, driven upstream from their ancestral home in Fluvanna County by the British in the 1700s, decided to follow a creek close by that eventually led them to Bear Mountain—about twenty miles northwest—where they have lived ever since.

We paddle back to the park and load the canoes for one more river stretch today, a few miles from Reusens Dam to Scott's Mill Dam, located right in the city and visible from Lynchburg's downtown. Again, there is no real put-in. But Rob has a friend with land on a pretty tributary—Harris Creek—and we maneuver our vehicles to a tiny spot on the bank, drop our canoes into the creek, and paddle out into the river. We head upstream with city homes and Riverside Park towering above us on the bluffs, circumnavigate Treasure Island (owned by Liberty University), and see—like a "Welcome to Lynchburg" sign—a beautiful bald eagle as we paddle back into Harris Creek to finish just as rain threatens.

As we load our boats on top of the cars, Ned and I comment that we've spent more time scouting put-ins and lifting boats on and off our cars than we've spent on the water today. But we've seen a part of the river that doesn't get much attention. A much better day than I thought it would be.

We notice a stone wall nearby and ask about it. It is an old support for a Southern Railway line made famous by "the Wreck of the Old 97," a notorious 1903 train disaster featuring a mail train that originated a few miles north before wrecking near Danville and killing eleven people. A song about the wreck is a country music classic, becoming the first million-selling country record in the 1920s. It has been recorded by dozens of artists—Johnny Cash, Woody Guthrie, John Mellencamp, Carolyn Hester, Boxcar Willie. No one yet has written a song about Frank Padget. If only I knew a songwriter . . . .

7

After our shuttle fest yesterday, we took Rob and his wife out to dinner to thank him for helping us figure out how to get through the "no-paddle stretch." We could not have done it without his local knowledge and adventurous spirit. We ate at a lively Italian place on a renovated bluff walk that Lynchburg has built high above the James. And the number of restaurants and bars, riverfront condos and apartments, and folks out strolling along the bluff walk makes me happy, especially as I think about how dramatically different this riverfront was a few years ago.

Virginia writer Earl Swift was unsparing about Lynchburg's inattention to the James, writing about a James journey in the 1990s: "We find Lynchburg built with its back to the river. The James is virtually invisible on the downtown waterfront, obscured by a shutter of railroad tracks, factories, hollow-eyed warehouses. Its weedy south bank is littered with old tires, cast-off machine parts and blowing fast food wrappers. . . . I find myself growing angry that a city spread along a glorious bluff-lined reach of river could forsake it so." Even his simple attempts to find a place to put his canoe in the water are thwarted by security guards, factories, chain-link fences, and debris.

In the twenty years since Swift took his trip, Lynchburg and Amherst County across the river have reconnected to the gem that is the reason for the city's location, the spot where early settler John Lynch opened a ferry in 1757. The Amherst side has a wonderful municipal park with ample river access. Lynchburg has built multiple river access points and started to reorient activity from suburban strip malls back to its beautiful hilly downtown.

Ned and I have a short day on the river, likely the shortest of my trip, from the base of Scotts Mill Dam into the heart of the city. Before we embark on it, we do a six-mile walk on a beautiful pedestrian trail that runs from downtown across the river onto Percival's Island, sitting in the middle of the river. The trail, lightly used on this hot morning by walkers and dogs, runners and bikers, stretches the length of the island and then crosses over into Amherst County where it continues downriver, pleasantly shaded along the bank of the James. It reminds me of Belle Isle in Richmond, another reclaimed island in a city that once turned its back on, but now celebrates, the river.

We leave my battered Old Town on the car today and use a different boat, a forty-foot, two-and-a-half-ton wooden batteau owned by the James River Association that is docked on the water in the Amherst County park directly across from the renovated shoe factory/ hotel where we've spent the night. Rob meets us there and we load up to motor to the last of the seven dams, not even a mile upstream. And he tells me that, once there, he'll take the motor out and I'll steer the batteau through a small rapid and back to the park.

Batteaux were the workhorses of the James before railroads supplanted them. The name came from the Huguenots, French Protestants driven from their country who settled in Virginia beginning in the late 1700s. Long, thin, wooden barges built to carry passengers and gear up and down the river and adjacent canals, these craft were steered by poles and sweep rudders both front and back. Skilled boatmen like Frank Padget were prized for their strength and courage. The boat builders were ingenious—often building batteaux with lumber cut perfectly so that—after a few trips—they could be disassembled and repurposed immediately to build a house or a barn.

I knew nothing about these boats when I moved to Richmond in 1984. But some enthusiastic river rats started an annual festival in 1985, a rolling weeklong river party every June where multiple batteaux negotiate the river between Lynchburg and Maidens Landing just upstream from Richmond. Participants build their boats, recruit a crew, and head downriver, camping along the way at many of the same spots where I will be when I return to the river in August. Their campsites are loud and raucous, with beer and live music ubiquitous. And the festival has taught current-day Virginians about this versatile watercraft and the role it played in life on the rivers of Virginia. Richmond even changed its city flag in 1993 to feature a batteau and boatman under a night sky filled with nine stars representing the states that were once part of Virginia territory.

As we motor upstream, Rob fills us in on a plan to reconfigure Scotts Mill Dam to create a whitewater boat channel. Lynchburg is not done with returning to the river and will continue to find new ways to highlight its defining feature. We cut the engine and I take the rear rudder, with Rob and Ned using long wooden poles to help with steering. It is a peaceful way to drift downriver, and we get through the one minor rapid without difficulty before arriving back at the park.

Ned and I each get in our cars to head back to Richmond. It's been a great spring week on the river and I'm ninety miles into my 350-mile journey. When the Senate goes into an August recess, I'll come back to Lynchburg and see how the heat of summer affects the river and this ancient mariner.

8

Forget cool and rainy. It's August now and the next stretch of the river will be ninety-five-plus-degree temperatures and low water. I have twelve days blocked off to travel the 145 miles from Lynchburg through Richmond. And then I'll return in October to finish the river from Richmond to Fort Monroe, hopefully in cooler fall temperatures.

The first four days of this stretch will be just Anne and me. We find ourselves counting the days to get back on the river after the fun of our Memorial Day weekend trip. I am locked in DC finishing up votes on a massive infrastructure bill and then setting up a second bill to finish after August recess—an investment in education, health, and climate resilience pursuant to a quirky Senate procedure called budget reconciliation. (Funny how the most partisan bills passed in the Senate are called "reconciliation" bills, but I will save that for another day.) We finish our last pre-recess vote around 6:00 a.m. I sleep for two hours, drive to Richmond, sleep a bit more, and pack up the car, and Anne and I drive two hours west to James River State Park, a beautiful park directly on the river about thirty miles east of Lynchburg. Our tent is up by 7:00 p.m., and the simple act of setting up camp in the humid heat has us drenched in sweat as we start to make our dinner.

Part of the fun of a trip like this is the variety of day's-end accommodations. So far, I have camped along the way at riverside campgrounds and I also luxed out with Ned in a beautiful hotel in Lynchburg. On this stretch, we are emphasizing state parks, using James River State Park as a base camp for four nights and then—after a three-night stay at a friend's farm in Scottsville—I'll set up for three nights at Powhatan State Park twenty-five miles west of Richmond. Using a base camp means more shuttling of vehicles to each day's start and finish, but it also means less packing and unpacking each day. Plus, since state park campsites all have convenient parking access, you can bring a lot more gear in the car for creature comforts to enjoy when you're off river.

Anne and I pass a pretty relaxed night in our well-used tent. We are in a primitive camping area—seven sites spread out through a hilly forest area near Branch Pond. There is no running water and just a simple pit toilet about one hundred yards from our campsite. We are the only campers in the whole camping area. We sleep in the tent without the rain fly attached and see bright stars through the tree canopy while attuned to all the noises in the forest that put one on edge for the first few nights of any camping trip.

I've talked about Anne's camping prowess. One of the many things that attracted me to her instantly when we met forty years ago was her delight at being outdoors in any conditions. And we've done a lot of camping over the years—while dating, as a young married couple, with our children, and on big neighborhood trips. She is better at most outdoor skills than me, particularly knot-tying. I exceed her abilities in only two areas—making a fire and quickly adjusting to sleeping on the ground. So her first night back in the tent after ten weeks is not her best. We are glad to get up with the sun and slowly make breakfast as we plot our first day back on the river.

Our stretch today is to head back to Lynchburg with our canoe, dropping Anne's car off at the Joshua Falls take-out spot. It's a long shuttle, and knowing that our arrival time was somewhat uncertain due to the Senate schedule, we've planned a relatively short day on the water, right about ten miles.

We get to Lynchburg and park near the JRA office. After visiting with them about various educational and research projects they are starting, we begin floating on what may be the summer's hottest day. The thermometer hits ninety-seven degrees and we are often in mid-stream with no shade to give us relief from the sun. Even the river feels like bath water in any section where the current is flat.

The one-hundred-plus-mile stretch from here to Richmond will be somewhat similar. The river gets wider as more tributaries enter. Having tumbled its way through the Blue Ridge Mountains, the drop now declines to a few feet per mile. Sometimes it seems like there is little current at all, with small ledges and rapids popping up every few miles just to keep you on your toes.

The scenery today is pretty on the left but developed on the right, with Lynchburg-area industries set along that bank. While the heat is seemingly perfect for time on the river, we only see one kayak all day. We do a lunch stop on a gravel bar near a small rapid, and the rushing water proves a good place to swim and cool off.

Anne is active with the binoculars today. She is rewarded with many sightings: bald eagles, ospreys, egrets, red-tailed and red-shouldered hawks, yellow-billed cuckoos, common mergansers, indigo buntings, kingfishers, red-eyed vireos, Acadian flycatchers, Eastern wood-peewees, sandpipers, warblers, wrens, chickadees.

I am struck by the number of bald eagles we see every day. Today we see many more eagles than boats, and that becomes my new definition of a really good day on the water!

Bald eagles are majestic in size and color, instantly recognizable by the dramatic white head and tail that develop by the time they reach about four years old. Females have an eight-foot wing span and males are slightly smaller. Eagles usually mate for life and return to the same place to breed year after year.

Anne fills me in on the history. At the time of European settlers, bald eagles in North America were most plentiful in Alaska and the Chesapeake Bay region. But they could be found in many locations—the Great Lakes, Florida, the Midwest, the Pacific Northwest. There may have been as many as one hundred thousand nesting pairs.

Over the centuries, development, hunting, and toxic substances decimated the population. As the eagles' nesting habitat declined and hunting took its toll, Congress took its first steps to protect the national symbol by passing the Bald and Golden Eagle Protection Act in 1940.

But the widespread use of DDT as a pesticide to control mosquitoes and other insects after World War II accelerated the demise of the species. DDT washed into streams and lakes and affected fish and aquatic plants. When eagles ate contaminated fish, the DDT caused their eggs to be laid with compromised shells that broke during incubation. By 1962, there were only 487 nesting pairs of bald eagles remaining in the Lower 48. And along the James River—once the nation's eagle epicenter—there were none.

In 1967, the secretary of the interior listed bald eagles south of the fortieth parallel as an endangered species. In 1972, the Environmental Protection Agency banned the use of DDT. The Clean Water Act, passed in 1972, began to improve water quality everywhere. And slowly, bald eagles have fought back. By 1995, the US Fish and Wildlife Service determined that the eagles were no longer endangered but merely "threatened." And by 2007, this hardy species was no longer endangered or threatened.

Today, there are more than three hundred nesting pairs of bald eagles along the James River and more than four thousand pairs in the Chesapeake Bay region. There are seventy thousand nesting pairs nationally, and together with unattached mature eagles and juveniles, the total population has quadrupled in the last dozen years to more than 315,000. This has happened at the same time as the North American population of other birds has dropped. That's a lesson preached loud and clear by the JRA—it's not uncommon to see one species recovering at the same time that apparently similar species are declining.

Still, environmental success stories like a healthy bald eagle population need to be told for many reasons. In a media climate driven by fear-inducing bad-news stories, we all know the real danger posed by climate change. But the absence of attention to the many environmental successes of the last decades—species resilience, successful battles against acid rain and CFCs, major advances in low- and no-carbon energy—can lead us to an outsized sense of despair. If we've innovated and regulated and invested our way to solutions before, we can do it again.

Anne and I are excited to see the Joshua Falls take-out on river right just so we can get out of the heat and back into our air-conditioned vehicles for the long shuttle back to James River State Park. The shuttle along back roads takes us by country stores, small rural churches, and serve-yourself farm produce stands. We take our time, grab some fresh vegetables to supplement our freeze-dried dinner, and eventually settle back around our tent, with the early evening bringing a coolish breeze as we enjoy a cocktail and prep for dinner. Still no one else in the campsite.

Thunder promises rain later tonight and tomorrow. We put the rain fly on the tent before turning in. Sore muscles from our day on the river, and a feeling of complete mental disconnection from the tumultuous floor session in the Senate that I left just yesterday, make the second night in the tent much more restful than the first.

9

Anne and I will do one of our longest stretches today—twenty miles from the Joshua Falls put-in to a take-out at Bent Creek, right where US 60 crosses the James River. It is a pristine section with no bridges and minimal development along the river. Also, in the general flatwater between Lynchburg and Richmond, this day's trip promises a little more whitewater excitement.

A word about put-in spots for anyone who wants to recreate some of this trip. I have been impressed over the years with the effort made by the Virginia Department of Wildlife Resources (until recently the Virginia Department of Game and Inland Fisheries) to create public access to Virginia rivers, streams, lakes, and the Chesapeake Bay. Driving on country roads, small brown signs advertising "Public Boat Landing" are common across Virginia. And—with the exception of the dam section above Lynchburg—the access points along the James are nicely spaced for planning anything from a short half-day fishing excursion to a long journey like the one we are on. There's usually a turnoff onto a paved or gravel road leading to a small parking area right on the riverbank. Normally a ramp is built from the parking area down into the river so fishing boats on trailers can be backed down directly into the water.

The river today lives up to its billing. Long pools with moving current end in ledges or rock garden rapids. I try to count the rapids and eventually lose count after fifteen. None are that challenging until a tricky ledge-and-rock combo shortly above the take-out. But they just make things interesting and keep you focused.

Yesterday was a one-boat day. Today the sun is not quite as hot and we see two boats in twenty miles. The eagles beat the boats again.

Being out here almost entirely on our own is peaceful. Anne and I talk a little bit about how I started canoeing. I knew people who canoed rivers in the Ozarks as I grew up in Kansas City but had never tried it. A few weeks after I switched from my public junior high school to Rockhurst, the Jesuit high school I attended at my parents' strong urging, I was home one day after school moping around. Most of the other first-year students had come from parochial schools and I didn't really know anyone. I was wishing that I had stayed with my old friends at Indian Creek Junior High.

The phone rang. It was Joe McKenzie, my shop teacher from Indian Creek, asking if I would go on a canoe trip in the Ozarks that weekend with him and two of my best friends, Ron and Jeff, who were still there. It was one of the best-timed calls of my life, and I agreed immediately.

Two days later, Joe drove us to the town of Eminence, Missouri, and set up camp at the confluence of the Current and Jacks Fork Rivers, part of the original National Wild and Scenic Rivers System created by Congress in 1968. It was a simple trip—camp on Friday, canoe nineteen miles on the Current on Saturday, camp again Saturday and then drive back home Sunday.

We got up Saturday morning and got a local outfitter to shuttle us and two canoes upriver. It was a beautiful fall Saturday with mist rising heavily from the serpentine stream as we drove the hilly route to the put-in. I'll never forget the feeling of launching the canoe into the river that first time. The feeling of the current taking over was powerful—immediately it was in control and I wasn't. I could paddle and steer and maneuver, but I was not in control. That same feeling still hits me every time I launch a boat into moving water.

The day was magical. The Missouri Ozark streams are often cold and swift because they are fed by massive springs that pump millions of gallons a day of cold water into them year-round. (Big Spring on the Current pumps thirteen thousand liters per second and is one of the largest single springs in the world.) There is not normally much whitewater, but the current pushes you along rapidly. The day passed in drifting, racing challenges between our two boats, a lunch stop on a gravel bar, and efforts to climb the bluffs that line the river. I also remember tipping the canoe—to Joe's chagrin—by leaning to avoid an overhanging branch. (Safety tip: you lean forward or backward to avoid a branch—not left or right.) By the end of that first trip, I was hooked on canoeing. Joe's call that day is still—many years later—one of the biggest influences any teacher has had on my life. I wasn't his best shop student. But he liked going camping and canoeing and may have intuited that I would be a little lonely trying to get used to a new school. We did a one-day trip and it not only lifted my mood but sparked a lifelong love of river trips.

Once I was home, I did exactly what I'd done after my first Boy Scout camping trip: urged my folks to take my brothers and me out to do it again. And indeed we did, as a family, with other neighborhood families, with high school friends as I grew to love Rockhurst and build up a good network of kids who loved the outdoors like I did. My parents even started to do canoe trips with their own friends.

By the time I got to college at the University of Missouri, I would look for excuses to go canoeing in southern Missouri and Arkansas, or even in small streams near Columbia if the rain brought them up enough. Spring break at Mizzou always involved a canoe trip I would plan for six to eight friends. And at Harvard, I found my way pretty quickly to nearby rivers like the Concord and Merrimack and convinced friends to come along.

Anne knew how much I loved rivers. As we were deciding whether to live in Kansas City or Richmond, she took me on a picnic on the James River right in the city where we could watch boaters maneuver the impressive wilderness whitewater that is a defining feature. The die was cast for Richmond that day and we've lived here more than thirty-five years now.

For the first Christmas we were married, her folks gave us the red Old Town Camper we are riding in now. It's a little beat up after decades of action—the canoe, not the marriage—but I wouldn't trade it for anything. (Neither the canoe nor the marriage!)

The canoe has been a companion throughout our life together, making moves with us and used often for day trips and longer excursions with our children. And Anne immediately loved canoeing the same way I do—enjoying everything from the planning of a trip to the total immersion in nature you feel as you paddle down wilderness streams far from the daily grind. Virginia has many amazing rivers and creeks, with enough mountains to create some challenging whitewater.

Our canoe is not technically a whitewater boat—it is really built for camping and can easily haul lots of camping and fishing gear. Despite its surplus of dents and scratches, I get two offers from folks along the way to buy the canoe. I ask, "This thing is thirty-five years old; why would you want to buy it?" The response both times is the same: "Old Town doesn't make those anymore, and they are great boats for carrying stuff."

We pull aside at a small development of about a dozen vacation homes sitting on a floodplain above the river in Appomattox County. Even though it's a Friday in August, we see no activity and so sit on the broad lawn beneath the homes to enjoy our lunch in the sun. We still have a ways to go, and as we finish lunch, we notice dark clouds starting to roll in. The weather calls for thunderstorms, so we better get moving.

The finish to the day is a race against the storm. The clouds darken; the wind picks up; we start to hear thunder. With each bend in the river, we hope to see the US 60 bridge that signifies the take-out. Now lightning starts to appear in the sky off to our northwest. Closer and closer it comes, and harder and harder we paddle.

Finally, we round a bend and can see the take-out a mile or so downstream. The rain begins, a windy downpour with lightning now disturbingly close. I see an empty campsite on river right and suggest to Anne we pull over to wait out the storm. She says, "No way, keep paddling." We get to the take-out just as the storm really throttles up. We barely get the boat to shore and hop in our car to retrieve our other vehicle when the sky opens. In the hour or so we take to drive upstream, retrieve my car at Joshua Falls, and then drive back to Bent Creek to pick up the boat, the storm pummels the area. As we drive the last miles to the park, there are trees down over the road and we have to pick a careful route around them. We can only imagine what we'll find back at our campsite with our tent under a tree canopy.

What we find is a campsite where everything we left out—camp chairs, bug candle, some clothes drying off from yesterday—is drenched and blown about. The tent is soaked on the outside but well staked and dry inside. There is nowhere to sit that isn't wet as we visit and then make dinner. But we're wet anyway, and our freeze-dried meal gets supplemented tonight with salsa that Anne made from local tomatoes a few days before the trip.

Around 8:30, the thunder starts up again, together with the wind. We load anything we can into the cars and then zip into the tent. It storms all night long. Except for a small drip from one part of the tent roof where the intensity of the rain causes water to pool, we stay dry. The sound is hypnotic, and—aside from wondering about how the campsite will look when we wake up—we get our best night's sleep of the trip.

10

It is still raining as I awake with the sunrise. The sound makes me want to just stay in the tent. And the prospect of making breakfast with everything soaked and rain still falling is not attractive. Then I have an epiphany—what we need is a diner!

The canoe is already on the car and the gear is all inside it. All we have to do is get our clothes on, get in the car, and go enjoy a hot breakfast before we get on the river for our fifteen-mile stretch from Bent Creek to the tiny town of Wingina.

I know this plan will be a winner with Anne. We would rather eat breakfast at a diner than have a gourmet dinner at a five-star restaurant. It's rare that we have the opportunity since we are so often in different cities—she is usually in Richmond during the week while I am in DC. But when we get the chance, we love it.

I find a place not too far away in the town of Dillwyn. It features home cooking and is an obvious favorite with local folks. At one point, a hearse pulls up and dark-suited employees of the local funeral home come in to get takeout orders. We show up dressed in swimsuits, T-shirts, and bucket hats and grab a table. The hot coffee, followed by corned beef hash and eggs, is the perfect way to celebrate a Saturday morning.

A table of local guys, a little older than Anne and me, keep looking over at us trying to figure out who I am. They haven't seen us here before. But they've seen us somewhere. I am unshaven, scraggly after a few days on the river, not dressed up. People who recognize me in a suit and tie often don't when I'm out and about.

That my wife relishes the simple pleasure of breakfast in a diner really captures her essence. When I met Anne in law school, an Appalachian-native Princeton grad whose dad was in politics, three things stood out about her immediately. First, she is deeply devoted to her friends and family. No one is more loyal than my wife. This was obvious in watching her interact with her friends four decades ago and still is today. She is the principal caretaker for her folks—now in their late nineties—and also spends significant time with her sister, diagnosed years ago with Alzheimer's. And even amidst intense career chapters—lawyer, judge, First Lady, cabinet secretary, college president—she always takes the time to be with those close to her, especially our children.

Second, Anne has a heart for the underdog. Anyone downtrodden or hurting finds a friend in my wife. Years after she left the juvenile court bench, I still marvel at her "caseload"—the sizable group of kids and adults she has come across in life who she still makes time to help negotiate the challenges they face. Mental health problems, financial woes, run-ins with the law, family dysfunction, educational stumbles, career advice—she is up for any of it. She will lend a hand or some funds and tough love too.

And finally—not so common among the denizens of Harvard Law School—Anne has a spiritual simplicity. For a whip-smart lawyer, my wife has a disposition very open to the joy of living. She can enjoy sophisticated arts and culture or an exotic vacation. But she takes even greater pleasure in walks, reading, sitting on the porch or by a fire, listening to music, local excursions, diners, bird-watching, getting ice cream, Minor League Baseball games, cooking a meal, bike rides, canoeing, time with friends.

There is an old-time hymn called "Simple Gifts" that I have always loved. But not until I met Anne did I really grasp its meaning—that it truly is a gift to be able to find joy in life's simple moments. So many people don't have it—they need stimulation or entertainment and fear boredom or quiet. Not Anne. She has the gift.

We finish breakfast, pay our bill at the cash register, shuttle the vehicles, and eventually put in at Bent Creek for a fifteen-mile trip. The first half of the trip reaches our camping spot at James River State Park. It is pleasant and crowded. It's a hot, sunny Saturday morning, and canoes, kayaks, and inner tubes populate the water—either doing seven miles to the park or even shorter two-mile segments between the upper and lower access points within the park. The trip is gentle and the scenery is pretty. It's particularly popular with families, and we see many who remind us of ourselves twenty years ago, trying to wrangle our three kids playing in the river.

As we reach the halfway point and pass the park, the trip changes dramatically. The river doesn't change but all the people take out at the park and we are alone for the last seven miles. We pass the spot where the Tye River enters on river left, a river that travels just thirty-five miles east from its stunning start at Crabtree Falls (a set of falls plummeting nearly one thousand feet from the Blue Ridge Mountains) to this confluence.

The Tye River Valley was the scene of one of Virginia's worst natural disasters. In August 1969, the remnants of Hurricane Camille dumped twenty-seven inches of rain here in three hours in the middle of the night as people slept. More than 150 people were killed by flooding and mudslides. We glide by the Tye today and it is a sleepy stream in the low water of summer.

Anne and I did a canoe trip on the Tye years ago. We were a young couple with one car and had to solve the shuttle problem. How to structure a twenty-mile day so that, when we reached the end of the trip, we could get the boat back on the car? I came up with a bright idea—we will bring a bicycle, drop it at the take-out point, drive the car and boat to the put-in, launch the canoe, and when we finish, I'll ride the bike back to the put-in, get the car, and then come back to retrieve wife and boat.

But the paddle trip took longer than we thought because we dawdled along the way. The sun was near setting when we finally got to the take-out. And then I hopped my bike to ride back to the car. I was tired. And sunburned. Soon it was dark. My bike didn't have a light. And I realized something—the Tye is a great river because it is full of whitewater. Whitewater happens when a river runs downhill. Which meant my bike trip was all uphill. By the time I reached the car, I was near collapse. And by the time I got back to Anne, she was sitting in the dark on our canoe, overturned next to the road, wondering whether I had abandoned her. I took her to a diner to appease her. And I've never tried that one-man shuttle method again.

Now we're older and wiser but still like to dawdle. Today we get our best eagle viewings. We find a riverside set of rock ledges and an adjoining gravel bar that is the perfect place to stop to eat lunch and swim. How relaxing. Until I remember racing lightning yesterday and look west. Sure enough, clouds are rolling in. We cast off and paddle as the skies progressively darken.

After ninety minutes or so, we make it to the final bend with our take-out bridge visible a mile ahead. Now the skies open up. No wind, no lightning. But the raindrops fall straight down with such force that the splashes they kick up in the river turn everything into a thick mist ten inches above the water's surface. It's like we're canoeing across dry ice while getting drenched by the storm.

When we take the canoe out of the water, we can hardly carry it up the ramp to the car against a cascade of rainwater flooding down the ramp. We're also under a bridge with water draining off it like a waterfall. But it's impossible to get any wetter than we already are.

We head back to the park and stop to say hello to two park rangers at the visitor center. One is helping a camper who has lost her car keys somewhere in the vast park or maybe in the river. The other is just back from rescuing an elderly couple who had been spooked by the storm while hiking and called the emergency line for help. Park ranger seems like a dream job to me, but it's not all fun in the outdoors. Anne and I tell them how much we appreciate what they do.

My favorite thing about having a title like "Senator" in front of my name is that when I say to these folks or others like them "Thanks for all you do," it makes them feel like they are truly appreciated. And they deserve to feel the gratitude of officialdom. The power of a thank-you works magic even if I am wearing a swimsuit and soaked after getting pounded by rain. Many people have photos with me in a suit and tie. But it's only a few who get pictures with me when I look like this!

11

We break camp and put in at Wingina today. It will be the last of the days that Anne and I canoe together by ourselves. Beginning tomorrow, other friends start to join, and then, in a couple of days, Anne will head back to work.

Wingina is an "unincorporated community" in Nelson County, too small to even be a town. It's little more than four connections with the outside world—a road, a river put-in, a rail line, and a post office attached to a now-closed general store. It is named for the werowance—the chief—of the Secotan Tribe who first confronted English settlers in the Outer Banks of North Carolina in 1585. He was assassinated by the followers of Sir Walter Raleigh the next year. Possibly out of respect for the indigenous population who lived here for centuries before the English arrived, the Richmond and Alleghany Railroad named this community Wingina as it started rail work here in the 1880s.

An unusual choice—a company naming a Virginia community for a chief the English had murdered in North Carolina three hundred years before. The names dotting the American landscape tell stories, many painful. How often do we just pass by without thinking about the meaning of these place names?

Though Wingina is largely forgotten today, his influence persists in everyday life. Raleigh's accounts of his expeditions to the Outer Banks described the territory occupied by Wingina as "Wingandacoa." Queen Elizabeth I, reading those accounts, may have combined that name with her own status as "the Virgin Queen" to name the English colony in the New World Virginia. Virginia schoolchildren are taught that our state is named after Elizabeth. But they are not taught that the name may also be a tribute to Wingina and the land itself.

Our trip today is without incident—gray skies provide relief from the sun, but there's no rain in the forecast. Our fourth consecutive day on the water has us in an easy rhythm of paddling, drifting, bird-watching. We see a group of kids fishing and learn that they are campers doing their own James River adventure with a few older counselors.

We spend some time today marveling at the change we've seen in Virginia during the thirty-seven years we've been in Richmond. A few weeks ago, Virginia transitioned from being the death penalty capital of the United States into an abolition state. That profound change, which would have seemed impossible when we moved here, and equally impossible when I was running my race for governor and getting blasted by television ads for my opposition to the death penalty, crystallizes the last twenty years of progress in Virginia. And at age sixty-three, we both have a dawning realization that we've contributed to some real change for the better in our state.

When we decided to marry in 1984, the choice between Richmond and Kansas City was hard. We are both close to our families and wanted to be near one or the other. And both cities are wonderful communities. But the tug to Richmond, besides Anne's superior negotiation skills, was our feeling, in the words of Jesus, that "the harvest is plentiful, but the laborers are few." There was so much work to be done here. And we, with the naivete of youth, believed that we could make a real difference in the direction of the Commonwealth.

For Anne, this feeling was very personal, having seen her father break one-party rule and then support school integration in 1970 and then face rejection by both parties and the electorate as he sought future elected office. For me, the motivation was less personal but no less passionate. The way I was raised and educated, together with my time in Honduras, made me choose civil rights advocacy as my life's work, with a "preferential option for the poor," in the words of Catholic social doctrine.

And we saw opportunity in Virginia. Though still too focused on the past, we could see evidence of a coming transformation. And without having any idea of the roles we would play, we believed our own skills, energetically applied, could make an impact. And so we started a very long journey together, two altruistic public-interest lawyers, to join efforts with others and make our state a more progressive, welcoming, dynamic, future-focused place. We wanted it to live up to the title it gave itself—Commonwealth. The wealth we hold should be held in common. All deserve a seat at the table.

That has been the mission during our marriage. And with fits and starts, rapids and long slack sections, we've seen our dream come true along the way. Just like a river trip, we're often unsure about what we'll see around the next bend. But that is exciting, too, and we've played a part in Virginia's progress that neither of us could have ever imagined.

There have been so many amazing moments. One of the most powerful was our work, beginning in late 2006, to help Barack Obama become president. I encouraged him to run and told him that I would do all I could to help him win. And I told him that we would work to make sure that his victory was because of Virginia rather than in spite of Virginia. Too much of our nation's progress toward the equality ideal over our 240 years has been in spite of Virginia. (Barack told me later that my early endorsement, as a brand-new governor of a state that had not voted Democratic since 1964, made him both appreciate my friendship and question my political judgment!)

When Virginia, the Capital of the Confederacy, delivered its electoral votes for Barack in November 2008, it felt like an amazing culmination of our near quarter century of work in Richmond. Anne and I did a press conference the next day at a Civil Rights memorial near the Governor's Mansion, and speaking from the heart, I said simply: "Ol' Virginny is dead." My reference to a recently retired state song that sugarcoated slavery made some of the old power structure mad but captured what Obama's election meant to today's Virginians.

Of course, 2008 wasn't the end of the journey. For those who think that presidential or congressional or governors' races are the ones that really matter, it wasn't until we finally took both Houses of our general assembly that our progress really took off: abolition of the death penalty, increase in minimum wage, LGBTQ+ equality, better-funded schools, support for ERA ratification, broader access to voting, protection for immigrants, meaningful climate and clean energy legislation—all while maintaining one of the best economies in the country. These achievements have happened since I began this Virginia Nature Triathlon a little more than two years ago. But the progress recently achieved was built on decades of foundational work.

And there is so much still to do. But Anne and I have full confidence in Virginia's direction. No longer do we worry that "the laborers are few." We have both mentored so many young public servants who have been staffers, volunteers, interns, colleagues, friends. These talented and diverse folks now populate elected offices, governmental posts, innovative companies, universities, and nonprofit staffs and boards all over the Commonwealth. Their passion makes me confident that our progress will continue long after I stop serving. Of course, we'll win and lose elections. The goal has never been to build a one-party state—Anne's dad destroyed one-party rule, hopefully forever, in the Commonwealth. But compared to when we came here to marry, most Virginians are looking forward now, not clinging to a false imagined past.

We reach Howardsville, another tiny community with a post office and country store, right at the spot where the Rockfish River enters the James. There must be some clear-cut logging upstream on the Rockfish because its waters are muddy with eroded soil. We get off the river with excitement because we are meeting Scott and Charles, my two buddies from law school, a few miles downriver. And, after four nights in a tent at a campsite with no running water, we are looking forward to hot showers and sleeping in a real bed, in Scott's family home, perched high on a bluff above the river.

12

We party into the night at Hermitage Farm in Scottsville. I have been in this spot on each leg of the trip—dropping Scott here to visit his mom, Judy, as we drove home from finishing the AT in 2019; spending the night here with the Nightwing crew as we traveled the nearby Blue Ridge Parkway last year; and now joining Scott and Judy, plus Charles and his oldest son, Jason, for two days on the river. It is a warm and welcoming home, and we compare notes about all that has happened in the last year.

Scott and his three siblings, and their many children, visit Judy often from all over the country. Anne and I pop in when we're in the neighborhood. She makes sure we are well supplied with a great breakfast before we load up the cars to head back to Howardsville. Today's float will take us by Scottsville, a charming small town on the river in Albemarle County. The river curves south at the town and Judy's farm is about a mile downriver on the right bank.

The trip is an easy one today, with mist on the drive to the put-in that abates just as we start. The cloud cover keeps intense sun down and it isn't as brutally hot as the first days of the stretch below Lynchburg. The only rapid of note is at Hatton Ferry, midway on the trip with a set of rocky ledges just upstream that pose a brief challenge at low water.

After four days of just Anne and me in our canoe, the day is enlivened by friends, including Charles's son Jason, who is a high school math teacher in Hanover, New Hampshire. Anne is on the Virginia Board of Education and teaches education policy at George Mason University. The chance to talk to Jason about his teaching and the circumstances faced by high school kids today is unique. We're in boats together for six hours, so he can hardly avoid our questions!

Jason went to Harvard as an undergrad and set his mind on being a math teacher and, hopefully one day, a principal or school superintendent. (He also took a year off college to work on my 2012 senatorial campaign—with his parents extracting a blood oath from me that I would make sure he returned to finish!) After teaching computer science at Yale and getting a master's in education at Harvard, he started his teaching career in the San Diego public schools, where he taught for three years in a low-income, primarily minority middle school. After moving cross-country to join a girlfriend pursuing a doctorate at Dartmouth, he now teaches at the public high school in Hanover. His current school is filled with kids whose parents are connected to Dartmouth. It is not so diverse, and the families are near the upper end of the income and education scale. His two teaching experiences cover a wide span of American public education, and his observations about the similarities and differences he has encountered are illuminating.

A principal similarity is related to the times. COVID has been hard on everyone, but I think it has hit young people especially hard. Missed classroom time, missed time with friends, missed athletic seasons and homecomings and proms and in-person graduation ceremonies. Anne sees it at George Mason, and Jason talks about this loss as a common experience in the two very different schools where he has taught.

An obvious divide is the sheer difference in opportunity available to kids. The differences between a crowded, low-income, inner-city school and an elite public school in a small, bucolic, university town are stark. Class sizes, teacher pay and turnover, the breadth of academic offerings—the schools could be on different planets. And it extends well beyond the classroom to the scope of extracurricular activities, field trips and enrichment experiences, parental and alumni engagement.

There is no way to standardize a one-size-fits-all American educational experience for every zip code, but the disparities are massive. You can usually make a prediction about student performance in any school by looking at the percentage of kids who are on free and reduced lunch due to low family income. And when you see outliers, especially schools filled with low-income kids who do unusually well, you usually find that it's because of an unusual degree of resources poured into that particular school.

Jason fills us in on other challenges, such as how to get diversity issues right, particularly in the relatively nondiverse school he is at now. If COVID has been tough for students, it has also been so tough for educators, administrators, school board members. Anne spends much of her time at the university educating future teachers, and we are always in awe of people like Jason who are so passionate about the profession.

Talking to Jason makes me reflect on how much I've relished working on educational issues at all three levels of government. I've pursued a simple philosophy—start earlier and go broader. Expanding high-quality childcare and early childhood education is a tremendous strategy for helping all students succeed—especially those who are at risk in any way due to low family income, disability, or lack of English language proficiency. And we need to go broader as we define educational success. The devaluation of career and technical education in favor of college and university degrees has, over many years, hurt individuals and the productivity of the American workforce. We are starting to improve in both these areas, but there is so much more to do.

We negotiate the rapids at Hatton Ferry and pull over on river right to have lunch, standing on the concrete entrance to the defunct ferry operation. The ferry began in the 1870s and was a wooden poled cable ferry. The ferry had no motor, instead relying on the river current and the ferry operator's use of long poles to push it along an overhead cable stretched seven hundred feet bank to bank. The wooden ferry was replaced by a steel one many years ago that could handle two cars per trip. I have taken it a few times when I've been in the area, but it shut down three years ago and a local historical society is trying to reopen it.

After lunch we resume the float and the conversation moves from policy to frivolity. We throw TV ad quotes from the past at each other and try to guess the product: "The cereal that's shot from guns," "Born in the land of sky-blue waters," "Stronger than dirt," etc. Soon we reach Scottsville and see two guys on the bank working to restore an old batteau. We pull over and chat with them about their plans to use the boat in this beautiful and relatively smooth stretch of the James to take tourists on short river excursions.

Scottsville was a boomtown along the river and adjacent canal beginning in the 1800s. Products from the fertile Shenandoah Valley would come to Scottsville for loading on boats heading downstream to Richmond. But when railroads came, the tracks were laid on top of the suddenly inefficient canal bed and the town's boom was over. Today the population is about six hundred, but a number of beautiful homes and a classic small downtown, together with proximity to Charlottesville and the University of Virginia, are starting to draw folks back.

About a mile and half below town, we get back to Hermitage Farm and haul our boats up into a cornfield adjoining the river. We trudge up a hill to the house and clean up for evening festivities. We expect the town to swell tonight with the appearance of a local community orchestra in a town park. Instead, a classic late-afternoon August storm washes out the concert and leaves folks from surrounding areas wandering the few blocks downtown looking for food, drink, and adventure. We get Chinese food and head back to the farm for another late-night discussion and sleep in a real bed.

13

Today is one of the prettiest stretches on the Middle James, from Scottsville to New Canton through a section known as Seven Islands. Anne will finish her six-day trip today and head back to work tomorrow morning. Scott, Charles, and Jason will do today's section and then head home—Scott and Jason to New Hampshire and Charles to LA. Because we are in an extended August recess, my goal is to stay on the river, joined by neighborhood friends, for another seven days to just below Richmond before returning to DC.

The river is wide and flat for the first half of the trip, joined by the small Hardware River on the left as we pass one of the pretty Virginia Wildlife Management Areas, public land holdings with limited facilities primarily designed to facilitate low-impact hunting and fishing. Anne and I manage in our trusty Old Town, Scott and Charles in a rented canoe, and Jason in a sit-on-top kayak. I decided a few days ago that my canoe needs a name, and we throw around ideas as we drift downstream.

Charles and Scott are the two people who have traveled with me on every leg of this triathlon. Charles brought his youngest son, Adam, and hiked for three days with me on the AT while Scott joined the last three days of that hike as I reached the Virginia-Tennessee border south of Damascus. Both were part of the Nightwing gang who did the bike trip last year. And as soon as that was done, they pinned me down on the timing of the river trip so that they could join as well. Their commitment—coming from far away to join the Virginia adventure—is notable and touching.

The heavy rain last night, together with rain upriver within the last few days, is pushing the river level and current up in deceptive ways. It doesn't seem any faster, and the first part of the day is absent of any meaningful rapids, but we find that we are making four to five miles an hour instead of the two to three that was the norm before today.

We hit Seven Islands and the wide river now starts braiding between multiple tiny islands—closer to seventy than seven—with each channel full of blind turns and whitewater. The narrow channels remind me of the river when we put in at Iron Gate. The islands are delightful as well, sand bars on the banks and then heavily wooded. This is probably the best wild camping section on the James, and it's obvious from stone campfire rings that many have figured that out. It is a warm August Tuesday, and we only see one other boat all day long.

We pull over on an island for lunch and wade into the water to cool off. I have to work to stand still against the strengthening current. We engage in a rock-skipping contest and I lose handily to everyone, with Jason winning overall.

It has been great to have Anne with me the last six days. Together with her joining me for the first three days in May, she has logged nearly 120 river miles, a third of the entire James. Anne is as close to these law-school buddies as I am. She knew Scott before I even met him at law school because Scott and Anne's sister were friends at Dartmouth. And as Anne's sister, Tayloe, has suffered early-onset Alzheimer's beginning nearly ten years ago, Scott and his wife, Mary (also a Dartmouth grad), have been so supportive. Anne's connection to Charles—she a college educator (and former college president) and he now a college president—gives them much in common.

These are not just individual friends but "couple friends"—we all value each other as individuals but also as married couples. Charles and Scott were both with us when we tied the knot in 1984. Anne and I attended Scott and Mary's wedding and then Charles and Cynthia's wedding, which took place on opposite coasts (California and Maine) one week apart in 1988. Friendship—a great theme of so much literature, including Thoreau's *A Week on the Concord and Merrimack*

Rivers—is usually the friendship of individuals. But there is a different friendship between couples, and then between couples and their children. Anne and I are blessed with a web of caring and intergenerational relationships.

When we reach New Canton, another place named for its post office without much of a town to speak of, we pull off the river and head back to Hermitage Farm to spend one last night before all head their separate ways first thing tomorrow. After another great Judy Brown meal, we gather into her living room to watch a movie. So many choices, but we decide on *The African Queen*. All right, our journey on the James is not quite so epic as Bogey and Hepburn's river trip. But the characters are as memorable!

14

We all depart Scottsville early, saying our goodbyes to each other and Judy. My trip today will be a beautiful and emotional one, from New Canton to the tiny town of Columbia. And my boat companion is my neighbor John. He has lived across the street for more than twenty-five years and worked in my Senate office as my state director during my first six years. He is also the best outdoorsman I know.

We begin paddling with John up front and me in back. He immediately asks, "What side do you like to paddle on?"

"I just paddle on one side until I get tired and then switch." I think he was hoping for a different answer. But we have been on many river trips together and fall into an easy rhythm. The current is still up and pushing us along nicely.

I wanted John with me today because we will do something special connecting to work we did together. When the trip ends in Columbia, we reach a spot where the Rivanna River enters on river left. It flows into the James at an angle, creating a triangular point of land with enormous history. Here was Rassawek, the ancestral headquarters village of the Monacan Indian Nation.

The Monacan were driven from Rassawek further west by the English in the 1700s. They have lived centered around Bear Mountain in Amherst County to this day.

When I moved to Richmond in 1984, I didn't know anything about Virginia tribal history. Aside from a vague and romanticized understanding of Pocahontas saving John Smith's life, I was without a clue. In 1990, I met Steve Adkins, a leader in the Chickahominy Tribe, and he began to educate me about indigenous Virginians. As with most interactions between Europeans and indigenous people, the history is painful. And there were a few peculiarities that explained why, though there are well over five hundred federally recognized Indian tribes, no Virginia tribe had yet been recognized when I moved here in 1984.

The tribes east of Richmond—generally part of the Powhatan Confederacy—spoke Algonquin and were loosely ruled by Chief Powhatan from his headquarters at Werowocomoco on the York River not far from Jamestown. The area around Richmond was somewhat of a no-man's-land between tribes, and upstream were the Monacan, a tribe speaking a different language completely, part of the Sioux people. Farther south in Virginia was the Nottoway Indian Tribe, whose members spoke an Iroquois language.

These tribes have lived intact in Virginia since before the English reached Jamestown. The Powhatan tribes entered into treaties with the English in the 1670s and lived side by side with their English neighbors in a handful of Tidewater Virginia counties. The tribes in western and southern Virginia lived in obscure areas and were discriminated against in virtually all areas of life.

When I met Steve, the story of these tribes—their resilience against adversity but the continuing refusal of the US to recognize them—was captivating and infuriating. Why no recognition? There were three principal reasons.

First, most federal recognition begins with a peace treaty between a tribe and the US government. The Powhatan tribes entered into treaties with the English long before there was a US government. And the southern and western tribes never entered into treaties. The fact that the Powhatan tribes made peace with the English—sovereign to sovereign—means that they receive a warm and dignified reception when they travel to England, even though they have been ignored at home.

Second, federal recognition is obtained either through a complex process administered by the Department of the Interior or by congressional resolution. Either path requires significant documentation. Most

Virginia tribal records were held in county courthouses that were damaged during the extensive Civil War battles in Virginia. The absence of documentation has greatly complicated tribal recognition efforts.

The crowning injustice was malicious destruction of Virginia tribal documents by state officials. Beginning in the 1920s, many Virginia officials and educational institutions embraced the eugenics movement. This embrace led to much evil—for example, the forced sterilization of women deemed insufficiently intelligent. One peculiar Virginia twist was the decision, by chief state archivist Walter Plecker, to categorize all indigenous people as "colored" citizens, thus pushing them into a de jure second-class status. For nearly forty years, he led a state effort to systematically change birth, death, and marriage records of all indigenous Virginians to rebrand them as "colored." There were even instances of indigenous people disinterred from all-white cemeteries and reburied in colored cemeteries. This massive state erasure of tribal records and identity—referred to by indigenous Virginians as the "paper genocide"—additionally served as a roadblock to full recognition of the tribes.

What has lack of recognition meant? Official Virginia policy toward its indigenous people has led them to be treated as second-class by their Commonwealth and country. Sometimes their treatment has been third-class. My friend Steve showed me a letter received by his aunt in the 1950s turning down her application to the state's "colored" nursing school because she was an indigenous person. With no white nursing program open to her, and no "colored" nursing program willing to accept her, the admissions officer advised her to move away from her home and seek training in Oklahoma or Minnesota.

The absence of federal recognition has deprived the tribes of federal funds decade after decade. And in a cruel twist, the Smithsonian holds many artifacts and bones from Virginia tribes. The tribes have tried for years to reclaim the bones for burial in accord with their own traditions. But the policy of the Smithsonian is to only return such bones and artifacts to federally recognized tribes.

Virginia tribes received recognition by the state beginning in the late 1980s. And they then began a slow move toward federal recognition. Educated about this history by my friend Steve, I began advocating for federal recognition of Virginia tribes when I was mayor of Richmond. I first testified before Congress to support these efforts when I was governor. During that time, I appointed Steve as the director of Virginia's state personnel agency, and he became the highest-ranking indigenous Virginian to ever serve in state government. But despite a concerted push, the federal recognition bill had moved nowhere when my gubernatorial term was done.

I never had designs to be a senator. When Senator Jim Webb decided in 2011 that he would not seek reelection, I was not inclined to start a new chapter after sixteen years in local and state politics. But one day I asked myself, "Do I have any unfinished business?" The stalled tribal recognition bill came to mind, along with two or three other items on my to-do list that I hadn't accomplished in the single gubernatorial term Virginia allows. The realization that I might be able to finish a few important, undone items was one key to my decision to run.

When I came to the Senate in 2013, my team and I went right to work with tribal leaders to finally gain federal recognition. My state director John, my chief of staff Mike, and four great policy staffers (Mary, Nick, Tyee, and Evan) pressed forward every year, confronting obstacles large and ridiculously small. In 2016, the Pamunkey Tribe received administrative recognition through the Department of the Interior. And in January 2018, Mark Warner and I stood on the floor of the Senate—with six tribal chiefs in the gallery—and watched as the body passed our bill unanimously. Now the Monacan, Nansemond, Chickahominy, Eastern Chickahominy, Upper Mattaponi, and Rappahannock Tribes were all finally recognized.

When we gathered with the chiefs minutes later to celebrate, I thanked them for never giving up and, in particular, for never giving up on us even as our efforts seemed painfully slow. Steve, now the chief of the Chickahominy Tribe, delivered a classic understatement: "We are very patient people."

Twenty-seven years in public life have given me the chance to do a lot of good for a lot of people. Few accomplishments have meant as much to me as working with our tribes to see that they were finally recognized. And today, more than three years after that legislative victory, I will meet with the Monacan to discuss their ongoing efforts to save their ancestral home.

John and I see the river bridge at Columbia around lunchtime and begin looking for the point of land where we will pull the canoe ashore to meet Chief Branham and other tribal officials. We find the spot, beach the canoe, and climb a bluff above the James and Rivanna confluence. We soon hear a four-wheeler coming to get us to take us to the road access where tribal leaders have arrived to talk. The land is undeveloped and the trails are so muddy today that no vehicles can easily get down to the river. So we agree to canoe to a take-out spot across the James and meet there.

As we sit in the shade eating lunch, Chief Branham tells us about a local government plan to build a large water treatment intake on the Rassawek site. The plan was barreling ahead until the Monacan, now armed with federal recognition, pointed out the historic nature of the land and serious inadequacies in some of the environmental studies of the proposal. The National Trust for Historic Preservation named Rassawek as one of America's most endangered historic sites in 2020. Now all sides are looking for a better alternative.

John and I say our goodbyes after lunch and stop at a gas station a few hundred yards from Rassawek to get a fill-up and Dr Pepper. The music playing inside is not from a country radio station as we would expect. It's a CD featuring Amharic singing. The owners are recent arrivals from Ethiopia. Ethiopian immigrants running the gas station in this tiny river town, less than a mile from the home of the first Americans, makes me marvel with pride at the multitude of stories our nation contains.

We drive to nearby Powhatan State Park and set up camp a few yards from the river. After a swim in the swift current, we are joined by two other neighbors, Tom and Mark, who will be with us for the next few days until we reach Richmond. We sit by our tents visiting late into the evening. The night is hot but the beer is cold! And with liquid inspiration, John comes up with the name for my canoe—Old Raggedy. It's a play on a Virginia mountain—Old Rag—that we've climbed together often. And a perfect name for a beat-up Old Town canoe piloted by an old and ragged boatman.

15

Today we have a fifteen-mile trip from the town of Columbia to Westview, a river side pull-off in Goochland County. Since we're staying at the state park for a few nights and have no need to break camp, it's easy to get on the river quickly.

Tom, Mark, and John all joined me on the AT two years ago. They are great friends and have been part of our neighborhood outdoor tradition for a long time. Spring break hiking trips in the Blue Ridge, an annual Memorial Day camping trip at Douthat State Park, and a summer canoe week—picking different Virginia rivers each year— formed strong bonds between us and our children.

Tom and I almost drowned once on a canoe trip on the South Anna River. It was an unusually warm February Saturday. We decided to do an impromptu twelve-mile trip through the fall line of the river, a delightful stretch of class-one to class-two rapids not far from Richmond. When we arrived at the put-in, we each had the same thought: *The water looks a little high*. But we were too macho to speak the thought out loud and hopped in the canoe with life jackets and paddles but no flotation.

The first miles of the trip were delightful, clipping along in the warm air. It being February, the water temperature was cold. Things turned bad when we hit the fall line, normally a set of pleasant rapids requiring you to pick paths between boulders. The water was so high that the boulders were now submerged and the river was a set of rowdy, rolling waves. We negotiated through the waves as best we could, but the canoe started to fill up with water and I had not brought anything to bail it out.

As we neared an old bridge, the canoe had taken on so much water that it sank. We clung to the submerged canoe and our paddles in the frigid water, sweeping downstream and trying to avoid getting caught up in any brush or rock piles. Eventually we maneuvered to an island midstream where we emerged cold and wet. Tom's glasses had been ripped off his face. We were shivering and still had about six hundred yards of the fall line section to finish. Tom told me that, as our boat was sinking and we were flailing in the water, I deadpanned, "I'm sure glad we didn't bring Anne and Carol on this trip." The attempt at gallows humor made him laugh even as we were fighting for our lives.

We emptied the canoe and prepped for the last stretch of rapids. Tom can't see well without his glasses so couldn't reliably scout from his front seat. But I said, "Just paddle like hell and I'll steer." We got through it, reached the take-out about thirty minutes later, and drove back to retrieve the upstream car. When we did, we spotted old guide-marks from Randy Carter on the bridge posts at the put-in. Carter was a river expert who would go around the mid-Atlantic marking bridge posts with river level markings and writing some of the first guidebooks about these streams. The zero mark would tell you if the river had enough flow to boat it. Each additional foot above zero was marked up until a top mark, above which it was deemed too high to float safely. Of course the river was running way above the "too high to float" mark. We saw that, busted out laughing, and—for the first time—each admitted that we had wanted to back out but were too stupidly macho to say so. I have never repeated that mistake and can't believe Tom has always been willing to canoe with me since that misadventure.

John and Mark were part of a week-long canoe trip that we used to take with our own kids and other dads and kids from the neighborhood. We would pick a different Virginia river each year (James, New, Maury, Shenandoah, Rappahannock) and head out with canoes and kayaks for a multiday adventure of paddling, fishing, and camping. One year, the latest *Harry Potter* book came out at midnight the night before we left for the trip. All the kids wanted their own copy, and we have great memories of all of them sitting around the campfire at day's end each with their noses in their books. I once nearly blew up the entire campsite by using too much white gas on a massive woodpile to start a bonfire. A picture was taken just at the moment when the fireball exploded, but I purchased it and the negatives and had them destroyed! A favorite game on the river was keep-away with a Nerf football—kids versus adults. Multiple boats formed creative offensive and defensive formations in moving water, and aggressive paddle use was fair game to scoop a ball out of the water or fight off an invading craft. Boat ramming was common—not all the dents in Old Raggedy come from rocks.

Today, Tom and I canoe in Old Raggedy (the same boat that survived our South Anna misadventure), and the other duo uses John's slightly newer Old Town Camper. Mine had sat behind my garage for many years before this adventure and John's was hanging up in the rafters of his garage. As much canoeing as we've all done, the sheer work of getting boats on and off cars, portaging around dams, and shuttling boats between put-in and take-out points has nudged all of us toward bicycling, running, or walking—all of which can be done right outside your door.

The logistics of each leg of my triathlon have been very different. On the hike, carrying everything with me and mostly hiking alone, it was just a matter of getting dropped off and then picked up days later. I did the forty-two days in five distinct segments—from three days at the shortest to fifteen days at the longest. As long as I could find water and a trailside town to restock food every five days or so, all was good.

The bike trip was the easiest because we found an outfitter who knew the area well. All we had to do was ride each day and a guide and support van carried our stuff and set up meal stops during each day's section.

The river trip has been the most logistically challenging. Planning each day's section involves a lot of calculation—How far can I go? What do I carry in the boat versus leave in the car? Where are put-ins and take-outs? Where will I stay? Who will be with me? How do we work the shuttle so that there is a vehicle waiting where we finish? And since so much of this river journey is new to me, and the current so variable based on fluctuating water levels, I frequently misjudge daily mileage and either arrive at the take-out much earlier or much later than I planned.

Today is a fast day. There is little or no whitewater on this stretch, but the upstream rain continues to really push water downstream, and we clip along. Most of the discussion is about our kids—all mid-twenties to midthirties—and the various joys and woes of young adulthood during COVID. Tom and Mark are grandfathers and proud of it. John and I are a little envious.

The heat is intense today, and that leads to a river trick that comes in handy in August. Since both banks are lined with trees, the passage of the sun across the sky usually leaves one side or the other in shade stretching twenty to thirty yards out into the water. We stay in the shade whenever we can, and it makes a huge difference.

We make good time to a small take-out at Cartersville for lunch and then eventually approach the take-out at Westview. The only challenge is not bypassing the take-out which is on river left just as a long island divides the river. If you failed to pay attention and cruised down the right side you would miss the take-out completely. But we are up to the challenge, exit without incident, and drive back to camp in time for a swim and another night of drinks, dinner, and gab. A storm starts rolling in around 9:00 p.m. and we quickly scramble into our tents. Today's trip goes into a sizable outdoor memory bank that the four of us share. And the days to come promise more memories.

!

It storms all night long. We wake to a misty morning with drizzle falling and everything except the inside of the tents soaked. The weather is perfect for our canoe stretch—clouds and drizzle will cut the August heat. But the prospect of making breakfast in the rain is depressing. We remember an enclosed picnic shelter up the hill from our primitive campsite, next to a gleaming new bathroom facility with hot and cold running water, a far cry from the dank privy one hundred yards away from our tents. So we drive up to the shelter and set up our stoves and breakfast food out of the rainfall.

I am using my trusty Jetboil stove that was a godsend on the AT and has been on this trip as well. An insulated container with a lid snaps down onto a small burner that has been screwed onto a fuel canister. The pieces are designed to fit together well and pack into the container when not in use. The contraption lights with no matches and boils a liter and a half of water in ninety seconds. I am doing my normal routine—making water for coffee for all of us before heating up more water for oatmeal. And we are talking about today's trip and the next two days that will take us into the City of Richmond.

When the water boils, I remove the container from the burner and begin to pour the first cup. But, in talking with my buddies, I have been careless with the container lid. It isn't snapped on tight. And so as I stand and pour, the lid falls off and the entire contents dump out right on top of my left foot, protected only by a rubber Croc water shoe. The pain is unbearable and I scream like an animal.

As I stumble around in pain, my first thought is fear that the boiling water might melt the rubber Croc to my skin. I instinctively perform a most unpleasant task—I reach down and rip the Croc off my left foot, hoping that it doesn't pull too much of me with it. Mark comes over with a bottle and pours cold water all over my foot. I sit down on a picnic bench unable to think straight.

After a few minutes, I gamely relight the stove to continue with breakfast and suggest that, after a little break, we should be able to continue. My friends look at me as if I'm nuts but humor me for a while. At first, pain isn't registering, but after about twenty minutes, it starts to seriously hurt. Mark and John pull gauze and tape from their first aid kits and wrap my foot. I can't even look at it yet but they say, "It's not pretty."

Damn it! I still have five days left on this stretch before I come back in October to finish. I have hiked the AT and cycled the Blue Ridge Parkway and Skyline Drive without incident. But now this? I keep trying to stand to see if I might be able to finish today at least. But the pain, as well as the dawning knowledge that a burn needs to be kept clean to avoid infection, eventually convinces me that I shouldn't get back on the river now. Tom, Mark, and John knew this as soon as they saw the burn happen, but they let me reach the conclusion myself. That's true friendship.

And these true friends, no doubt disappointed themselves that the trip is being cut short, tell me to sit and sip my coffee in the shelter while they go break camp. They take down the tents and load everything into our cars and then come to retrieve me. I go to a twenty-four-hour doc, hoping that the burn isn't so serious that I need to go to a hospital.

The doctor on call takes one look at my foot—which I now see is red and covered with massive blisters—and tells me that it's serious, but the fact that blisters are forming and I can feel pain is actually a good sign. My mind is toggling back and forth between listening to her medical advice and thinking about how to shift my schedule so I can finish the river journey.

I eventually get home to good nursing from Anne. I am heavily medicated and the pain in my foot is now a steady throb, with only occasional bursts of more intense pain. I sleep for a while. When I wake, I see that Tom, John, and Mark have come by to unload all the gear from my car and take the canoe off the roof rack.

I realize something. My friends have been great about joining me along the way. I have been thrilled to have them and they have a good time together. But as I near the end of my three-year adventure, there is a new motivation. They come with me not only to enjoy the outdoors but because they are actively invested in helping me finish the improbable journey I started in 2019. When I told them what I was planning to do, I am not sure any of us thought I could finish. But why not give it a try? Now that I am close, they are not just solid outdoor companions but guardian angels for the trip itself.

I can't even wear a shoe for nearly a month. (I have to preside over a pro forma session of the Senate one day and likely make history as the first senator to do so in flip-flops.) I visit the Senate doctor's office a week after the burn happens. When I unwrap my foot, the attending physician stays silent for about thirty seconds before saying , "I didn't know hot water could do that. Gasoline or wax, yes. But that is a most impressive burn."

I hear the same diagnosis a few weeks later when I get an appointment at the burn center at Virginia Commonwealth University to make sure my foot is healing. I had second-degree burns from the base of my toes up to my ankle, with some third degree burn spots in the area where the water first hit. Thank goodness there is no burn on the sole of my foot! But the healing is coming along fine. The doc tells me that I will have obvious scarring and "no future as a footwear model." Oh, well—when one door closes, perhaps another opens. Except now I have to figure out how to scramble and finish the trip. To paraphrase the famous saying, "Life is what happens when your plans fall through."

16

I get back on the water on a Sunday in mid-September, three and a half weeks after the burn. I missed out on five days of my planned route. I replace them with today and then, hopefully, four days later this week when the Senate is in a brief recess for the High Holy Days. That will catch me up and enable me to finish during an October recess before the air and water temperatures get too cold. It'll be tight, but still doable. My buddies are as flexible as can be and we all adjust.

My foot is healing but not there yet. I put on a clean gauze bandage and ointment each day and am still wearing flip-flops. And to make matters worse, while the river is cleaner than it once was, there have been a few instances recently where sewage overflows occurred due to faulty wastewater treatment systems nearby. I won't be doing any intentional swimming and will have to monitor my foot during the next stretch to make sure it doesn't get infected.

My friend Ned, who bravely traveled with me earlier as I negotiated around all the dams above Lynchburg, becomes my companion again today. We drop his car at Maidens Landing and drive back upriver to Westview. Ned is a rock-and-roll encyclopedia with a phenomenal memory for lyrics. As we pull up to the river to put in, we hear the opening chords of one of our favorite songs on the radio—"Waterloo Sunset" by The Kinks—and burst into laughter as they sing about a dirty old river. A good reminder to keep my foot as dry as I can.

The trip today is divided into two segments—about two-thirds of the mileage is above Powhatan State Park where we camped a few weeks back. There are three boat landings on the water as the James passes the park on the right-hand side. Our plan is to pull out at the quiet middle landing and have lunch at the modest campground there before heading downriver to the Maidens take-out.

The first stretch of the trip is like so many upriver. Where are the people? It is a beautiful, sunny, temperate September Sunday. There is no one else out here. We don't see other boats; we don't see people fishing from the banks. The parking lot where we put in is empty. Ned and I talk about work and family as we drift along—the water clear and fish very visible today.

Since I was last on the river, I've been in DC working heavily on Afghanistan issues. Joe Biden made the right call to end US military operations after twenty years. The US has invested enough in Afghanistan, and the next chapter has to be on the shoulders of Afghans. But an unwise peace deal by the previous administration—negotiated between the US and the Taliban without including the Afghan government—and the Biden administration's overly optimistic view on Afghan military capacity have led to visible tragedy as the US withdraws. We stage a near-miraculous rescue of 125,000 Afghans—seventy-five thousand to the US and fifty thousand to other countries. But we tragically lose troops during the withdrawal, and the scenes of chaos as the Taliban reasserts control over the country are painful.

Virginia is the arrival point for most of the first wave of Afghan immigrants, and I have visited an initial processing center at Dulles Airport and then three Virginia military bases where Afghan families go to await resettlement processing as they move on to the challenges of life in a new country. I find myself wishing that more Americans could see the amazing effort to resettle the families and the gratitude that so many feel to have a new chapter of life here. (On my first visit, my foot is still recovering and I am a little self-conscious about wearing flip-flops but immediately notice that my footwear matches the Afghans' preference.)

The effort to help these families establish new lives in the US will be massive, and Virginia—along with Texas and California—is the top choice for many as an ultimate home. When I was born, one out of one hundred Virginia residents had been born in foreign countries. Today the number is one in nine. But don't get this wrong: the successive waves of immigrants from all over the world have not *hurt* the state but have tremendously *benefited* it. Over the same period of time, Virginia has grown from one of the nation's poorest states into one that is high-income and economically dynamic. Regional inequities exist, but the state is doing so much better with the influx of immigrants. And the regions with high immigrant populations tend to overperform. There's a lesson there. Afghan families will face challenges just as all immigrants do. But I have no doubt that they will work toward success and add to our Commonwealth and country.

We reach the park and eat lunch at the picnic table in the now-empty campsite where Tom, Mark, and I camped a few weeks ago. A simple lunch and two ice-cold beers are savored in the shade. A few folks walk by, using Powhatan State Park's superb trail network. Ned engages all of them in conversation, as is his delightful habit. Anne and I like to come here and walk while looking for birds. We saw our first orchard oriole here.

I am happy to see that the low use of the river above the park now changes. Many people put in canoes, kayaks, or large inner tubes at the upstream end of the park, near a sizable parking lot, and float either to the downstream end or all the way to Maidens Landing where our car is parked. It is good to see so many enjoying it.

As we paddle downriver after lunch, with no rapids to speak of, I get my rhythm back after my layoff. I find myself excited at the prospect of reaching Richmond later this week and then beginning the closing phase of my trip: the nearly one hundred miles of the Lower James, a widening tidal river all the way to the Chesapeake Bay. Thinking about arriving by water in Richmond reminds me of moving here to marry Anne in 1984—knowing only one person in the whole state, with the high hopes of youth about what life might bring. Ned and his wife, Patty, were the first friends I made after I moved here. It is fitting that the final leg of my Nature Triathlon is the one that will bring me home.

A shape appears in the water ahead moving toward us. We can't figure it out. As we draw nearer, we realize it's a swimmer, moving steadily upstream, with no obvious support boat helping him out. We salute him. Going downstream is work enough for us.

17

Today is a mostly flatwater stretch from Maidens to Watkins Landing. It's the final day on the river before I reach my hometown of Richmond.

The three friends who helped me through my burn and had their own trips cut short as a result are joining me variously over the next few days to get more river time. Mark is with me in the front of the boat today. He is a former county parks official and has been a frequent companion on outdoor trips. His son Peter has been a longtime friend of my two boys. I'm in good hands as we start in a light rain.

The stretch today has three points of interest. There's a set of rapids about two miles downstream from the put-in that are formed by the ruins of the old Maidens Dam. All the guidebooks I read suggest that they shouldn't be much trouble. Mark and I pass one bass boat just above the rapids with two guys fishing. They ask where we're going, and when we tell them Watkins Landing, they express amazement that we would go that far on paddle power without a motor. It's only about twelve or thirteen miles, but we modestly feign manly courage and paddle on. Maidens Dam proves no problem.

The second place we await is a bit of a mystery. There are two Virginia prison farms on opposite sides of the water in Goochland and Powhatan. (Obviously, you don't pick up any stray hitchhikers on the riverbanks here!) And there is a bridge across the James connecting the two prisons, described in one guidebook as a "low bridge, or low-water, or underwater bridge, depending on water levels." No matter how much I research in my canoe books and online, I can't find out how "low" this low-water bridge is. Can we go under it? Do we portage around it? Does the river, when high, go over it? We don't know.

It's a little rare nowadays not to know how serious an obstacle might be. When I started canoeing as a kid, it was pretty common to get on streams in the Ozarks without any map or guidebook. You'd figure out two roads that you could use as put-in or take-out points and put your boat in the water with a possible surprise around every bend. The movie *Deliverance* from my teenage years summed this up—a river trip was an unpredictable voyage into wilderness. (Our trip will hopefully be a little more predictable, but you get the idea.)

It's so much easier now. Not only are there good guidebooks about most Virginia streams (H. Roger Corbett's *Virginia Whitewater* is the best for adventures in the Commonwealth), but with social media, people post trip descriptions, video clips from their adventures, and helpful advice about where to put in, where to stay, where to get supplies. All this makes planning easier, even if, like today, I'm traveling a stretch where I've never been.

The minor mystery of not knowing what the low-water bridge will be like makes me think about my favorite river adventure of yore, John Wesley Powell's descent of the Colorado River through the Grand Canyon in 1869. Powell was an amazing figure, a New Yorker whose family transplanted to the Midwest when he was young. As a teenager, he walked across the state of Wisconsin, boated the length of the Mississippi and Ohio Rivers, and became deeply interested in geology. An abolitionist, he joined the Union Army at the start of the war and worked his way up to colonel. He lost his right arm in the Battle of Shiloh in 1862 . . . but stayed on and kept fighting anyway in battle after battle until the end of the war. He returned home and lectured on geology at Illinois Wesleyan and Illinois State Universities.

In May 1869, Powell recruited a band of adventurers to descend the Green and Colorado Rivers. They had no good maps or guidebooks, just survival skills and wooden boats. Led by Powell, they took three months to travel through some of the most outstanding scenery and fearsome rapids on earth, finishing their trip in August, with four of the crew having quit and walked out along the way. (Three who left near the end of the trip were never found.) After two months boating from Green River, Wyoming, the expedition arrived at the beginning of what we now call the Grand Canyon near Lees Ferry, Arizona. Powell wrote: "With some feeling of anxiety, we enter a new canyon this morning. Below us are the limestones and hard sandstones which we found in Cataract Canyon. This bodes toil and danger." But on they went.

Years later, after he realized what he had done, he punched up the prose: "We have an unknown distance yet to run, an unknown river to explore. What falls there are, we know not; what rocks beset the channel, we know not; what walls ride over the river, we know not. Ah well! We may conjecture many things."

I can hardly imagine the courage of Powell and his crew. He was famous for battling the river during the day and then climbing the canyon walls, carrying a sketchbook so he could draw pictures of the sedimented rock formations that delighted his geologist imagination. All with one arm!

To go into such dangerous territory without knowing it seems insane to me. Maybe had he known it, he wouldn't have gone. An awful lot of good in the world gets done by people who are so naive that they don't know how hard something will be.

River travel is a different experience today—you pretty much know in advance if there's a spot where you'll hit trouble. As we round a corner on the river, we spot our low-water bridge and see that it is easily ten feet over the water surface at its late summer low level. It's a one-lane bridge with no railing—probably scary to drive over—and could indeed be under water in winter or spring. Today, though, we drift under easily.

We now enter a special stretch of islands with fun rapids and eddy below one particularly nice drop to eat lunch on a large, flat rock jutting into the river. Mark and his wife, Eliza, have just had another grandchild, and I get a proud picture display. We take and send selfies to make friends and family jealous. We've seen only one boat all day and several bald eagles.

We reach the take-out in the early afternoon and a dad is putting a small fishing boat on the water with three kids scrambling all over him and each other, in and out of the boat and in and out of the water. Our most likely river stewards are those who catch the bug as children. Mark and I visit with them briefly and drive home talking about river trips years ago with our own kids.

18

I reach Richmond today! I haven't set any speed records getting here, but that's not been the point of the trip. My neighbor John and I will begin at Watkins Landing, canoe a completely flat stretch that is essentially a lake formed by the backwater of Bosher Dam, portage around that to a stretch of slightly swifter water until a second portage at Williams Dam, and then finish with a fun whitewater run to Pony Pasture, a popular city park. The trip totals about thirteen miles.

The James in Richmond has been such a part of my life. Kansas City is a river town, at the junction of the Missouri and Kansas Rivers, but these were never recreational streams growing up. We loved traveling three to four hours to the Ozarks for canoe trips, but there was something immediately magical about coming to Richmond and seeing how many cars were fitted with rooftop racks for canoes and kayaks due to whitewater access right in the city.

Riverside trails, parks for picnicking and sunbathing, fishing, great canoe segments on the James and nearby rivers (Appomattox, South Anna, North Anna), raft trips through the class-three to class-four rapids on the fall-line section in downtown Richmond—these became an integral part of our life as a couple and then as a family. Our children all grew up going to a camp on Belle Isle right in the middle of downtown where they learned to kayak and rock climb. The river—so much cleaner than when Anne lived here as a girl—became very much part of our kids' extended backyard.

I remember how nervous and excited I was to embark on marriage, a career, and a new home all at the same time. We've built a community of friends through work, church, nonprofit organizations, and neighborhood activities. I worked at two private law firms, mostly trying civil rights cases for people who had been victimized by housing discrimination. Anne helped low-income folks with their legal needs as a staff attorney at Central Virginia Legal Aid Society.

We each slowly built up reputations as solid trial lawyers—Anne winning major class-action cases for public housing tenants, home-owners victimized by mortgage loan fraud, and food stamp recipients denied benefits due to unacceptable bureaucratic delays. She also helped start a successful volunteer lawyer program that extended the work her legal aid office could do. And she did all this while juggling the responsibilities of motherhood as our children were born—first Nat in 1990, then Woody in 1992, and finally Annella in 1995.

I shared last meals with two clients right before they were executed in the place that has used the death penalty more than any American state. My peak case was winning a one-hundred-million-dollar jury verdict of national significance against Nationwide Insurance for redlining minority neighborhoods in Richmond and all over the country in the issuance of homeowner's insurance.

Our kids grew up attending local public schools, loving the river, and each forging their own paths. They brag about Richmond and always seem to be excited at new things going on when they come home to visit.

I imagined when I moved here that we might go back to Kansas City one day, but our love for Richmond was instantaneous and unbreakable. Virtually all the US senators from Virginia during the time I have been here have chosen to live near DC. But Richmond is home, so I live here and have a small condo in DC about a mile from the Capitol where I stay during the weeks the Senate is in session.

There are many reasons we love Richmond—friends, our parish, history, diversity of people, beautiful architecture, great food and culture scenes. But the natural opportunities offered by the James, as well as proximity to mountains and the ocean, are the heart of its attraction for us and for so many others.

John is a superb river guy due to tutelage from his father, the former superintendent of the Virginia Military Institute. His son Johnny and our daughter, Annella, were inseparable as kids. We have fun talking as we maneuver the flatwater stretch to Bosher Dam. Beautiful large homes appear on river right, many with luxe docks, as we enter the western part of the Richmond metro area and we see a few powerboats and paddleboards out on a nice fall day.

The dam is about sixteen feet high and dates all the way back to 1823. It was rebuilt in 1885, and its original purpose was to divert water into the navigational canal that was constructed to allow boats to bypass the whitewater rapids on the fall line in Richmond. As the canal fell into disuse, the dam has been subsequently used to produce hydropower and divert water from the river into Richmond's water treatment plant, a few miles downstream on river left.

We have never portaged Bosher before and drift nearer and nearer to the drop looking for a spot to pull out on river left. Finally we see a muddy path and pull over. It's one hundred yards up a path to a fish ladder. This was built when I was mayor to help American shad find their way back to traditional spawning grounds that had been blocked for nearly two hundred years. We pull out the cooler and rest at the lip of the dam enjoying lunch.

We take our time watching a blue heron fishing and eventually put in below the dam. We maneuver a nice stretch to and under Willey Bridge and then Huguenot Bridge enjoying some light rapids and watching for our next portage. The Williams Dam (most call it "Z-Dam" because of its zigzag shape) runs from the south bank to an island in the middle of the river and then cuts in a diagonal direction to the north bank, where it serves to funnel water into Richmond's water treatment system. The right side of the dam has a fish notch cut that seems innocent enough to boaters wanting a little fun. But it has a nasty hydraulic, and its placid look is deceiving. Many have died here over the years.

We make way for the island and do a two-hundred-yard portage, putting in below Z Dam just after a group of college kids in inner tubes set off for Pony Pasture, probably a half mile downstream on river right. The rapids start to pick up here and I tell John, "You take the back now." He is a better boater than I am, a nimble halfback to my straight-ahead fullback, and he steers us through the boulders and ledges with ease.

We pull the boat up at the access point at Pony Pasture. The parking lot is full of people enjoying the river and great network of trails in the city's James River Park, the most-visited park along the river's 350-mile length. It's a delightfully diverse crowd all drawn to the water like a magnet on a pleasant Friday afternoon.

19

It's early Saturday morning when Anne and I head back to Pony Pasture to meet our friends Bob and Liz for one of the most remarkable stretches of the entire river: the fall line of the James.

The fall line describes the point in many mid-Atlantic rivers where an upland region meets the coastal plain. Rapids and waterfalls are common on rivers and streams crossing the fall line. Many cities were settled just below the fall line of major streams, as the turbulent water usually marked the end of easy navigation upriver from the ocean. Washington, DC, is just below the Great Falls of the Potomac, Fredericksburg below the fall line of the Rappahannock River, Petersburg below the fall line of the Appomattox River. Here, the James River tumbles through a seven-mile stretch of whitewater right within the city of Richmond. Below the fall line, just under Richmond's Fourteenth Street Bridge (also called "Mayo Bridge"), the rapids end and the river becomes a tidal stream for its last one hundred miles.

I met Bob more than thirty years ago. He was a sharp young college graduate from Charlottesville working on an historic Virginia campaign: the election of L. Douglas Wilder as the nation's first African American governor. He was also an ace whitewater C-1 boater (a specialized canoe purpose-built for rapids) and had also done raft guiding in western North Carolina. He and I have done some good kayaking and canoe trips over the years. Bob went to Yale Law School after Governor Wilder's term, met Liz there, and then came back to Richmond, where they have both been active in civic and political life here. They are about ten years younger than Anne and me and have always been very gracious in supporting my political career.

When I tell Bob about my James River journey and seek his help, he volunteers to steer us through on a four-person raft he and Liz use often with their kids. He has the raft inflated and ready to go where they live just above Pony Pasture Park. After drinking coffee and catching up on work and family, we walk down a hill, hop in the raft, and push off.

The rapids along this stretch increase in complexity—Pony Pasture, Choo Choo, Mitchell's Gut, First Break, Hollywood, Pipeline. The two toughest—Hollywood and Pipeline—are solid class-four rapids and can be even tougher in high-water conditions. I have canoed most of these rapids but not Hollywood or Pipeline—my boat would immediately fill up with water in the ledges and waves and tip or capsize. It's good to be in a raft with a skilled leader like Bob. It's a warm day, and we see many others out along the river.

As Anne and I became active in law practice and civic life, we also threw ourselves into Virginia politics as volunteers on state and local campaigns. The Wilder election when I met Bob was a huge point of celebration for us. Nat had been born just a few days before that frigid January 1990 inauguration. I remember Anne going with her parents to the swearing-in to see history made while I did my first solo babysitting in front of the television watching Governor Wilder, a grandson of enslaved people, take the oath of office.

I grew up in a very apolitical family, but being part of the Holton family and hearing about her dad's political career—while doing my own work on civil rights issues as a lawyer—motivated me to run for city council in 1994 after I had lived in Richmond for ten years. (I had to ignore Linwood's advice as he told me that local politics was "the graveyard for any good politician"!) I began representing a very diverse part of the city: all or parts of thirteen different neighborhoods, containing some of Richmond's largest mansions and also its largest public housing community.

I ultimately was elected to four two-year terms on the council and was chosen by the council to be Richmond's mayor for the last two of those terms. My time of service was July 1994 through September

2001, when I resigned while in the last weeks of my campaign to be lieutenant governor. It was a time of intense work as the city fought back against decades of disinvestment and population loss similar to that experienced by cities around the country. Cutting crime, building schools, redeveloping downtown, restoring the river, reclaiming thousands of blighted buildings all over the city—the everyday work was meaningful, though far from glamorous.

My colleagues varied from skilled to troubled, and often both at once. Along the way, through hard work by many during those years and since, Richmond has experienced a real renaissance. No longer is it a city in decline. The population is growing, our arts and culture scene is vibrant, the economy is more dynamic, and outdoor assets like the James are a defining part of the city's brand.

After our second child was born, Anne worked a part-time schedule, still doing high-impact litigation for low-income folks. But when our daughter was born in 1995, she took a multiyear leave of absence from law practice. Local judges who admired her courtroom skills asked if she would accept occasional calls to be a substitute judge, and she sat on the bench a few days a month during the stay-home period. When she returned to practice in early 1998, state legislators encouraged her to submit her name for a permanent position on the city's juvenile court bench. One of the best twenty-four hours of our life as a couple came about when she was sworn in as a judge one afternoon in June 1998 and I was elected mayor by my city council colleagues the next morning. We were both forty years old and had seen fourteen years of steady work in our hometown open up truly amazing leadership opportunities for us.

That was nearly twenty-five years ago, and we are still both humbled and amazed by the way Richmonders have encouraged and helped us along the way. Whatever project we put our efforts to, we have no trouble finding willing assistance from our friends and neighbors. People just treat us as they always have—calling us "Tim" and "Anne," rarely using any title—and that's just how we like it.

I have been particularly touched by the gracious support I've received from our city's African American majority population. There are too many examples of this support to count, but one stands out and for me summarizes them all. When I threw my hat in the ring to be mayor in 1998, the mayor was chosen by a city council that was predominantly African American. During the hundreds of years that Richmond had a majority white population, there was never an African American mayor. The city became majority Black in the 1970s and some tough voting rights litigation ensued over efforts by the city's white majority to slow down the growth of African American political power. Finally, in 1977, the city had its first African American mayor, the civil rights lawyer Henry Marsh.

My predecessor chose not to run again in 1998, and that left an opening for the mayor's job. I told my colleagues that I would seek the position, and there was significant discussion in the two months between council elections and the swearing-in about whether a majority Black city that had only recently been able to gain power in proportion to their numbers should select a white mayor. I attended a candidate forum before the city's premier African American political organization, and right before I spoke, a council colleague gave a very impassioned speech about why the city should have a Black mayor. I stood up in front of the large and suddenly quiet audience and opened my comments with "I guess my stealth campaign to be mayor without anyone realizing I'm white has been a big bust." It was the only perfect ad-lib joke of my life, and the crowd erupted with laughter. A few days later, Henry Marsh, by then a state senator, weighed in to support me, and my council colleagues elected me by a vote of 8–1.

This experience captures so many others for me—being treated with respect and affection by African Americans who themselves had often experienced disrespectful treatment from whites. Being welcomed in our predominantly Black parish so many years ago made me think about the sole Black family that attended my Kansas parish growing up. My memory is hazy—I hope they weren't treated poorly, but I doubt they were made to feel so welcome.

Living in a community that has been so defined by race—one of the largest slavery markets in the country, the Capital of the Confederacy, the intellectual home of the Lost Cause myth about the Civil War and massive resistance to school integration—means that issues of race and tolerance are always very close to the surface. My own understanding of the many privileges I was both born with and granted along the way has been so deepened because of where I live. And I still experience new epiphanies about the long road to the equality all were promised in a Declaration of Independence written by a Virginian who could not live up to his professed ideals. Our nation still suffers from that malady. I do feel a sense of progress—I've seen it all around me. But there are continued reminders of the vast amount of work remaining.

The Hollywood Rapid is named after a nearby riverside cemetery where Jefferson Davis, dozens of Confederate generals, and eighteen thousand Confederate enlisted men are buried, together with Presidents John Tyler and James Monroe (both of whom enslaved people) and many other people from prominent Richmond families. These reminders of our history are all around us—challenging, confounding, and motivating. The rapid is a steep drop, with a jutting rock just to the left of center in the water and an extended ledge blocking the right side of the flow just below the drop. It is adjacent to Belle Isle, a former prison camp for Union captives, now a gathering spot for picnickers and sunbathers who are always alert to laugh at any boat mishaps. Bob points out that the water level is just about as low as he's seen it. In higher water the current is more dangerous; in lower water the rocks are more dangerous. Pick your poison! But he tells us what to do and steers us cleanly through.

Bob is the CEO of the state's primary electric utility, and his office is right on the river near Hollywood. He is renowned in the city for occasionally kayaking—and even paddleboarding—downriver to work. He and Liz entertain us by describing their parental duties later today:

309

escorting a daughter and friends to a Harry Styles concert in DC, two hours north. We are so illiterate in pop culture that we have to ask who Styles is (even though he shares my wife's birthday, as I later discover).

After a flatwater stretch, we pass under two pedestrian bridges and near Brown's Island, a beautiful park between the river and the city's restored canal system. As mayor, I led the city's 2000 millennium New Year's Eve fireworks display from this island and cut the ribbon for our canal restoration here. Everything along this stretch brings memories personal and political.

Bob lines us up for the set of rapids and ledges that lead to the Pipeline, a set of large drops on river left adjacent to a wastewater treatment pipe. The skyline buildings of our city tower above us— Richmond might be the only major city in the country with natural class-four whitewater in the heart of downtown. We go through the Pipeline drops so fast that I can hardly describe them, and suddenly we find ourselves in slack tidal water. We pass a cross on the bank that commemorates a visit paid to this spot by Christopher Newport shortly after Jamestown was settled in 1607. This dramatic spot was already a small trading community of indigenous Virginians, a dividing line between the Algonquin tribes downstream and the Sioux tribes further upstream.

We reach a take-out at Mayo Bridge, pull the raft out of the water, and lug it up to Bob's car, where we deflate it and pack it in for the drive home. A few other kayakers are using the take-out as well. For a few hours, we've had a wilderness experience in the heart of our city—far away mentally from our daily cares even though we are so close to our houses and offices. Where else do wilderness and a city coexist so beautifully?

20

My park director neighbor Mark and I put-in the water at the Mayo Bridge in the midafternoon with the tide running against us. Our goal is Osborne Landing, a public marina and boat landing about a dozen miles downstream.

I've never read a tide chart before. I'm not a sailor and don't frequent oceangoing boats. All my canoeing over the years on Virginia rivers has been above the fall line, immune from the push and pull of tides. On this pleasant Sunday, we each have the afternoon free, so regardless of tide, that is why we are out here now.

We pass Manchester Docks on river right. This was the landing site for hundreds of thousands of enslaved men, women, and children who were gathered in Richmond and then sold off to white families farther south. Richmond was the largest slavery market in the country from 1830 to 1860. The Docks is also the start of the Richmond Slave Trail, a self-guided walk to sites connected with the monstrous institution— Lumpkins Jail, the site where enslaved people were held before sale; the African Burial Ground; the First African Baptist Church. Along the walk is the Richmond Slavery Reconciliation Statue of the triangular slavery trade between Liverpool, England; the Republic of Benin on Africa's west coast; and Richmond.

The trail is powerful but also betrays continuing ambivalence over how, or whether, the story of Virginia's role in slavery will be told. There are numerous informative exhibits along the trail, but it's not kept up to the same standard as other trails in the city. A long-discussed plan to build a museum telling the story of American slavery along the

Richmond Slave Trail is in limbo, further reflecting the difficulty we still face in confronting painful truths about our country.

We work hard to paddle downriver and feel the effect of the wind and tide against us. The tidal push and pull will get stronger and stronger as I get closer to the ocean. I realize that I will need to consult a tide chart and time my paddling with outgoing tides from now on. Friends have told me I should switch to a sea kayak in this tidal stretch, but I will use Old Raggedy as long as I can.

The James is wide and flat as we pass by industrial buildings, warehouses renovated into condominiums and apartments, and the Richmond wastewater treatment plant (we paddle by opposite river from its outflow). On a sunny afternoon, we see many pleasure boaters and Jet Skiers zipping up and down the river and have to adjust often to maneuver through their wakes. We watch cyclists riding on the Virginia Capital Trail.

My time in state government was full of projects and priorities. It started on a fun note—my wife, Anne, in her judge's robe administering the lieutenant governor oath of office to me before a huge crowd on the Capitol grounds in 2002.

I worked to dramatically expand pre-kindergarten for four-year-olds around the state, build up our state university system, expand housing and health insurance options for Virginians with disabilities, ban smoking in restaurants and bars, and slash our unacceptable infant mortality rate. And we won recognition as the best-managed state in America, the best state for business, and the best state to raise a child. We were able to celebrate the four hundredth anniversary of the English settlement of Jamestown by welcoming Queen Elizabeth and Prince Philip to the capital in May 2007.

Of course, there were hard times. Anne and I had just landed in Japan on a trade mission in April 2007 when we received word that there was a shooting underway at Virginia Tech. We raced to the airport and flew back home to comfort the families of thirty-two people who were slaughtered by a disturbed young man who should never have been allowed to purchase the firearms he used to kill others. Jet-lagged, I spoke to the Tech community right after Easter with an unanswerable question from Scripture: "My God, my God, why hast thou forsaken me?" I continue to interact with students and faculty members who were injured or had friends and relatives killed that day. The raw emotions have not dulled, and I still get overcome at random times as I think about the lives lost, and the many more damaged, by that tragedy—as well as all the gun violence I saw in Richmond neighborhoods when I served at the local level.

I was particularly proud of Anne's work as First Lady, the only person who has ever lived in the Virginia Governor's Mansion as a child and then as an adult. She made the hard decision to step down from the bench so that she could throw herself into her new role and made it her focus to reform the state's foster care system, which she had come to know so well as a juvenile court judge. She still has kids she met when they were in foster care—now grown adults—who come to her for wise counsel.

My children had heard for years about the pranks Anne and her siblings played on everyone at the mansion when she was a kid. Had we realized that they would have had the same experience, she probably wouldn't have shared those stories! They adjusted well to the three-mile move from our neighborhood to the Mansion and had many experiences that we'll always remember. But I'll never forget the look of relief on their faces the day my successor was inaugurated and we returned home. They were overjoyed at the prospect of no more living in the bubble of security and public scrutiny! I love that my children want to chart their own paths rather than expecting us to clear the way for them.

Near the end of my term, in late 2009, I did what all outgoing governors do—chose an artist and sat for my official portrait that now hangs in the state capitol. Most governors do something in their portraits to capture an important essence of their term. I decided to have my picture painted in an outdoor setting, leaning against a tree with the James River in the background. We had worked hard to preserve open space, invest in sewage treatment upgrades, expand state parks, and protect critical species that were at risk—blue crabs, the native Virginia oyster, rockfish, menhaden. So a portrait featuring Virginia's land, water, trees, and sky seemed natural.

Mark and I experience a truly amazing example of species restoration today, somewhat accidentally. It is mid-September, and I had not originally planned to be on the water this month. I had planned a long August trip and then a finishing week in October. But my foot-scalding took me off the water early last month and I had to scramble to find a few September days to make up for lost time. Thank God for the unexpected change in plans!

I look downriver as we paddle and see a large splash of water six hundred yards ahead, near the Richmond Marine Terminal, a city-owned port on the James for barges bringing goods up and down the river from the international port in Hampton Roads. It looks like the plume of water created by a Jet Ski, but since it doesn't continue, that can't be it.

As we keep paddling, I start to see more and more of these splashes, closer and closer to the boat. And it dawns on me—we are right in the middle of the fall spawning season for sturgeon, which hits its peak for about ten days in September each year. These fish are living fossils and have hardly changed over hundreds of millennia. They live in the ocean and then come to spawn in the freshwater rivers where they were born. They can grow to fourteen feet long and weigh up to eight hundred pounds. The males leap out of the water and belly flop back in, either to attract females or maybe just to have fun. We see thirty-five to forty strikes today and some of the sturgeon look to be easily eight feet long. The closest strike happens about fifty yards from the canoe. They could easily knock the canoe over if they landed nearby but we needn't worry about them—they eat small fish and plants along the river bottom. Still, it's hard to believe they can grow so large and live so long by eating such small things.

Sturgeon were decimated by overfishing in the late 1800s, their eggs a desirable caviar. And it was long thought that they were extinct in the James River. But in the late 1990s, some enterprising naturalists offered a bounty of fifty dollars to anyone who could catch, tag, and release a sturgeon in the James. The angling community loved the challenge and caught and tagged so many that they had to reduce the bounty to twenty-five bucks and then eliminate it entirely. But the experiment at least proved that sturgeon were not gone.

During my first year as governor, a big group of stakeholders—the US Fish and Wildlife Service, the Virginia Institute of Marine Science, the National Oceanic and Atmospheric Administration, the US Army Corps of Engineers, the Virginia Commonwealth University Rice Rivers Center, and the James River Association—started a collaborative effort to restore the Atlantic sturgeon population in the James. The effort has involved construction of experimental spawning reefs and other strategies to protect and grow the population of this magnificent fish. The James River Association calls it "the Great Return," and it is powerful to experience it up close for the first time.

Mark and I are entertained by these strikes all afternoon, and we eventually reach Osborne Landing, which is busy today with powerboats coming in and out of the public marina. As we arrive, a couple, each in kayaks, is getting on the water, and they ask us with excitement, "Did you see any sturgeon?" We point them upriver and assure them that they will experience quite a show.

Just then, we look up and see a massive oceangoing ship head downstream. We passed it earlier at the Port of Richmond, and it is now loaded and underway. I compare the scale of the ship with Old Raggedy and realize that while this section of river may lack whitewater, there will obviously be new challenges to negotiate in the days to come.

21

I am finishing the trip in mid-October during a Senate recess. I hope to reach Fort Monroe in six days. The air and water temperatures are cool but not cold. Weather forecasts vary this week—some sun, some rain, and hopefully not too much wind.

For the first time, I have asked one of my staffers to travel with me. Mike is my chief of staff, an excellent outdoorsman, and has put up with and helped facilitate this three-year journey. It only seems right to ask him to join me as I near the completion of this adventure.

I met Mike when he was deputy campaign manager during Mark Warner's successful gubernatorial campaign in 2001. I was running for lieutenant governor that year and we struck up a friendship. I asked him to run my own campaign for governor in 2005 and he accepted, putting together a near-flawless effort that wiped out a polling deficit in the last weeks of the campaign to win a decisive victory. He ran other campaigns in successive years, and when I was confronted with an unexpected Senate opening, I asked him to come back and run my 2012 campaign. He did it again and then became my chief of staff in the Senate. He is a consummate team builder and has forged a great Senate office.

When I told Mike about my Virginia Nature Triathlon idea, he had other proposed uses for my time! But he got into the idea when he saw what it meant to me. It even awakened a dormant hiking bug in him; he's started checking off sections of the AT with one of his brothers. Mike is ten years younger than me, and he and his wife, Dani, have two daughters who are transitioning from high school to college. With years of attending his daughters' multiple sporting events nearing an end,

I think he's happy to find his appetite for outdoor adventures renewed as he has more time to indulge it.

We put in the water at Osborne Landing on a cool Monday morning. Nobody else is around. Our goal is to head downriver, passing a big power plant at Dutch Gap, canoeing under Varina-Enon Bridge, and working our way downriver to a National Wildlife Refuge, Presque Isle, that sits as an island in the James. We'll explore that a while and then finish by boating to Hopewell, the city that the Union Army used as its headquarters in the closing phase of the Civil War.

Mike's presence means we talk about work a bit as we paddle. I am in an unusual position in the Senate. I am in my twenty-eighth year in public life, and the fact that I have been a mayor, governor, national party chair, and VP nominee makes me somewhat of a senior statesman in both the Democratic Party and the Senate. But, due to strict seniority rules in the Senate Democratic caucus, I am not a committee chair and likely won't be. I am not in formal Democratic leadership—the endless fundraising and the need to put everything in "Democrats are good, Republicans are bad" lingo doesn't match my strengths.

My value in the Senate is my ability to forge consensus across the aisle and my willingness to help broker peace when disagreements break out among my Democratic colleagues. I work hard to do these things—occasionally even succeeding! Being in a time in my life where I have no desire or need to outperform others often gives me a path to finding a solution. And Mike is extremely adroit at helping me get things done.

One of the true blessings in the Senate is working in an environment surrounded by altruistic young people. About 60 percent of my staff are younger than thirty-five. Many come to the Hill right from college, thinking about public service careers and hoping to learn. Mike and I agree that our responsibility to them is to offer a work experience that will equip them with greater skills without dampening their altruism. We have a huge ability to impact young people when we do our jobs right. We don't always think of that responsibility in the press of a day's work, but we try to remind ourselves of this key part of the job.

I have been happy in the Senate, although my friends point out that I could be happy anywhere. I've made significant policy difference in many areas—pediatric cancer research, mental health resources for our frontline health care workforce, fighting to reduce unemployment among veterans and military spouses, raising the federal tobacco age to twenty-one, strengthening support for career and technical education, igniting congressional interest in reclaiming decision-making on war and diplomacy from the executive branch. I've been able to address two key areas of unfinished business from my work in local and state government—recognition of our tribes and being part of the movement that achieved marriage equality. And I've used my missionary work and Spanish fluency to work closely with our Latin American immigrant communities and draw more attention to US diplomacy in the region.

I've done some real good. But—if I'm honest—I have to also acknowledge a feeling of incompleteness. When I left the mayor's office, I knew that both the workings of city government and the quality of life in our city were better because of my seven-plus years. And I felt the same about my eight years in state government—that the workings of government and quality of life for Virginians were better when I left than when I started. But my time in the Senate has coincided with Donald Trump's depredations, a once-in-a-century pandemic, an increasingly out-of-touch Supreme Court, and a first-ever domestic attack on the Capitol. I can't say that the nation or the Senate are better off than when I came here in 2013, though I hope to be able to say that one day. I feel as if we're still being tested, like Job, to determine our faithfulness to democratic values.

As I've been toiling in the Senate, my wife's public service career has really hit warp speed. Anne finished her time as Virginia's First Lady and then embarked on significant work to spread her foster care reform successes nationally with the Annie E. Casey Foundation. Much of that reform work involved creating specific programs at community colleges—in Virginia and nationally—for kids aging out of foster care.

In 2013, Governor Terry McAuliffe asked her to become his secretary of education and she performed that role with her trademark blend of passion and smarts.

I've often thought that, had I been elected vice president in 2016, it would have been harder for Anne to take on some of the responsibilities she has been able to embrace in the years since. She would have been fantastic in the indeterminate role of VP spouse. But her work there would have always been seen through the prism of her connection to me. Now, she shines on her own. So many people who first came to know her through my elected positions see her clearly for the exemplary leader she is.

I also wouldn't have been able to concoct and complete this multiyear adventure had I been VP. But the door to future footwear modeling would still have been open!

We pass a huge coal-fired power plant on the water at Dutch Gap, likely to convert to natural gas within a few years. The industrial buildings hulk over the river. Less than a mile downstream, we pull over at a small dock that is part of Henricus. This is a Chesterfield County park featuring a restoration of the small English settlement, established in 1611, where Pocahontas married John Rolfe. That union helped pave the way for peace between Virginia tribes and the English, although that peace developed in often-violent fits and starts until treaties were finally reached in the 1670s. As we stand on a bluff overlooking the river, reading historic markers about Pocahontas and the village, we realize that it is Indigenous Peoples' Day.

We get back in the canoe and keep downstream, seeing multiple pairs of bald eagles as we negotiate past riverside forests and farms. And we duck and dodge barge traffic, too, learning to pull far over near the bank to avoid the wake from these oceangoing vessels. Around lunchtime, I spot the horseshoe bend in the river that signifies arrival at Presque Isle. The Lower James coils like a snake—here the Corps of Engineers dug a shortcut, leaving the former farmland of Presque Isle cut off as an island in the middle of the river. The property was donated to the state in the 1950s and is now a 1,300-acre federal wildlife refuge, a beautiful spot to see migratory bird life.

When we pull up at the dock, there is a small chain on the ramp to shore with a sign that says "Refuge Closed." Maybe it is closed due to the federal holiday, or, more likely, its isolated position means that it is not normally staffed during the week. But Mike and I decide that, as a member of the Senate Budget Committee, I need to do a "fact-finding" visit. We step over the chain, carry our cooler up to a picnic table, and enjoy a lazy lunch while watching birds circle all around us. What a pleasant way to spend a day.

The weather starts to change a bit and we still have to paddle across wide-open water to Hopewell, a city on the south bank of the James where the Appomattox River enters the James. Wind is in our face and the tide that was outgoing this morning is incoming now. We can see the city and the confluence where the city marina is located. But we make slow headway toward our goal. Finally we cross under the Route 10 bridge on the western end of the city and pull Old Raggedy out of the water.

We'll start back here tomorrow, but now Mike and I are thinking the same thing: *Let's check our emails, texts, and voice messages!* Even on a federal holiday, they've piled up. We spend the late afternoon catching up on the work we've missed today before joining Anne for dinner.

22

Mike and I head back to Hopewell on a cool, breezy, and drizzly morning. Fog sits low to the ground. We carry our boat to a small city park on the water and prepare to put in where our first task is to canoe across the mile-wide channel from south bank to north. (From this point on, the river gets so wide that I'll stick to the north bank the rest of the way.)

A guy up early fishing sees us and asks, "Are you guys really going out in that?" (I think "that" refers to both our canoe and the crummy weather conditions.) When we tell him we are, he says, "Wait, I have to film this on my cell phone!" Though we are not intending to entertain, we shove off and he stands there filming until the mist swallows up our red boat.

Hopewell is an industrial town that was long an environmental disaster. Pollution from plants here and in Richmond essentially closed the river to swimming and fishing all the way to the bay for many years. Patient implementation of the Clean Water Act, passed in 1972, has been a godsend for the river. When we reach the far shore, it is a low marshy forest that seems on a different planet than the industrial shoreline we just left.

As we head downriver, we approach Benjamin Harrison Bridge, a vertical-lift bridge built across the James in 1966. I say to Mike, "I wonder if they even use the lift anymore?" Almost instantaneously, a foghorn sounds and the center section begins to rise. Cars stop on the bridge to wait. But there's no boat. We think it must be a monthly test to confirm all is in good working order.

Just then—and a little too close for comfort—an oceangoing ship comes out of the fog behind us heading downstream. We paddle furiously to get closer to shore and watch it glide beneath the bridge—moving quickly but not spreading too large a wake. We cruise beneath the fixed section, watching the ship disappear downriver and the center bridge section quietly descend.

We are heading to a lunch stop at the Rice Rivers Center, a multidisciplinary research site operated by Virginia Commonwealth University on land donated by the Rice family, dedicated local philanthropists. We are scheduled to meet with a variety of the researchers from the university and also the US Fish and Wildlife Service to hear about ongoing projects.

We make good time as the rain stops and fog clears and arrive about forty-five minutes ahead of schedule. I put the time to good use looking for a place to stay tonight. We are now in Charles City County and I have been calling local B and Bs in this rural county for the last few days to find a place to stay for the next two nights. I haven't even been able to get anyone to pick up a phone, and the messages I've left have not been returned. Finally, on my fourth call, I hear a pleasant voice greet me. I say that I am canoeing down the river and hope to stay for two nights. The woman on the other end of the line says, "Let me look at the book." I hear pages turning. She tells me that one of her four rooms is taken but the others are available. I notice that her North Bend Plantation is only about ten minutes from where I will finish today and tell her I should arrive by 5:00 p.m.

Now the scientists arrive with box lunches. After a brief walking tour of the center, we sit in a wooden classroom cabin built right over a marsh and talk about what they are working on—sturgeon and shad restoration, the health of migrating prothonotary warblers, how marshes like the one we are looking at contribute to water and air quality. Much of the university work is federally funded and our agencies cooperate well with VCU. I admit to the local Fish and Wildlife chief—who gives us a great report on restoring freshwater mussels at a nearby federal fish hatchery—that Mike and I stepped over the "Refuge

Closed" sign yesterday at Presque Isle to poke around the preserve. She laughs it off.

When we leave after lunch, one of the researchers walks us down to the dock and tells us that there is very little development for the next thirty to forty miles. "You'll be seeing it almost the way John Smith did," he says.

And he's true to his word. We pass by Westover and Berkeley Plantations, impressive plantation homes built in the 1700s, looking much like they did then. I've only visited Berkeley once, and I came in from the nearby Route 5, essentially approaching the back door of the mansion. They were built to be seen from the river and they are striking when viewed from the water. But other than these two historic homes, there is little development as we make our way downriver. We pass Herring Creek and see it snake away through marshes to the north—I need to come back and explore more.

This is all part of the Captain John Smith Chesapeake National Historic Trail, one of the two water trails designated as part of the National Historic Trails network that includes the Appalachian Trail, the Pacific Crest Trail, and so many others. John Smith was the true hero of the early Jamestown settlement, the one with survival skills and street smarts who could always figure a way out of a jam.

Smith lived an amazing life even before he came to Virginia in his midtwenties—fighting as a soldier in Europe. He was captured and sold into slavery there, followed by a daring escape. On the voyage from England in 1607, his headstrong actions got him imprisoned on board for attempted mutiny. But when the settlers arrived and opened a letter they carried from the Virginia Company designating the community's first governing council, all were amazed that Smith was one of the chosen leaders. This likely spared him from hanging.

While at Jamestown, Smith led two expeditions from 1607 to 1609, covering nearly three thousand miles in a thirty-foot boat with a small crew exploring the Chesapeake Bay and its many tributaries, including the James. His detailed observations of the region, interactions with the area's indigenous tribes, and his careful mapmaking gave the English world its first clear description of the Chesapeake watershed. As I maneuver the Lower James, the National Park Service has installed signage and exhibits at public access points to explain aspects of the Smith expeditions.

Smith learned the Algonquin language spoken by area tribes and led the village's interactions with indigenous Virginians. He was famously kidnapped at one point and taken to Werowocomoco on the York River: the headquarters village of Powhatan, the werowance of the Powhatan Confederacy. In his telling, he was at the point of being executed when the chief's young daughter, Pocahontas, rushed to him and saved his life. The accuracy of the story is questioned, but it is clear that his interaction with Powhatan and Pocahontas initiated a period of friendlier relations between the settlers and tribes. Smith was injured in a gunpowder accident in his canoe (important safety tip!) and left Jamestown in 1609, never to return.

Later in life, Smith explored the Northeast, drew the first detailed maps of the region, and gave it the name New England.

As I think about John Smith's three-thousand-mile exploration of the Chesapeake or John Wesley Powell's first descent of the Colorado River, my own Virginia Nature Triathlon seems puny. But might I defend myself? Powell and Smith deserve awe for exploring this alien uncharted terrain. I have explored the "faraway nearby." (I acknowledge Georgia O'Keeffe here—whose beautiful painting *From the Faraway Nearby* has long called to me.) Most people can't go to alien lands. But all have access to the faraway nearby—the deep exploration of places close at hand.

Mike and I reach Lawrence Lewis Jr. Park on the left bank, a delightful riverfront park donated to Charles City County by a local family who my wife knew as she was growing up. Mike will head down the road to William and Mary to have dinner with his college-age daughter, and I head off to North Bend Plantation before meeting my friend Chief Steve Adkins of the Chickahominy Tribe for dinner at a local restaurant.

I find North Bend—an old plantation home built by the Minge family in 1819 and named for a bend in the James River that I will paddle tomorrow—a few miles from the county courthouse. I walk in the front door wearing swim trunks, a T-shirt, and a bucket hat, feeling a little out of place among the heirlooms and dark furniture. I call out and an older woman—maybe in her eighties—comes out from the kitchen. "I'm Ridgely, but everyone calls me Nanny," she says. "And you call me Nanny, too, because when you're here, you can do no wrong."

I apologize for being dressed so raggedy but she waves me off, explaining that many of her guests show up in bicycling clothes due to the nearby Virginia Capital Trail. She shows me to my room, and I shower and change quickly before going to meet Chief Adkins.

Steve is the longtime friend who first educated me about Virginia tribal history and worked hard for years to help the Virginia tribes attain federal recognition. The recognition vote was nearly three years ago and we tour a plot of land on the James River that the tribe has recently purchased. I talk to Steve and other tribal leaders about how the interaction with the Bureau of Indian Affairs, the Indian Health Service, and other federal agencies has proceeded. The process of starting the sovereign-to-sovereign relationship has its bumps.

We head for dinner at Cul's Courthouse Grill, a converted 1870s-era general store owned by Cul and his mother, Bonnie. This is *the* gathering spot in Charles City, a very unique small community of indigenous people, African Americans, and white folks, most of whose families have lived nearby forever. The Virginia Capital Trail has added a new stream of people into the clientele here, and it's always interesting to see the mix of locals and visitors when I am able to visit. Former governor Doug Wilder lives nearby and is such a regular here that he has a sandwich named after him!

The dinner and conversation are relaxed, with Bonnie going table to table beaming with pride at the collection of folks who are here on a Tuesday night in October. There is usually music on weekends and Anne and I love the welcoming vibe.

I depart for North Bend and find Nanny in the kitchen talking to the other two guests staying with her tonight. They are retirees from the Midwest and are on a long driving tour to see a sibling in Virginia. We ask them about their lives and the husband says he had a long career working for the Indian Health Service. Nanny and I ask in unison, "Do you know about our tribes?" He looks surprised at the question, and it's clear that he hasn't heard about the recognized tribes within a few miles of here. Nanny and I both begin to excitedly share all we know about the Chickahominy.

23

I am meeting my friend Tom today. He is one of the neighbors who helped me out when I was burned a few weeks back. It is his seventieth birthday, and we'll canoe from Lawrence Lewis Park to the Chickahominy River, finishing off with a birthday dinner in his honor.

I slept like the dead at North Bend last night and come down early for breakfast. Nanny has made an egg casserole, bacon and sausage, and homemade biscuits. Coffee and fresh fruit are plentiful. Her other guests are sleeping in, and the two of us visit during breakfast.

When I met Nanny yesterday, she often mentioned her husband, George. I wondered if he was out working on the farm but learn this morning that he died fifteen years ago. She moved to North Bend when they married in 1958. They raised four children and have four grandchildren, all living nearby. Nanny tells me she runs North Bend as a B and B "when she wants to," only taking reservations by phone and only answering the phone when she is in the mood for company.

North Bend played an important role in Civil War history. In the Union's Overland Campaign in 1864, the farm—then owned by the Wilcox family—was seized by the Union and this house was occupied by General Philip Sheridan. Union engineers constructed a 2,200-foot pontoon bridge here that they then stretched across the James River. For two days that June, more than 100,000 Union troops, 56,000 horses and mules, 2,800 head of cattle, cannons, food, ammunition, and other equipment crossed south by pontoon bridge and boat to lay siege to the city of Petersburg, a critical rail junction thirty miles south of Richmond. Civil War–era trenches are still visible on the farm, and the house contains fascinating memorabilia of this time. The farm has been on the National Register of Historic Places since 1989.

George's family, who are related to the local Harrison family that produced two presidents, purchased the farm in the early 1900s. During their marriage, he farmed the land and Nanny worked as a nurse practitioner in the area, eventually retiring after many years working at a nearby state mental hospital.

Nanny tells me a powerful story as we linger over coffee. In the year 2000, she was "thirsty" for the word of God. She and George had raised their family in nearby Westover Episcopal Church, which dates back to the 1630s. But she was missing something. One day she prayed, asking God where he wanted her to go.

The next day, she was driving down a local road and saw a sign for nearby Liberty Baptist Church. She had passed it many times before without thinking about it, but that day the sign was adorned with a red banner that read "Praise-and-worship Wednesday nights, all are welcome." She had an immediate feeling that her prayer had been answered.

Nanny came to a Wednesday service and was warmly received. She slowly became a regular at this small African American Baptist congregation—first on Wednesday nights and then on Sundays too. George began worshipping there as well. And soon, in Nanny's words, "God had given us a new family."

In 2002, Nanny conferred with family and invited the Liberty congregation and its pastor, Reverend Johnson, to hold its Sunday service on the lawn at North Bend. At the close of the service, George and Nanny, their four adult children and their spouses, and their grandchildren stood before the congregation and asked them for forgiveness for the sin of slavery practiced on their land and in the Harrison family. (The Minge family that built North Bend enslaved about eighty people there until David Minge took them to Maryland to release them in the 1840s.) Reverend Johnson and the church family granted the forgiveness that had been sincerely sought.

George died a few years later. His funeral service was held at Westover Episcopal, where generations of his family are buried. Reverend Johnson preached the eulogy. Nanny has worshipped at Liberty for more than twenty years now.

I head off to meet Tom with my emotions full at Nanny's story. I didn't just get a bed and a breakfast—I got a powerful inspiration. Tom and I put in at Lewis Park, and as we paddle down the North Bend, we see Bonnie from the Courthouse Grill on her nearby dock with a cup of coffee in hand. I told her last night what I was doing, and she said she would watch for me on the river today. We wave and press on, feeling turbulence in the outgoing tide as it makes a sharp right bend heading downriver.

I tell Tom about Nanny's story and marvel at the way this river trip—indeed, the entire adventure—has been peopled with friends and family I am close to, but also folks I encounter by chance for the first and possibly only time. Tom is a spiritual guy—the first person to tell me about Thich Nhat Hanh—whose notion of a "walking meditation" has inspired me throughout this journey. Tom appreciates Nanny's story.

I am fascinated by Nanny's description of being "thirsty for God" and asking for something, though she knew not what she sought. That something became a banner hanging on a sign she had passed for years; that banner led her to a Wednesday night prayer service; that service led her and George to a new church; that church became a new family; that new family led her own family to seek reconciliation and forgiveness for the slavery once pervasive here and all over Virginia.

As we talk about it, I am struck that most prayers fall into three categories: *please*, *thanks*, and *why*. Nanny was offering a *please* prayer; her willingness to ask for direction *and then listen for an answer* fundamentally altered her life. Listening for guidance amid the rush of life is so important. While I intended this three-year journey to be a celebration of twenty-five years in public life, part of it was also motivated—like Nanny's journey—by a *please* prayer. As I turn sixty, I want fresh inspiration for the next chapters in my life.

Tom and I round the downstream side of North Bend, passing low marshes filled with beautiful cypress trees, and eventually near a place called Sturgeon Point. Even though we are past the peak spawning season, many sturgeon are still here. We saw this yesterday on a computer screen at the Rice Rivers Center, where they track tagged sturgeon in the James. The researchers even renamed two of the fish—commonly given numerical designations—Mikey and Timmy. And we see a few splashes indicating that these magnificent creatures are still active in October.

We stop for lunch at a tiny park—Fort Pocahontas—and sit on a dock watching the tide running strong. The fort was an earthen enclosure built in 1864 by African American troops under the command of General Edward Augustus Wild. In May of that year, 2,500 Confederate troops under the command of General Fitzhugh Lee attacked 1,100 African American Union troops here and were soundly defeated in the Battle of Wilson's Wharf. It was the first combat encounter between Robert E. Lee's Army of Northern Virginia and African American troops. Fitzhugh Lee, Robert E. Lee's nephew, was thought to be in line to replace the recently killed General J. E. B. Stuart and was humiliated by being defeated by the smaller African American force. Stuart was replaced instead by another leader, General Wade Hampton. Lee later led the last cavalry charge of the war near Farmville and served as Virginia's governor from 1886 to 1890.

We still have miles to go to reach the Chickahominy River that enters from the north and forms the boundary between Charles City and James City Counties. And our take-out is a good way up the Chickahominy at a county park. We bear down as the tide goes slack and now starts to push against us.

All along this trip I've dealt with the anticipation of arrival, the belief that our take-out is just around the next bend. And I'm often wrong! We do, however, finally arrive and then head to Indian Fields Tavern, a longtime restaurant in a farmhouse that was itself part of a plantation. We sit outside on a delightful fall evening and toast Tom's seventieth birthday, reminiscing about a camping trip we took ten years ago to celebrate his sixtieth. I started today learning from a new friend and spent the day on the river celebrating an old friend. Is there a better way to spend a day?

24

I'll paddle by myself today. I have breakfast with Nanny, and we're each glad to have a new friend. I tell her, "I never would have met you if you hadn't answered the phone just a few hours before I showed up."

"It was meant to be," she says. Then, as I leave, she adds, "Make the family proud."

I depart, promising to bring Anne back to meet her.

I go back toward Chickahominy Riverfront Park, quite a ways up the Chickahominy River, requiring backtracking to get back on my route. But I see a gated golf-course community right on the point of land where the rivers merge. It has a marina. Maybe I can put in there?

I pull up to the gate and ask permission to put in the canoe and leave a car there for a few hours until I can come retrieve it. No dice.

"The marina is only for residents," the guard says, but as I turn away, he adds, "Wait a minute; aren't you Senator Kaine?" I turn and smile, certain I'll now be granted admission to the marina. "I sure am."

Instead, he asks, "Can I take a selfie with you?" We take a selfie— but still no admission to the marina. Grrr.

I put-in back at the Riverfront Park and paddle for about thirty-five minutes on the Chickahominy to reach the James. Today I will paddle down past the Jamestown-Scotland Ferry and historic Jamestown Island to Kingsmill, a large residential development on the river where a longtime campaign staffer lives with her family. Jenny has promised me a good bed, hot shower, and homemade dinner tonight.

Nanny's work to make sense of the slavery history on her farm makes me think about my journey in a different way. All along the route— from my first steps at Harpers Ferry, to the ruins of freedmen cabins along Brown Mountain Creek, to the once-segregated campgrounds in Shenandoah National Park, to the plaque honoring the enslaved boatman hero Frank Padget, to Manchester Docks in Richmond, to the plantations along the James—the impact of slavery and legally enforced degradation of African Americans has been in plain sight. And I can't help think, *What if slavery as we know it never existed?*

In June of 2020, I made a speech on the Senate floor where I said, "We didn't inherit slavery; we created it." My comment drew much squawking from people who pointed out the global history of slavery and the references to slavery in the Bible. Of course I knew those things. But absolutely nothing compelled slavery here—in Virginia, in America.

The first enslaved people to come to Virginia in August 1619 were captured off a Portuguese slaving ship by English pirates aboard *The White Lion* and were later dropped off at Fort Monroe along with other items seized in that raid. The Virginia settlers inventoried and paid for what they received, including "twenty and odd" Africans.

From the moment these "twenty and odd" human beings arrived in Virginia, they were question marks. Because they were taken away from their homes against their will, while in transit, they were enslaved. But on Virginia soil in 1619, there was no such thing as slavery. No English statute allowed slavery. English common law did not allow slavery. The charter granted to the Virginia Company made no mention of slavery. The Virginia legislature was formed the same year the first enslaved people arrived and did not pass any law even referencing slavery until 1659. What was their status in Virginia?

English law *did* allow indentured servitude. Someone could be brought to Virginia and, over a period of years, work off the cost of passage and then be freed. More than 50 percent of the Europeans who came to the English Colonies before the Revolutionary War came as indentured servants. By 1619, many white indentured servants lived here, hoping to work off the cost of passage and then begin life free in the New World. There is evidence that many of the first Africans in Virginia were treated as indentured servants in accord with English law. While they didn't volunteer like their white brethren, their passage had been paid by the settlers who bought the contents of *The White Lion*. Many did work for a period of years and then gained freedom, marrying, having children, owning land.

But subtly and slowly, the founders of this country created an American institution of slavery that had not previously existed in English law. Wills might pass African indentured servants as property, but not white indentured servants. Criminal punishments against servants attempting escape started to show a race differential—white servants would have their indenture extended by a few years, while African servants would have their indenture converted into a lifetime status.

Slowly, the conversion of the status of Africans and their descendants from servants to enslaved people began to be formalized in statute. Massachusetts was the first colony to legally allow and protect slavery in 1641.

It's unrealistic to expect that the English settlers in 1619 would have treated the "twenty and odd" Africans in accord with today's notions of equality. That's not my "what if" question.

But what if the English founders of our country had simply followed English law of the day? What if they never created the legal institution of slavery? What if they had treated Africans as indentured servants, able to earn their freedom after a period of years? What if they had allowed children born to Africans on Virginia soil to be free, rather than assign them—and their successors for all eternity—the status of "slave"?

There was nothing rosy about indentured servitude, and it was eventually outlawed by the same Thirteenth Amendment that banned slavery. But you could generally find a home, live where you wanted, save money, marry, own property, form a family that couldn't be disrupted at someone else's whim. All these were open to you so long as the work got done. Also, you were not subject to beatings or rapes with no legal consequence. Most importantly, you knew you would be free one day with the ability to build wealth and pass it down to your children.

If Virginia's founders had just treated the first Africans in accord with the English law of the day, the new nation would have seen the robust growth of a free African American population—intact families, land and business ownership, infinitely fewer scars from the whip, infinitely fewer rapes of captive African women. Citizenship to all born here. And with no slavery, no Civil War.

American slavery was not a "necessary evil," as some claim. It was an intentional choice and required a perversion of the existing English law that settlers brought to Jamestown.

It is a particularly haunting fact that a key driver in the formalization of American slavery was the question of how to treat children. An adult was one thing. But the early Virginians had to decide how to treat the newborn children of Africans—free, indentured, enslaved? And they were confronted with another commonly occurring question: how to treat the children of African women who had been raped by the English men who enslaved them.

I break from this reflection as I approach the Jamestown-Scotland Ferry, a large ferry taking vehicles back and forth across the wide James just upstream of Jamestown Island. A bridge extends from the shore into the river until the water is deep enough for the ferry to pull up to the large dock. The bridge looks very low. Can I paddle under it, or do I need to paddle out into the channel and dodge the ferries going back and forth?

I get closer and closer to the bridge and see vehicles parked on it, waiting for the ferry, wondering what the hell I am doing. It will be a very tight fit. I paddle hard twice and then lean forward as flat as I can on the boat, scraping through with inches to spare.

Downstream from the bridge, I first reach Jamestown Settlement, a state-run re-creation of the first English settlement with extensive programming about the lives of the settlers, local indigenous people, and Africans who were there. And then immediately adjacent is Historic Jamestown in the Colonial National Historical Park, the well-preserved actual site of that first settlement, still undergoing ongoing archaeological exploration. I have been to both sites many times—to learn and also to officiate at the state's official commemoration of the four-hundredth anniversary of settlement when I was governor in 2007.

But I've never seen these sites from the water. It is different to approach them in a canoe on the river, as so many did for so long. Tourists at each site look at me with curiosity—other than the massive ferry crossing there are no boats out today. The views from the water make plain the growing danger that sea level rise poses to the existence of the island on which the archaeological site lies. Some estimates suggest it will be entirely underwater by the end of the twenty-first century.

The settlers who established a first English community here at Jamestown also began a legislative body, the General Assembly, in 1619. Because the English Parliament was disbanded by Oliver Cromwell in 1653, Virginia claims its House of Delegates as the oldest continuously operating legislative body in the western hemisphere. And the assembly grappled with a case here in 1656 that demonstrates the degree to which slavery was still a fluid status in formation nearly forty years after the arrival of the first Africans.

Elizabeth Key was born in 1630 to an African mother just down-river from here. I knew nothing about her until I began planning my river journey. Her father was Thomas Key, a wealthy planter and member of the assembly. Key was married and denied paternity of Elizabeth, but a lawsuit in 1636 concluded that he was Elizabeth's father. He then arranged for Elizabeth to be baptized, provided her financial support, and placed her with another planter, Humphrey Higginson, in a nine-year indenture. (These seemingly "responsible" actions separated the six-year-old Elizabeth from her mother, likely for the remainder of her life.) Under the indenture terms, she would be freed when she turned fifteen.

Higginson transferred Elizabeth's indenture to John Mottram, who moved his family to then undeveloped Northumberland County, about fifty miles north of Jamestown. Many years later, Key was still working for Mottram and had never been freed. A sixteen-year-old indentured servant who may have had rudimentary legal training, William Grinstead, arrived from England to serve a period of years with the Mottram family. He began a relationship with Elizabeth, and they had a son. But they couldn't marry—both because of questions about her status and the terms of his indenture.

Mottram died in 1655, and his administrator classified Elizabeth and her son as property of the estate. Grinstead filed a freedom suit arguing that she and their child should be freed by contract (she had worked past her indenture), status (she was the daughter of a free Englishman who thus inherited his status at birth), and faith (she had been baptized a Christian). Elizabeth won her case in the trial court but lost it in a higher court that ruled her enslaved because of her mother's race. The case was appealed to the assembly and eventually resolved in Elizabeth's favor on the original grounds. She and her son were freed and Mottram's estate was ordered to reimburse her for holding her past her contracted indenture. Once Grinstead completed his indenture, he and Elizabeth married, had another child, and purchased land together. Theirs might have been one of the first recorded marriages in English America between an Englishman and a woman of African descent.

How had I never known about Elizabeth Key until this trip? Her story contains multitudes and sums up so much about the origins of our nation: slavery and freedom, cruelty and love, power and powerlessness, family separation and family formation, laws, lawyers, legislators, courts.

The aftermath of the story is illuminating and tragic. The Virginia General Assembly began passing laws to "fix" the legal ambiguities revealed by the Key case and other freedom suits. They authorized slavery for the first time. They clarified that baptism as a Christian provided no path out of slavery. Virginia became the first American colony to ban marriage between white and Black persons, regardless of their status.

In a particularly cruel twist, the assembly acted in 1662 to overturn longstanding English law by establishing that a child born in Virginia inherited the status of their mother, not that of their father. This consigned all children born to enslaved mothers to perpetual slavery, regardless of paternity or proportion of European ancestry.

And it accomplished another goal—freeing white fathers from acknowledging those children as theirs, relieving them of the burden of providing financial support that was previously required by English law. The new law was basically a license for white men to have sex with enslaved women and avoid legal consequences. And if this sex led to childbirth, even better in their minds; they would have more enslaved people to work or sell. Other states followed these Virginia statutory "innovations," and American slavery hardened from a nascent and evolving status into an ironclad prison for millions lasting another two centuries.

I reach the eastern end of Jamestown Island, an undeveloped stretch of beach and marsh far from park amenities and tourists. I pull my boat out of the water and sit on a driftwood log. It is pristine, quiet, and I see little development. The water gently lapping at the sand, the current rolling by, the wide tidal channel with forests on the distant shore—this place doesn't look so different than it must have looked four hundred years ago. Elizabeth Key almost certainly passed this place. I think about Elizabeth and my new friend Nanny and feel some connection between them—one fighting for her freedom from slavery and the other fighting for a different freedom, a spiritual liberation that comes from seeking reconciliation and receiving forgiveness. I encountered both women on this journey and don't believe that's an accident.

I enjoy this tranquil place but wonder whether future generations will be able to sit and enjoy it or whether rising sea levels will deprive them of the opportunity. I gaze across the water and think of the old spiritual "Deep River," a seemingly simple song about life and death, Earth and heaven, home and exile, also with a coded reference to captivity and freedom:

> *Deep river, my home is over Jordan.*
> *Deep river, Lord, I want to cross over into campground.*
> *Oh don't you want to go to that gospel feast?*
> *That promised land where all is peace?*

I take a picture and send it to my dad—today is his eighty-seventh birthday. I cast off downriver and reach the Kingsmill community in the midafternoon. Jenny and her family greet me, and I see that she has bought me a dress shirt. Why? My staff has decided that I need to do television interviews later today and tomorrow morning about some political crisis du jour. Jenny's family loves boating on the James, and I entertain them with stories of my trip. They laugh particularly hard when I tell them about being turned away at the marina this morning.

25

I have a long day today—more than twenty miles paddling solo from Kingsmill past Fort Eustis, a large Army base on the north bank, and into Newport News, one of the cities in metropolitan Hampton Roads that marks the end of the river. The river is miles wide here but I am blessed with near perfect weather, outgoing tide, sunny and seventy degrees and no wind. The water is like glass as I depart early in the morning.

As I paddle, I begin to see the Navy ghost fleet anchored in the middle of the James. This is a fleet of decommissioned Navy ships awaiting sale or salvage. When I was governor, the fleet was nearly one hundred ships but over the years it has been whittled down to fewer than ten. I did reach out to base security at Fort Eustis yesterday to let them know I would be paddling by. I didn't want anyone suspecting a lone canoeist to be some threatening kook. They told me they would watch for me and alerted me that there might be some "special forces" training going on at the ghost fleet. Sure enough, as I get closer, I can see helicopters around the ships with SEALs dropping into the water nearby. I keep my distance.

The base security boat comes up on my left quickly, slowing down to avoid any wake that would swamp a member of the Senate Armed Services Committee. I talk to the crew for a bit as they drift near me and they are impressed that I've made it this far. Probably even more impressed that I've done the trip in this sixteen-foot canoe. While I saw many canoes on the Upper James, I haven't seen a single other canoe in the water since I hit the tidal section in Richmond. Powerboats, barges, ships, Jet Skis, and a few sea kayaks. But a canoe is rare in this big water.

Canoes have been developed and used all over the world. The design is pretty consistent—a narrow boat pointed at both ends and open on top. One or more paddlers, either seated or kneeling, face the direction of travel and use a single-blade paddle to propel the boat. Some are outfitted so that they can use small motors or even sail power. But the primary engine is human energy and a simple paddle.

The word *canoe* comes from the word *canoa*, a term adopted by the Portuguese and Spanish from a Caribbean Arawak word (*kanawa*) for a boat commonly used there. Canoes from as early as 8000 BC have been found in archaeological excavations. And they were in early use all over the world—Europe, Africa, South America and the Caribbean, Canada, the Pacific Northwest. A common style was a dugout canoe—a hollowed-out tree trunk much used by indigenous people in the Chesapeake region. Lighter canoes were made by stretching bark from birch trees over a light wooden frame.

Modern canoe design is simple and elegant. I have become a master at getting my plastic composite boat on and off the roof rack of my car, often by myself, because there's a yoke strategically placed in the eighty-pound canoe that enables me to tote it perfectly balanced over my head. And, on days like today, when I am paddling by myself, the boat design allows me to flip the boat backward and paddle from the front seat.

I paddle south for nearly three hours toward the point of land where the river wraps around Fort Eustis and orients to the east. When I round the point, the sight is magical. I am still many miles from my destination, but now I can see the towering cranes at the Newport News shipyard glinting in the sun. I feel like Dorothy glimpsing the spires of the Emerald City after her long journey to see the Wizard of Oz. And, as if on cue, I begin seeing dolphins surface ahead of me, playing in the calm water. They are pretty common in the Chesapeake Bay, but I am still nearly twenty-five miles from the bay and I've never seen them this far upriver. I keep trying to get close enough to get a good picture but they stay about one hundred yards ahead of my boat as if beckoning me onward.

I still have a long paddle to clear Fort Eustis but the sight of the city motivates me. I decide to skip lunch and just keep paddling as I begin seeing the western neighborhoods of Newport News along the riverbank. And I now keep my eyes out for friends who will join me to make sure I don't mess things up in the last day and a half.

Frank and Mark are neighbors in Richmond who both spend time in Virginia Beach, Virginia's largest city, where the Chesapeake Bay enters the Atlantic. Frank owns Richmond's premier foreign-auto repair shop and Mark is a lawyer who was my chief counsel when I was governor. They both love fishing and were more than a little skeptical when they heard that I was going to try to reach Fort Monroe in a canoe. So they gathered with the other guardian-angel neighbors one night a few weeks ago on my back porch, spread out a detailed navigation map, and helped me figure the most likely route. And—good friends that they are—they declared themselves up for an expedition, volunteering to accompany me in Frank's Boston Whaler as I negotiate the the big water near the shipyard and into the bay.

I send them periodic texts about where I am and soon see them pulling close. I still have about seven miles of paddling to reach a marina where we will dock for the night before the finishing stretch tomorrow. Mark hops in the canoe and we paddle downriver together with Frank tailing us a few hundred yards away. Mark is still very connected to state politics and we kibitz about local and state elections coming up in a few weeks. Frank pulls up on occasion to tell us our land speed, and our slowing pace makes it clear that the tide is now switching against us.

We are paddling toward the James River Bridge, a nearly five-mile-long crossing from Newport News south to Isle of Wight County. When first built in 1928, it was the longest bridge in the world. It was replaced in 1982 and has a center lift section like the Benjamin Harrison Bridge we passed a few days back. The marina is just at the downstream foot of the bridge. We finally arrive after a long haul. Now I notice that Frank has borrowed a two-person sea kayak from a friend and strapped it onto the front of his boat just in case I need it on the last day.

We head across the road to the Crab Shack on the James, one of my favorite restaurants in Virginia, built right on the river and known for crab cakes and peel-and-eat shrimp. We enjoy a great meal and check into a nearby hotel. My son Nat is driving down from DC tonight to join me for the last day. The weather report does not look good. I push that out of my mind and relish the thought of finishing up the journey with family and friends tomorrow.

26

I wake before dawn on October 16. Today is the anniversary of the John Brown attack on Harpers Ferry in 1859. I began my Virginia Nature Triathlon on the Bloody Stone Steps in Harpers Ferry nearly thirty months ago. John Brown tried to ignite the spark that would destroy slavery there. Today, I hope to reach the place where enslaved people were first brought into our Commonwealth and country. It is also a place that became pivotal in the destruction of American slavery.

Nat arrived late last night. He transitioned from active-duty Marine officer to reservist about a year ago and now has a challenging day job with the Department of Homeland Security. He is a superb whitewater kayaker and has also done basic ocean sailing and boating during his ROTC days. Having him in the boat today gives me confidence.

The route is straightforward. It is about five miles from the James River Bridge southeast to the Monitor-Merrimack Memorial Bridge-Tunnel. During most of this stretch, we will pass the massive Newport News shipyard where nuclear submarines and aircraft carriers are built and maintained. Just before the MMMBT, we also pass the Port of Virginia facility that loads coal mined in Appalachia onto oceangoing ships. The massive scale differential between our boat and the ones at the shipyard and port is head-spinning.

Once we paddle through the cut where the tunnel drops below the river, we turn northeast for a seven-mile paddle to Fort Monroe. The main Port of Virginia container loading facility and the Norfolk Naval Shipyard, the largest US Navy base in the world, will be on our right during this closing stretch, the city of Hampton on our left. We will finish by paddling through the cut in the Hampton Roads Bridge Tunnel and find our way to a small beach next to the marina at the fort.

Twelve miles sounds simple enough. But the water is big and the ships are bigger. As we leave the hotel, it is clear that the weather is not friendly. The wind is picking up, and—great—we see that a small craft advisory has been issued for the James River and Chesapeake Bay today. We are definitely a "small craft."

As we arrive at the marina, a Virginia Marine Police officer is exiting his car to board his boat and patrol the river. He looks at us, starting to take the canoe off the car, and says, "You're going out in that?" The guy in Hopewell who said it a few days ago seemed amazed but this law enforcement officer seems truly worried. I tell him I've come down the entire river and this is the last day to finish. He sees our determination, pauses, and tells us what radio channel he'll be on "when you need me." He is somewhat relieved to hear that Mark and Frank will be nearby in the Boston Whaler, even though it also qualifies as a "small craft."

The marina is a set of docks sheltered by a stone enclosure that keeps wave action down where the boats are moored. Nat and I make a game-time call to skip Old Raggedy today and use the borrowed sea kayak. It is a molded plastic boat with low sides and holes in the hull to drain water. Two padded seat backs attach to the boat and we both use double-bladed paddles. We each put on our life jackets, grab a water bottle, and push off.

As we exit the stone enclosure into open water, my first thought is, *There's no way we can do this*. The wind is blowing hard from the southeast, right in our faces. The water is choppy and irregular. Even the sound of the wind and waves is intimidating. But Nat sits right in front of me, power paddling forward with no apparent concern.

After about eight hundred yards, I see why everyone suggested I use a sea kayak in the lower river. It sits low in the water and hardly has any sides to speak of—more like paddling a large heavy surfboard. Because the center of gravity is low, it's hard to tip and very easy to steer. Thank goodness it's not a cold day. The kayak is unsinkable. Unlike a canoe, it doesn't take on water—water washes over the boat and drains immediately through the holes in the hull. If you do flip— and we sure might—it can be easily flipped back upright in seconds.

As we head toward the MMMBT, we see massive subs and carriers in the shipyard to our left. I alerted shipyard security yesterday to watch for us, and we see a boat patrolling nearby, aware of us but not coming close. Mark and Frank maneuver a few hundred yards away, and watching their fishing boat rock up and down makes clear that this is no pleasure cruise for any of us.

Even in an outgoing tide, it takes us more than two hours to paddle the five miles to the MMMBT. This structure, opened in 1992, is a 4.6-mile-long bridge over the James, with a center section where the road drops down into a tunnel to allow ships easy passage through a main channel. The only benefit of being out in the water on such a windy day is that there is no boat traffic at all. We needn't worry about having to maneuver around ships and barges.

The bridge is named after the two ironclad ships that skirmished near here during the Battle of Hampton Roads in May 1862. The Confederate Navy seized a Union shipyard in Norfolk at the start of the war and turned a partially destroyed wooden ship, the USS *Merrimack*, into an armor-coated hulk called the CSS *Virginia*. The Union accepted an odd design from a Swedish-American engineer and built the USS *Monitor*, essentially a revolving armored gun turret sitting on a flat deck barely out of the water. After a first day in which the *Virginia* wreaked havoc on Union wooden ships, the *Monitor* appeared on day two and the two ironclads fought to an essential draw. But the battle changed the future of shipbuilding—wooden ships were out for war fighting, and armored ships became the new standard.

Nat and I notice the turreted office structures built on each side of the tunnel. We've driven through it many times. But from the water, the structures have the appearance of two ironclads facing each other. You notice things from the water that you don't see on land.

As we come through the cut and turn north toward Fort Monroe, the wind is mostly now at our backs instead of blowing in our faces. We can see the multistory Hotel Chamberlin in the distance dead ahead, a historic hotel (now a senior apartment building) adjacent to Fort Monroe and an obvious landmark to steer us home. The wind picks up, but now the clouds blow out and sun shines around us. We are soaked, and my stinging eyes let me know that it's all salt water now.

This stretch of water, where the James, Elizabeth, and Nansemond Rivers all come together, is called Hampton Roads. The term *roads* is an old English phrase, short for "roadsted"—meaning a body of water sheltered from rip currents, spring tides, or ocean swells. It is one of the largest natural harbors in the world. It's about four miles wide and enters the Chesapeake Bay between Fort Monroe, on the left bank, and Sewell's Point, on the right bank.

With wind and tide at our back, we really cruise now, and it almost feels like we are surfing the last miles. The wave action is very irregular and we nearly flip over a couple of times. But Nat knows how to do a high brace from his whitewater kayaking and keeps us upright. Mark and Frank pull near and tell us that our land speed has more than doubled after the turn. (They also point out that Nat seems to be doing most of the paddling!) They snap pictures of us with massive warships in the background.

We make the last seven miles in about ninety minutes. As we near Fort Monroe, we start to see sailboats coming out of the marina— the start of a midday Saturday regatta. They are leaning heavy into the wind and some come very near us, having a hard time steering precisely in the southeaster. Nat and I maneuver through the cut in the Hampton Roads Bridge-Tunnel and turn into a protected harbor at the fort, dodging sailboats still maneuvering out into Hampton Roads. And then we see the small sand beach that will mark the end of our trip.

Old Point Comfort is a bit of land jutting into the water that marks the entrance into Chesapeake Bay. The English stopped here in 1607 as they arrived in Virginia before proceeding forty miles upstream to settle in Jamestown, thought to be safer there from the Spanish navy. But the strategic location of the point meant that it was occupied and used as a fort to protect the entrance to Hampton Roads. The English built Fort Algernourne and then Fort George on this spot, and the fort was greatly enlarged by the US military and renamed Fort Monroe in 1834. A young West Point graduate and engineer, Robert E. Lee, helped with final phases of construction of the massive fortification. It is a six-sided stone fort surrounded by a moat, the largest of its kind ever built in North America.

So much has happened here. The "twenty and odd" Africans whose arrival paved the way for American slavery and were sold to English settlers here in 1619. But just as the beginnings of American slavery are connected to this place, so was the destruction of the tragic institution.

Fort Monroe was held by the Union throughout the Civil War, facing across the water to the southern side of Hampton Roads under Confederate control. In May 1861, barely a month after the first shots at Fort Sumter, three enslaved workers—Frank Baker, James Townsend, and Sheppard Mallory—who had been "leased" by those who enslaved them to help construct Confederate fortifications at Sewell's Point rowed a skiff over at night and sought asylum at Fort Monroe. The base commander, General Benjamin Butler, allowed them to stay, rejecting requests from his opposing Confederate general that the enslaved men be returned. He made them work, referred to them as "slaves," and paid them no wages until September, when Navy Secretary Gideon Welles dictated that these "persons of color, commonly known as contrabands," should be paid a salary and food ration for their work. This led more and more enslaved people to escape and seek refuge with Union soldiers.

Word spread throughout the South and estimates are that more than ten thousand enslaved people began their path to freedom as "contrabands," still eighteen months before the Emancipation Proclamation was issued. Many of the self-emancipated men joined the Union Army. By war's end, more than 10 percent of those who had served in Union uniform were African American.

After the war, Jefferson Davis was imprisoned at Fort Monroe for two years. And the Grand Contraband Camp that had grown up near the fort became a community that, together with the American Missionary Association, helped birth Hampton University.

The fort was in use by the US Army until 2005, when it was closed as an active-duty military post and deeded back to the Commonwealth of Virginia. I was governor then and worked with local officials to develop a plan to reclaim it to community use. I urged President Obama to designate the historic fort as a national monument and he did so on November 1, 2011. The extensive military housing on and around the fort was renovated under the direction of the Fort Monroe Authority and is fully occupied. Commercial operations like the marina, The Chamberlin, restaurants, and microbreweries serve area residents. Miles of beach and walking trails are now accessible to all.

I interrupted my AT hike in August 2019 to visit this place and participate in the federal commemoration of four hundred years of African presence in the English colonies that became the United States.

I have asked the head of the Fort Monroe Authority to meet our intrepid foursome today for a brief tour. Glenn was an area legislator who accepted the leadership role in the Authority when he finished his time in public office. He has the zeal of a missionary about this place and stands waiting for us on the beach as Nat and I arrive, trailed by Mark and Frank, who pull past to dock at the marina. Glenn and staff from the authority and National Park Service will show us the recently discovered site of the original Fort George, discuss the potential reno-vation of the Old Point Comfort Lighthouse, and describe the African Landing Memorial that will be built to the Africans who arrived in 1619 and all who followed them. This powerful site is still not known to enough people.

We paddle the kayak onto the beach and Nat steps out. I am in the back of the boat and ready to make a triumphant exit, paddle aloft, to celebrate the end of my 1,200-plus-mile journey. I step into the knee-deep water. The hours of fighting choppy waves have completely knocked out my sense of balance and I collapse backward into the harbor. I try again to stand, falling back once more. Glenn laughs from shore, capturing it all on video.

In a few minutes, I will change into dry clothes, take the tour with Glenn, thank my friends for providing a support boat (and kayak) at the end of my journey, and drive home with Nat to tell Anne all about it. But I've just completed my river sojourn, finishing up in a wild storm. This is the first time I've gone into the water involuntarily the entire trip! I started my Virginia Nature Triathlon soaked by spring rain at Harpers Ferry and end up soaking in saltwater at the end. I stop thinking about the things I have to do next and just float on my back, looking up at the blue sky.

AFTERMATH

Less than two weeks after I finish my river trip, I get a text from Anne to call her ASAP. I exit a staff meeting and call to find out that her father, Linwood, has died. We celebrated his ninety-eighth birthday together last month. Neither of us has lost a parent before. Lin's death was peaceful, thank God.

As the child living closest to her parents, Anne is swept up with organizing memorial services, working with her siblings to convince her mom to move into a nearby assisted-living unit, worrying about the endless details of estate administration, and cleaning out her folks' house. The family agrees to have memorial services right before Christmas so all can come back home to celebrate Lin's life and then spend the holiday in Virginia.

Lin was my political hero because of his courage in integrating Virginia schools at a time when the powers that be were fighting so hard against racial equity. He was a most unusual man for his era and his public service example, together with his wife's own advocacy for good, have left a strong mark on Anne and her siblings, and also on the ten Holton grandchildren. His morning wake-up call of "It's opportunity time!" still motivates this extraordinary family.

A few days after Lin dies, Virginians go to the polls and narrowly elect a Republican governor, also flipping control of one Virginia House from Democratic back to Republican. It wasn't my preferred outcome, but it reminds me of Lin's political mission to make sure that Virginia had competitive two-party politics after decades of single party rule. That seems safely guaranteed into the future.

In mid-November, as we near our thirty-seventh wedding anniversary, I arrange a weekend away for the two of us in the mountains of Western Virginia. Anne is juggling a lot and deserves a break. So we book two nights at a beautiful inn in Clifton Forge and drive there on a perfect Friday afternoon. It is the very last gasp of fall warmth, and temperatures will drop steadily over the next few days.

We do have one task for the weekend—finishing the James River. When we started our trip in May—Anne and I together with Annella and Fern—we put in at the first public access point on the James. But that access point was seven-tenths of a mile downstream of the point where the Jackson and Cowpasture Rivers come together to form the James River in the town of Iron Gate. The actual confluence is inaccessible, on private land with no road access. I want to do that stretch today to truly say that I completed the whole river. And since I started the river with Anne, I want to finish the journey with her too.

I look carefully at the maps of the area and see that there is a public access put-in on the Cowpasture River a few miles upstream from the confluence. I'm a little surprised that I hadn't noticed it before. So Anne and I pull our car into the tiny parking lot there and unload Old Raggedy. No one else is on the water. The daylight hours are dwindling. A late-afternoon sun sparkles on the river.

Our trip is just a little over two miles on the Cowpasture and then the short bit on the James to reach the place where we started nearly six months ago. In the quiet of the trip, punctuated by some minor rapids, we talk about Anne's dad and his legacy, both within the family and across Virginia. In the rush of things to do since his death two weeks ago, it's been hard to step back and just reflect. This afternoon on the river, and the downtime for the rest of the weekend, gives us the chance to do that.

We reach the spot where the crystal-clear waters of the Cowpasture merge with the dark waters of the Jackson River, stained by effluent from the paper plant fifteen miles upstream. This is where the James River begins. The demarcation between the different-colored streams is clearly visible hundreds of yards downstream. We arrive at our take-out spot after one last tricky rapid, pull the canoe ashore, and commence a walk back along country roads so we can retrieve our car.

Finishing our trip at the beginning of the James reminds me of the unbroken circle of a river—continually running to the sea and continually replenished at its origin.

Anne's family gathers for Lin's funeral services in December. There is a small, private service in an Episcopal church near the Chesapeake Bay where Lin and Jinks lived. And the next day, there is a larger service at a Presbyterian Church in Richmond that the family attended when Anne's dad was governor. Every living Virginia governor is present—from Governor Wilder, the grandson of enslaved people and now the senior member of our small club at age ninety, to Governor-Elect Youngkin who is still a month away from inauguration. Lin's favorite scripture—the story of the Good Samaritan—is the gospel reading. Anne's brothers, Dwight and Woody, give powerful tributes, and there are also heartfelt messages from ministers, civil right leaders, and journalists who discuss Lin's legacy. We sing a beautiful Carter Family song about life, death, and family—a favorite from Lin's Appalachian region. Anne's ninety-six-year-old mom is a trooper—kindly welcoming all even though she's a little confused by the loss of her husband and the throng of well-wishers.

The family collects at our Richmond home to mourn and celebrate together. They have come from around the country and world, from as far away as Alaska and Germany—kids, in-laws, grandchildren, nieces, nephews, Lin's sole remaining sister. My own parents have traveled from Kansas City to be here with us. We huddle around the firepit in our backyard telling stories and playing music—daughter Annella on mandolin, son Woody on guitar, cousin Roger on guitar, cousin Billy on violin, me on harmonica. At some point we realize that it's the largest gathering of Anne's family since all came to Richmond sixteen years ago when I was inaugurated governor. Many were together fifty-two years ago when Lin was inaugurated governor. As I look at the illuminated faces around the fire, I think of the song we sang a few hours ago at Lin's service—"Will the Circle Be Unbroken," about seeing loved ones again—and find myself asking that same question.

At peace amidst the loss, I think: *Yes. Undoubtedly, yes.*

EPILOGUE
2022

When I began thinking about this journey in 2018, I didn't know that, over its course, I would live through a global pandemic, my own COVID and long COVID experiences, a global economic shock, a violent attack on the Capitol and our democracy, two impeachment trials forced by shocking presidential misbehavior, and a dramatic set of actions and reactions to America's continuing struggles with racism. The journey, as I conceived it, was fundamentally about celebrating the *past*—my twenty-five years in public life—and finding motivation for the *future*. I now see that the trip was equally about the *present*.

Never before in my life could I have taken the journey that I took during this season of my life. Work, children, campaigns, and so much else would have made this impossible until now. And never before in my life had I needed a journey like this as much as now. Never before in my life had the challenges of the present posed such a threat to my lifelong assumptions about our country.

When I started this journey, I didn't know that I needed emotional and spiritual refuge in the tumult of the day; that I needed to find in the timeless cycles of nature an antidote to the daily news cycles of politics; that I needed to connect to a deeper sense of our nation's beauty to counter my sadness over its recently polarized ugliness; that

I needed to look anew at the relationships that really matter to me and devote more time to them; that I needed to be out among Virginians in an approachable and unscheduled way, not insulated by staff or the formalities of the office I hold; that I needed to think about the arc of my own life and realize emotionally what I've always known intellectually—that a title is temporary and public office is a wonderful chapter of my life, but not my life itself; that I needed to root my daily life in things that last.

When he was nearing eighty, English philosopher Bertrand Russell wrote the essay "How to Grow Old." A friend hearing of my trip shared it with me a few weeks after I pulled ashore at Fort Monroe:

> Make your interests gradually wider and more impersonal, until bit by bit the walls of ego recede, and your life becomes increasingly merged in the universal life. An individual human existence should be like a river—small at first, narrowly contained within its banks, and rushing passionately past rocks and waterfalls. Gradually, the river grows wider, the banks recede, the waters flow more quietly, and in the end, without any visible break, they become merged in the sea and painlessly lose their individual being. . . . The man who can, in old age, see his life in this way, will not suffer from fear of death, since the things he cares for will continue. And if, with decrease in vitality, weariness increases, the thought of rest will not be unwelcome. I should wish to die while still at work, knowing that others will carry on what I can no longer do and content in the thought that what was possible has been done.

Letting go of ego and seeing your own efforts as "merged in the universal life," connected to the work of others, and carried on by others, is something to aspire to. I began the journey wanting to find motivation for continuing my public service. I've found multiple reasons to keep serving others. Indeed, the chaotic events of the last several years have increased my awareness of the urgent stakes involved. But—just as important, especially for this particularly challenging time—I've also embraced a sense of satisfaction in what I've been able to do and accepted the inevitability, indeed desirability, of one day passing the work on to others. It will pass on unfinished, as it must. The work of caring for others is never finished.

The year 2022 starts with an unforgettable, slightly scary, and ultimately comical event. I leave Richmond to drive to DC on January 3 for a meeting on voting-rights legislation. A light snow and road signs urging caution warn me to be alert but don't discourage someone used to driving in snow. But soon, the snow turns to ice and a series of mishaps leads thousands of us to be stuck on I-95 overnight with temperatures in the mid-teens.

The trip to DC—normally two hours—takes twenty-seven hours. Thank God my Nature Triathlon has conditioned my body to survive—I get by with a Dr Pepper and one orange. The latter is a gift from a family returning from a Florida vacation; they offer their holiday oranges to stranded folks on the highway.

To keep from running out of gas during multiple-hour standstills, I run the engine and heater for ten minutes at a time and then hunker down in my coat for an hour or more until it gets too cold. I finally make it to an open gas station as the traffic moves from a dead stop to a crawl.

When I at last arrive in DC, I am surrounded by press who have followed my travails via social media put out by my staff. The resulting attention—more than I get for legislative accomplishments—says something about the state of American politics. More than one of my colleagues expresses wonder that I didn't pull senatorial rank to get help while I was stuck.

We pass one year of the Biden administration. I am proud of the good we have done—enacting a comprehensive COVID-relief bill by a single vote and passing the nation's largest infrastructure bill in a generation. I appear at an event on the banks of the James River in Richmond with federal officials to talk about using the infrastructure investment to make the river even cleaner. And I help pass meaningful legislation to provide mental health services to our frontline health professionals.

We finally resolve Democratic divisions to pass the Inflation Reduction Act by a single vote, advancing a clean-energy economy and providing health care protections, particularly for seniors on Medicare and coal miners, many in Virginia, afflicted by black lung disease. We find bipartisan accords on gun safety, protecting veterans and investing in research and American manufacturing.

The Monacan Tribe receives good news—the plan to build a water intake facility on the Rassawek site where John and I stopped months ago is scrapped and the community commits to a different site that will not interfere with their ancestral home. The Chickahominy Tribe works with Virginia to purchase a site sacred to them on the Chickahominy River, a few miles upstream from where it enters the James. The federal recognition of tribes that we worked on for so many years has elevated respect for these first Virginians and opened up new possibilities for them.

In a sobering parallel, the National Trust for Historic Preservation that helped advocate for saving Rassawek places Jamestown Island on its 2022 list as one of America's most endangered sites. Will we succeed in saving Jamestown from sea level rise as we helped save Rassawek from development?

The Senate confirms Ketanji Brown Jackson as the newest Supreme Court justice. When I started law school, the only woman justice at the Supreme Court was a white marble statue on the steps outside the building. Now, four of the nine justices are women. That this has happened in the course of my legal career is powerful.

My Virginia Nature Triathlon pushes me to be more active in efforts to protect public lands and celebrate Virginia's remarkable history. I introduce two bills to establish wilderness areas in the George Washington and Jefferson National Forests in Western Virginia and two bills to establish heritage areas on the Northern Neck of Virginia and around the Great Dismal Swamp. I begin work with Maryland senators to consider establishing a national recreation area encompassing the many historic sites surrounding the Chesapeake Bay. My staff and I also convene stakeholders to form a national trails bill that will commemorate the centennial of the AT.

And we pass a most important civil rights statute guaranteeing marriage equality. That I'm here to cosponsor this bill is a sweet feeling, making up for the many days in the Senate when progress seems painfully slow.

The run of achievements beginning in late 2021 with the passage of the infrastructure bill helps lift my own mood about the Senate and the state of the country. The first two years of the Biden administration have shown real legislative momentum. I feel a sense of pride about being here at this moment, playing a meaningful role in major accomplishments.

All my leadership experiences—mayor, governor, and senator—have occurred during times of crisis. I don't get the reins during smooth times. Fighting crime and disinvestment, governing during economic downturn and gun violence tragedies, legislating during a pandemic and political turmoil—these have been my local, state, and federal assignments. But in the ups and downs of this journey, I start to see that as my unique strength. I can keep a steady hand on the tiller and find a way forward even when—especially when—times are tough.

This epiphany—that the many blessings and experiences of my life have prepared me to stand up for people in hard times—sticks in my brain as I contemplate whether to run for another term in the Senate. From my time in Honduras, to tough civil rights cases, to mourning with families stricken by gun violence, I seem to do my best when times are worst. Gutting through the many challenging moments of this three-year journey reminds me of this. It's a strength likely to be needed even more in this high-stakes season in American life.

We celebrate Thanksgiving with Anne's mom at her nursing home, and three weeks later, she is gone at age ninety-seven. I watch Anne, for the second time in a year, help comfort a parent in the last weeks of life and then spring into action organizing a family reunion to mourn their passing and celebrate their life. Jinks was an amazing woman—going from Roanoke to Wellesley during World War II and then joining the CIA in Europe and Washington for five years until she met her husband at a hometown Christmas party. She embraced her roles as wife, mother, First Lady of Virginia, and community volunteer with gusto, only showing signs of slowing down in the last two years of her life. I've always seen my wife as much like her mother. The last year has made me see Anne in a new way: exemplary daughter.

In the Senate, we fall short on our effort to protect voting rights and remain far away from necessary reforms of our immigration and criminal justice systems. The mounting evidence of climate change is seen in extreme weather events all over the world, including sea level rise along our coast and severe rains and flooding that repeatedly hit Appalachia. Our infrastructure bill and Inflation Reduction Act demonstrate an America willing to take big steps forward to lead on climate, but questions hang in the air: Have we started too late? Are we doing enough?

The COVID situation improves, takes a turn for the worse with delta and omicron variants, and then begins a steady improvement again as we pass the million-death mark. The economy starts to roll, but job and wage and GDP growth also come with growing inflation. An isolated and delusional Vladimir Putin seeks to distract the Russian people from the country's own deep internal problems by invading Ukraine. President Biden understands the value of alliances and is able to forge a strong coordinated response of Western democracies against the brutal and illegal war. But my gut tells me that a multidimensional war between authoritarian and democratic societies will be a defining challenge for years and decades to come.

That battle—between authoritarian realpolitik and democratic ideals—is also underway at home. We see it in the refusal of many to accept election results and the efforts to restrict voting rights in states under GOP control. We see it in a Supreme Court—warped by two stolen seats—that ignores a century of constitutional doctrine and clear popular sentiment in restricting women's reproductive freedom. We see it in elected officials trafficking in "replacement theory" and manufacturing fear over critical race theory. And we see it in an endless cycle of mass shootings.

The nation maneuvers through another election cycle—they all seem existential now. Since I'm not on the ballot, I spend our October recess campaigning for Virginia congressional candidates and—extending my new annual adventure tradition—break free for five days to bikepack with my son Nat from Pittsburgh to DC on the Great Allegheny Passage and C and O Towpath. Our bad luck with weather holds and we get blitzed by Hurricane Ian wind and rain but love our time together.

The election confounds polls and pundits who are sure that the Democratic Party in power will suffer a disastrous midterm setback. We narrowly lose the House of Representatives—including the painful loss of one of our three Democratic congresswomen in Virginia—but maintain a Senate majority. Races across the country for governors and state legislatures show real strength for Democrats. Six very diverse states hold referenda on abortion rights, and each one votes in favor of women's rights to make reproductive choices without unnecessary interference by government. Donald Trump contributes mightily to the Republican underperformance by backing many substandard candidates who lose winnable races.

The results say something positive about the American voter. Some factors—low approval ratings for President Biden, inflation, the traditional midterm blues for the party holding the White House—lead folks to predict a Republican wave. But it doesn't happen. Voters look past temporary concerns and see the world's greatest democracy threatened by extremism. And they stand up and speak out.

I think about how to best summarize life in our country during the course of my journey. The word that pops up is *humbling*. The Capitol attack, the pandemic death toll, political division—all have been humbling. The word is from a Latin root—*humus*—meaning *ground*.

Humility can be a door to something better. The gospels of Matthew and Luke teach that "whoever exalts himself will be humbled, and whoever humbles himself will be exalted." Can humility be a virtue in politics? We politicians want to boast of ourselves, and our nation, being "indispensable" or "exceptional." But so much spiritual wisdom assigns humility a primary place. If true for individual character, can it be untrue regarding national character? Can a nation—our nation—be strong and lead while maintaining a humility about our own imperfections? Such an acknowledgment can be an antidote to complacency and provide motivation to learn from others and always strive to improve.

If I were to summarize the journey itself, the word *humbling* would not be the first to enter my mind—but *grounding* would be. And being more grounded is well worth 1,200-plus miles exploring Virginia by foot, bike, and canoe over the last three years. I believe I'll need that grounding in the years ahead.

There is one visible change to go with the spiritual grounding. Life has left its marks on me. I had to wear a brace on my feet when I was a kid, and it dug scars into my skin just above both ankles. I bit through my upper lip playing tackle football in the backyard and still have an awkward bump there. A car door slipped from my hand once in the rain and slammed into my face, scarring me just below my left eye. I am still experiencing bizarre nerve tingling 24/7—a long COVID symptom that may never go away.

My riverside burn from a few months back is healed, but the top of my left foot is discolored red and brown. The doctor at the burn center said they could do something to make the scar less visible. But hiding imperfection seems contrary to my journey's lessons. And the scar is already fading.

I earned it. I think I'll keep it.

ACKNOWLEDGMENTS

I undertook this Virginia journey to inspire my future public service. I wrote up this journal as a gift to all who have adventured with me along the way. You are too numerous to name but many of you appear in these pages. Words can't convey how much you mean to me—I've tried my best.

I thank Virginia writer Adriana Trigiani for believing in this book after others were skeptical. She sent it to a wonderful agent, WME's Suzanne Gluck, and suddenly *Walk Ride Paddle* had a champion. Suzanne and Austin Ross at Harper Horizon have improved it in ways large and small.

I do have to single out Anne, though she insists that I've written too much about her already. I wouldn't have started the journey without her and wouldn't have completed it without her. The best days of the journey were the ones when we were together. But even those great days will certainly be eclipsed on journeys to come.

Planning the Virginia Nature Triathlon was facilitated by these books:

Walk

Appalachian Trail Thru-Hiker's Companion, Appalachian Trail Conservancy, 2018

Appalachian Trail Thru-Hike Planner, Appalachian Trail
Conservancy, 2015

Appalachian Trail Data Book, Appalachian Trail Conservancy,
2019

K. Powell, *The Anguish of Displacement*, UVA Press, 2015

S. Eisenfeld, *Shenandoah*, University of Nebraska Press, 2014

Guide to the Appalachian Trail, Potomac Appalachian Trail Club,
1959–60

Ride

E. & S. Skinner, *Cycling the Blue Ridge*, Menasha Ridge Press,
2020

A. Yarsinke, *Blue Ridge Parkway Through Time*, Arcadia
Publishing, 2018

Paddle

A. Woodlief, *In River Time: The Way of the James*, Algonquin
Books, 1985

J. Bryan, *The James River in Richmond*, Charles Creek Publishing,
1997

E. Swift, *Journey on the James*, UVA Press, 2001

H. R. Corbett, *Virginia Whitewater*, Seneca Press, 2000

E. Grove, *Classic Virginia Rivers*, Howling Wolf Publications, 1992

R. Hambrick, *Transforming the James River in Richmond*, History
Press, 2020

P. Rouse, *The James: Where a Nation Began*, Dietz Press, 1994

B. Deans, *The River Where America Began*, Rowman &
Littlefield, 2007

Two nonprofit organizations, the James River Association and
the Appalachian Trail Conservancy, have been particularly helpful in
offering advice and support during this journey. Proceeds from this
book will be shared with these dedicated nature advocates. (I'm also

sharing proceeds with the Richmond Area Bicycle Association "Bikes for Kids" program.)

I hope some might use my book, and these resources, to replicate the journey. Or—better yet—be inspired to create your own. There is so much great travel literature about distant lands. But all can benefit from a deeper exploration of the faraway nearby.

I have to acknowledge the many privileges—health, wealth, time, supportive family and friends and the self-confidence they've nurtured—that enabled me to tackle this adventure. Living in Virginia is a privilege—such amazing places, people, and history within easy reach of my home. As I finish writing up my trip, it strikes me that the whole manuscript is a love letter to Virginia, the home I adopted in 1984 when I moved here to get married.

One last acknowledgment must be made. The form of this book—a day-by-day account of a journey with each day containing details of the trip with reflections both connected and tangential—is a tribute to Thoreau's *A Week on the Concord and Merrimack Rivers*. That work braids together travel, nature, religion, literature, politics, human nature, friendship, philosophy, and an extended elegy to the brother who accompanied Thoreau on the river but died before the book was written.

My favorite passage from the book is Thoreau grappling with the challenges of keeping a journal when surrounded by beauty and too absorbed in it to pick up a pen. But, years after the river trip, while he sojourned at Walden Pond, he did pick up a pen and created a beautiful account of this journey of a lifetime:

Unfortunately many things have been omitted which should have been recorded in our journal, for though we made it a rule to set down all our experiences therein, yet such a resolution is very hard to keep, for the important experience rarely allows us to remember such obligations, and so indifferent things get recorded, while that is frequently neglected. It is not easy to write in a journal what interests us at any time, because to write it is not what interests us.

Whenever we awoke in the night, still eking out our dreams with half-awakened thoughts, it was not till after an interval, when the wind breathed harder than usual, flapping the curtains of the tent, and causing its cords to vibrate, that we remembered that we lay on the bank of the Merrimack, and not in our chamber at home. With our heads so low in the grass, we heard the river whirling and sucking, and lapsing downward, kissing the shore as it went, sometimes rippling louder than usual, and again its mighty current making only a slight limpid trickling sound, as if our water-pail had sprung a leak, and the water were flowing into the grass by our side. The wind, rustling the oaks and hazels, impressed us like a wakeful and inconsiderate person up at midnight, moving about and putting things to rights, occasionally stirring up whole drawers of leaves at a puff. There seemed to be a great haste and preparation throughout Nature, as for a distinguished visitor; all her aisles had to be swept in the night, by a thousand hand-maidens, and a thousand pots to be boiled for the next day's feasting;—such a whispering bustle, as if ten thousand fairies made their fingers fly, silently sewing at the new carpet with which the earth was to be clothed, and the new drapery which was to adorn the trees. And then the wind would lull and die away and we like it fell asleep again.

ABOUT THE AUTHOR

Tim Kaine has served people throughout his life as a teacher, civil rights lawyer, and elected official. He is one of only thirty people in American history to be a mayor, governor, and United States senator. He lives with his wife, Anne, in Richmond, Virginia.